COMPLETE GUIDE TO
COMPACT
HANDGUNS

*Other Stoeger books
by Gene Gangarosa Jr.:*

MODERN BERETTA FIREARMS

P.38 AUTOMATIC PISTOL — THE FIRST 50 YEARS

COMPLETE GUIDE TO SERVICE HANDGUNS

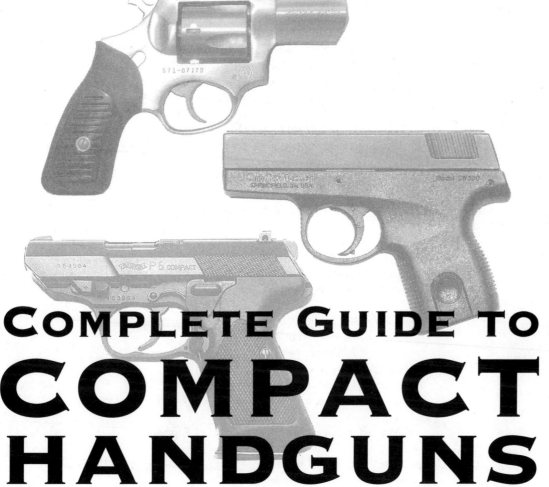

COMPLETE GUIDE TO
COMPACT
HANDGUNS

BY
GENE GANGAROSA JR.

 STOEGER PUBLISHING COMPANY

I dedicate this book to my family

COVER DESIGN and PHOTOGRAPH:
Matt C. Wells and O. Ray Wells
BOOK DESIGN and DIGITAL PRODUCTION:
Loretta Luongo Associates

FRONT COVER:
The compact pistols pictured on the front cover are (left to right) the Glock
Model 19, the Smith & Wesson Model 4013 and the
SIG-Sauer Model P230.

Publisher by Stoeger Publishing Company
5 Mansard Court
Wayne, New Jersey 07470

International Standard Book Number: 0-88317-203-8
Library of Congress Catalog Card No.: 96-071002

Manufactured in the United States of America

In the United States, distributed to the book trade and to the sporting goods
trade by:
Stoeger Industries
5 Mansard Court
Wayne, New Jersey 07470
Tel.: 201-872-9500 Fax: 201-872-2230

In Canada, distributed to the book trade and to the sporting goods trade by:
Stoeger Canada Ltd.
1801 Wentworth Street, Unit 16
Whitby, Ontario, L1N 8R6, Canada

PREFACE

Large, military-style revolvers and automatic pistols may be easier to shoot accurately and more powerfully, but it's the small handguns that are carried around and used primarily for self-defense. A gun that's too large to carry and conceal probably won't be close at hand when it's needed; but then, relatively small pistols almost always invite compromise, sacrificing caliber choice and striking power. They also have shortened grips, undersized sights and low-profile controls, all of which reduce their handling qualities compared to full-sized pistols. But when it comes to preventing a criminal assault, or stopping one that's already begun, a small handgun can quite literally prove a lifesaver. As the old saying goes: "A .25 in the pocket beats a .45 in the briefcase every time." And because of recent improvements in bullet design, the low-powered .25 ACP and .32 ACP cartridges have become much more effective, thus creating renewed confidence in small, lightweight automatic pistols.

This book (and its companion volume, *The Complete Guide to Service Handguns*) presents a practical resource for the average person who seeks a reliable handgun. Literally thousands of models, both new and used, are available in every size, shape and caliber. The purpose of the two-volume *Complete Guide to Handguns* series is to examine and explain the many choices available, and to help prospective buyers decide whether a given handgun is serviceable, affordable and appropriate for their needs. In this volume, you'll find photos of each handgun along with its specifications, including most importantly its width and height—the two dimensions most critical for concealed carrying of the smaller guns. In addition, the book provides an overview of each gun's operating and safety features, plus test-firing results of several hundred automatic pistols, derringers and revolvers—far more than any book of its kind. Even if a certain model is not featured specifically in this edition, a closely related model or variation is most likely covered. Exotic collector's items—those that readers are unlikely ever to see, much less shoot—are not included.

The *Complete Guide to Compact Handguns* covers both smaller models, many of which can be carried in a pant or jacket pocket, and larger handguns in small caliber for target or outdoor sporting use—or, in an emergency, for self-defense. The book leads off with two sections on revolvers: the classic models, some of which date back to the late 19th century, followed by modern small-caliber revolvers in common use. The automatic pistols begin with the classics such as the Beretta Model 1934 and the famous Walther PPK; this is followed by small-caliber/backup pistols in .22, .25, .32, .38 and .380 calibers. Finally, there's a section on larger-caliber compact models in 9mm, .40 S&W and .45 ACP, and important chapters on safety, carrying, and disassembling.

A word of caution about owning and firing handguns of any kind. No amount of intelligent training and preparation will automatically confer a measure of self-protection or a competitive trophy. Safe handling procedures are a must for those who aspire to be careful, responsible handgun owners. Those who are first-time handgun owners must carefully read the owner's manual that comes with each gun. If the gun is a used model with no owner's manual, the manufacturer or importer can probably supply one. Also, check with a local gun store or firing range about joining a firearms safety class sponsored by the National Rifle Association.

ACKNOWLEDGMENTS

No book of this magnitude can be the work of a single individual. My deepest thanks and gratitude go to my family— my lovely wife, Lynn, and our children, Megan and Tyler— without whom nothing I've done would be worthwhile. Next, my thanks to the terrific people at Stoeger Publishing Company, especially Robert Weise, former executive vice-president, David C. Perkins, his successor, and Bill Jarrett of Stoeger's wonderfully talented editorial team. I am also deeply grateful to the many businesses and individuals who have given generously of their time and resources to help make this book possible.

BY AND ABOUT
THE AUTHOR

I have enjoyed shooting since I was a little boy, and all my early exposures were to long arms. The first handgun I ever fired was the Colt M1911A1 during my service with the U.S. Navy, in which I served from 1977 to 1981 as a helicopter air crewman. Although my squadron's primary mission was antisubmarine warfare, I also did a considerable amount of rescue and intelligence-gathering work, which I personally found most gratifying. Naturally, I had occasion to work with my standard Navy firearms and for a time carried a Walther P.38 as my personal sidearm. Since my collateral duty was intelligence, I had considerable exposure to firearms used in various countries.

As a rescue swimmer, I flew in several rescue sorties for which I received letters of commendation. We were not technically at war during my enlistment, but the cold war was raging and I was involved in a supporting role during the Iranian hostage rescue attempt in May 1980. Afterward I attended college and commenced a teaching career. I began writing firearms articles a number of years ago and have since written well over 100 of them, along with several books (this is my third book).

Because of the circumstances under which I first began using handguns in the Navy, I've leaned mostly toward the service-type automatic pistols and revolvers; I think, therefore, primarily in terms of each gun's usefulness in self-defense situations. I believe that we live in a world in which it is often easier and more natural for evil to triumph— at least temporarily— over good. In such a world, it is prudent to take all appropriate safety precautions, and in some professions and circumstances it may be appropriate for law-abiding citizens to arm themselves. I oppose gun control, basing my position on the belief that human beings should be treated as responsible moral agents and should be made to face the consequences of their actions. Thus I consider the punishment of criminals a much more effective crime-fighting tactic than outlawing guns or their law-abiding owners who pose no threat to society. In my opinion, when society learns to punish malefactors swiftly and effectively, things will improve.

Regarding handgun selection, I've gravitated mostly toward the major gun types over the years and feel that almost all of them will do the job as long as the owners are well practiced and pay close attention to what they are doing. When testing a gun, I always assume it has something to offer. I work hard to discover its good points and try to be as open-minded as possible. I also believe that subjectivity and ego have no place in gunwriting; I have no personal axes to grind and am always willing to listen to other points of view. So be it.

CONTENTS

1. CLASSIC COMPACT REVOLVERS 11

2. COMPACT REVOLVERS 27

3. CLASSIC COMPACT PISTOLS 63

4. SMALL CALIBER/BACKUP PISTOLS 101

5. 9MM, .40 AND .45 CALIBER COMPACTS 203

   HANDGUN SAFETY 279

   CARRYING A HANDGUN 281

   DISASSEMBLING COLT MODEL 1903-TYPE PISTOLS 284

   INDEX 285

1. CLASSIC COMPACT REVOLVERS

CONTENTS

Charter Arms Bulldog 12
Colt Detective Special 14
Smith & Wesson Chiefs Special Model 36 . . 16

Smith & Wesson (cont).
Model 60 18
Safety Hammerless 20

The classic "compact" revolvers discussed in the following section have stood the test of time and by and large are still available. Such small revolvers as the Smith & Wesson "Lemon Squeezer" date back to the late 19th century, while others like the Model 60 were introduced as recently as 1965. And even though they are considered "old," many out-of-production models continue to serve their original purposes more than adequately. Most so-called "Classics" were made in enormous quantities— in the hundreds of thousands, or even in the millions in some cases—and thus spare parts needed to maintain them are often still available. Strong caution is urged, however, in using these handguns. Before firing any old gun, no matter how advanced its design or how impeccable its reputation, the owner must first have the weapon thoroughly inspected by a qualified gunsmith who is familiar with its design. Even then, it's a good idea to limit such older guns to standard factory ammo, especially the milder loadings.

CHARTER ARMS BULLDOG

When Charter Arms introduced its .44 Special Bulldog model in 1974, it was the largest-caliber revolver in the company's line. It remained in production until Charter Arms failed and was then revived by Charco (Ansonia, CT) in 1993.

The Bulldog can serve as a service revolver, an undercover or back-up, a civilian's concealed-carry piece, or a police undercover and off-duty gun. It has played its most celebrated role as part of the anti-hijacking Sky Marshal program. On the other side of the coin it was the gun used by serial killer Sam Berkowitz, better known as the "Son of Sam," during his reign of terror.

During the 19th century, in their attempts to combine a large, heavy cartridge with a relatively small frame and short barrel suitable for concealed carry in an overcoat pocket, several manufacturers made so-called "Bull Dog" revolvers. These included guns made by Forehand & Wadsworth (1875 to 1890) and Johnson, Bye & Company (1881 to 1882), both American-owned and operated in Worcester (MA). Britain's Webley No. 2 revolver (1878 to 1914) and its many copies out of Belgium were also known as Bulldog revolvers. Smith & Wesson (Springfield, MA) also promoted a .44 Russian caliber version of its famous Safety Hammerless revolver in 1886, but the project never went beyond a single prototype. In any case, ample historical precedent exists for combining a heavy, powerful cartridge with a lightweight, compact frame. In fact, some of these 19th-century "Bulldogs," notably the Webley, had impressive production runs.

Because of its many built-in compromises, the Bulldog remains a controversial handgun. Built on the same frame used on all Charter Arms' revolvers—including the small Undercover and Off Duty models—it's considered light for the cartridge it fires. Recoil is therefore pronounced and durability compromised. On the other hand, armed with suitable ammunition the gun offers a high level of power for its size and weight. The .44 Special cartridge is certainly more lethal than a .380 ACP round, for example, and yet the Bulldog is not much larger and certainly no heavier than many pistols firing .380 caliber ammo.

Of two basic Bulldog models, the older ones feature an ejector rod (located beneath a 3-inch barrel) exposed at the front. Its Patridge-style front sight is more suited to a target pistol; the grip is either a checkered wood-type or neoprene. Newer Bulldogs—the kind now offered by Charco—sport a 2 1/2-inch barrel with a protected ejector rod and a ramp sight that's less likely to snag on the draw than the hooked sight found on earlier models. The new Bulldogs also feature an improved neoprene grip that enhances recovery from recoil, a critical factor in controlling this lightweight gun.

Because the .44 Special cartridges are so large, Charter Arms/Charco has wisely limited the contemporary Bulldog to a 5-shot cylinder. On earlier Bulldogs, the cylinder could be opened by pulling forward on the exposed ejector rod or by pushing the cylinder release forward. Right-handed shooters often removed the release latch on these early Bulldogs for fear the latch might cut their thumb upon recoil. Left-handers often bypass the release altogether, mostly because it's so poorly placed, and simply use the ejector rod to open the cylinder. With the shrouded ejector rod found on newer models, only the cylinder release method will open the cylinder for reloading. Like most modern revolvers, the bulldog has a transfer-bar safety mechanism that prevents the hammer from reaching the firing pin

The Charter Arms Bulldog offers an impressive level of firepower (five quick rounds of the respected .44 Special) in a compact, lightweight gun weighing less than the Walther PPK. This Bulldog Pug (above) offers a shrouded underbarrel ejector rod and neoprene stocks.

until the trigger is pulled all the way to the rear at the moment the gun is fired. The pin itself is made of a beryllium-copper alloy said to allow unlimited dry firing (i.e., pulling the trigger on an unloaded firing chamber). While this may be a useful feature for practice, just be sure the gun is unloaded before pulling the trigger!

While the Bulldog boasts a decent trigger pull, reasonable sights and acceptable accuracy, the only serious weakness is its recoil. The .44 Special in a lightweight gun is a handful that many shooters find excessive. Also, the ejector rod, even on the early models, is too short to extract the cartridge casings fully. After firing all five rounds in the cylinder, the shooter must then turn the barrel up to remove the expended rounds before reloading—just as in a Smith & Wesson J-frame or other snub-nosed revolver.

To sum up, the Bulldog offers a higher level of power than most guns its size. But because of its strong recoil, it's a gun that every prospective buyer should test-fire before making a commitment.

CHARTER ARMS BULLDOG

Manufacturer	Years Produced	Caliber/Capacity	Dimensions
Charter Arms Corp. Stratford, CT (now Charco, Inc. Ansonia, CT)	1974–Present	.44 Special/5 rounds	Barrel Length: 3.0" O.A. Length: 7.75" Height: 4.9" Width: 1.45" Weight: 19 oz. (unloaded); 22 oz. (loaded)

COLT DETECTIVE SPECIAL

Although Colt introduced its Detective Special in 1927, it was for the first 40 years of its long production run merely a Police Positive Special with a 2-inch barrel. By the time Colt ceased production in 1986, production of the Detective Special exceeded 400,000. Wisely, Colt reintroduced the same basic gun to rave reviews in 1992.

Of several major variations, the first were the pre-World War II guns, which many collectors still consider the most desirable. In the post-World War II era, the Detective Special was produced with a slightly shortened frame from 1966 on; and in 1971 Colt changed the front sight from a hemisphere to a ramp, which was retained on new-production models.

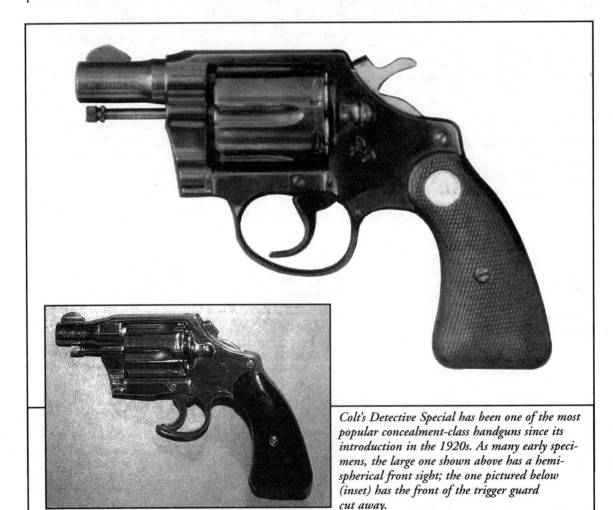

Colt's Detective Special has been one of the most popular concealment-class handguns since its introduction in the 1920s. As many early specimens, the large one shown above has a hemispherical front sight; the one pictured below (inset) has the front of the trigger guard cut away.

The Detective Special reintroduced in 1992 features improved neoprene stocks. The relieved area at the bottom offers a better grip for the pinky finger.

The Detective Special proved highly accurate. This five-shot offhand group, fired from 25 feet, all in double action, measures 2.2 inches across.

The Detective Special is a bit larger than Smith & Wesson's competing J-frame series of small revolvers, making it an easier gun for large-handed shooters to hold. In fact, the grip, whether the old wooden style or the contemporary rubber type, is noticeably more comfortable to hold and shoot than is the tiny J-frame grip. Another advantage gained by the Detective Special's slightly increased size over the S&W's J-frames is its cylinder, which holds an extra round, giving it six shots before reloading instead of only five.

Balanced against these positive qualities is the Detective Special's loss of concealability compared to the smaller Smith & Wesson guns. Still, Colt's classic revolver shoots well for such a small gun, yet is rugged enough to handle hot +P .38 Special rounds.

COLT DETECTIVE SPECIAL

Manufacturer	Years Produced	Caliber/Capacity	Dimensions
Colt Industries, Firearms Div. Hartford, CT	1927–1986; 1992–Present	.38 Special/6 rounds	Barrel length: 2.1" O.A. Length: 6.6" Height: 4.6" Width: 1.4" Weight: 22 oz. (unloaded); 26 oz. (loaded)

S&W CHIEFS SPECIAL MODEL 36

In 1949 when Smith & Wesson decided to expand its product line aggressively, its dynamic president, Carl Hellstrom, sent out the word to develop a new small revolver. It was to feature a small frame, called the J-frame, carry a 5-shot cylinder and include a coil mainspring to reduce costs. At first, Smith & Wesson saw the J-frame as a compact yet powerful revolver for use by off-duty police and plainclothes officers; but this versatile little handgun has enjoyed much more widespread applications. It has also armed aviators, various military organizations, police forces and thousands of civilians the world over. The original J-frame revolver (also known since 1957 as the Model 36) has inspired a whole family of small revolvers made by Smith & Wesson, not to mention a host of copies and competitors. The first J-frame revolver was completed in October 1950 and was unveiled to the public soon after at the annual conference of the International Association of Chiefs of Police. It was there that the new revolver received its permanent name: Chiefs Special.

Various options have been offered in the Chiefs Special line by Smith & Wesson, including a choice of blued or nickel finish, round or square butts, and 2-inch or 3-inch barrels. Other modifications have included an improved thumb latch and hammer linkage, plus alterations to the side plate and trigger guard. Amazingly, even a target model with adjustable sights has been produced.

Among the numerous variations of the Chiefs Special is the Chiefs Special Airweight, which S&W introduced in 1952. Originally, this small revolver, which weighed less than 11 ounces unloaded, featured an aluminum-alloy cylinder and frame. Although it was rejected by the U.S. Air Force, Smith & Wesson kept the gun in production. When its cylinder construction was changed to steel in 1954, the gun was renamed the "Model 37 Chiefs Special Airweight." This excellent handgun weighs six ounces less than

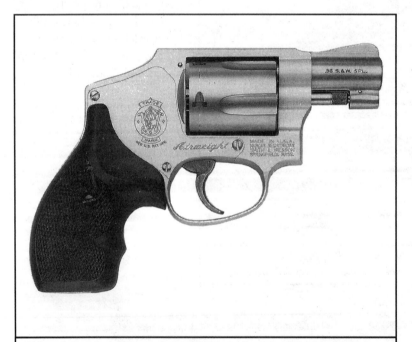

Although Smith & Wesson discontinued production of the Model 42 in 1974, the company revived its design in the early 1990s as the Model 642 Centennial Airweight, which is still prospering.

the all-steel Chiefs Special. Earlier, in 1952 when Smith & Wesson celebrated its 100th anniversary, the company introduced an updated version of its legendary "Safety Hammerless" revolver. Appropriately named the "Centennial," it was, from 1957 on, also called the Model 42, which featured a concealed hammer and a grip safety. Although Smith & Wesson discontinued production of the Model 42 in 1974, Smith & Wesson revived its design in the early 1990s and it has prospered ever since.

An odd-looking Chiefs Special variation appeared in 1955, when Smith & Wesson introduced the Bodyguard, featuring a hammer shroud that gave the revolver a humpbacked appearance. Only the tip of the hammer appeared above the shroud for thumb-cocking the

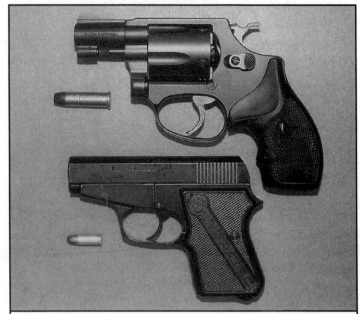

While small automatic pistols like Intratec's Pro-Tec (bottom) are more compact and concealable than J-frame revolvers, small revolvers like the Model 37 (top) have greater power and are usually more reliable.

hammer for single-action shots. Assigned the designation "Model 38" in 1957, the Bodyguard has earned its reputation as a premier pocket handgun. Another Chiefs Special variation—the Model 60—appeared in 1965 and was the first handgun made almost entirely of stainless steel. A separate discussion of this gun follows.

When placed in the hands of a skilled shooter, the Chiefs Special and other Smith & Wesson J-frame revolvers can be quite accurate. The Chiefs Special is a particularly demanding handgun to shoot, thanks to its tiny sights and stocks, short barrel and heavy trigger pull. Recoil is severe, too, particularly with +P ammunition. Still, with practice the Chiefs Special and the other Smith & Wesson J-frame revolvers are excellent small revolvers that can be carried where larger guns cannot.

To make these small wonders more pleasant to shoot, numerous after-market accessories exist for the Chiefs Special. The excellent Boot Grip, designed by Craig Spegel, is highly recommended. It makes the little J-frame revolvers much more comfortable to shoot without adding excessive bulk as do so many after-market stocks. Federal Cartridge Company's "Nyclad" brand of ammunition is also effective for small Smith & Wesson revolvers. It's relatively mild to shoot, and yet, because of its efficient hollowpoint design, achieves good expansion even in short barrels. The exotic MagSafe round, which is loaded with tiny pellets in an epoxy core, is even better in close-range emergency self-defense situations (although it's also appreciably more expensive). For rapid reloading, HKS's speedloaders are worth trying; the Model 36-A will fit any Smith & Wesson J-frame as well as the similar Charter Arms and the Taurus .38 Special 5-shot revolver.

Compared to automatic pistols of the same size and weight, the Chiefs Special carries a more potent cartridge and is definitely more reliable in operation. When not scrupulously maintained, small automatic pistols tend to jam, whereas the Chiefs Special requires minimal maintenance. The sole shortcoming, aside from those listed above, is its limited ammunition capacity of five shots in the cylinder. That's a small price to pay, however, for such an excellent compact handgun.

S&W CHIEFS SPECIAL MODEL 36

Manufacturer	Years Produced	Caliber/Capacity	Dimensions (2-inch barrel)
Smith & Wesson Springfield, MA	1950–Present	.38 Special/5 rounds	Barrel Length: 2" O.A. Length: 6.5" Height: 4.4" Width: 1.3" Weight: 20 oz. (unloaded); 24 oz.(loaded)

S&W MODEL 60

Prior to Smith & Wesson's introduction of the Model 60 revolver in 1965, stainless steel had been used occasionally, but only for individual parts. No gun had ever been made wholly—or even mostly—from stainless steel. Thus did the Model 60 represent a major innovation in gun manufacture. Today, dozens of guns follow the lead of the Model 60 with their all-steel composition. For that reason, even though the Model 60 is identical to the earlier Model 36 Chiefs Special in every detail except for its finish, the Model 60 is worthy of a separate entry.

The big advantage of stainless steel over conventional blued steel, or even a nickel finish, is its superior resistance to corrosion and easier maintenance. While not entirely rustproof, a stainless steel gun is much more forgiving of neglect than a blued steel gun. A second advantage of stainless steel in a small gun like the Model 60 is that its bright finish makes the gun look bigger—hence more intimidating—than it actually is.

Smith & Wesson began development of the specialized tooling needed to make the stainless parts of the Model 60 in 1964. Production began in May 1965 and the world first saw the new revolver in October, when it was unveiled at the annual conference of the

Smith & Wesson's Model 60 was the first gun in the history of firearms to be built almost entirely of stainless steel.

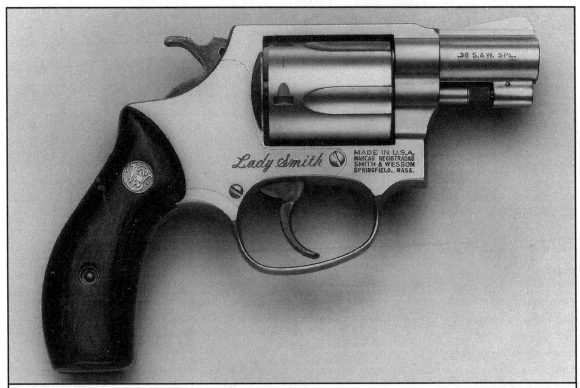

Not for women only is the Model 60 LadySmith with satin stainless steel finish, casehardened trigger and hammer, and 2-inch barrel.

International Chiefs of Police, just as Smith & Wesson had announced the first Chiefs Special 15 years before. The company quickly accumulated a tremendous backlog of orders for the Model 60. Many purchases were made by U.S. soldiers and airmen in Vietnam, who liked the gun's compact dimensions and rust-resistant finish.

At first, Smith & Wesson made the Model 60 with a bright polished stainless finish, but in late 1966 this was changed to a satin finish when policemen objected to the shine. Smith & Wesson was glad to make the switch, because the bright finish required a great deal of polishing and was expensive to manufacture. That same year, the Model 60 became available with a color casehardened trigger and hammer.

Although Smith & Wesson has a winner in the Model 60, its trigger pull is not quite as smooth as the company's carbon-steel J-frame revolvers. The Model 60's chief attraction, of course, is its rust-resistance, making it a sensible choice for warm, humid climates or for coastal areas exposed to salt air.

S&W MODEL 60

Manufacturer	Years Produced	Caliber/Capacity	Dimensions
Smith & Wesson Springfield, MA	1965–Present	.38 Special/5 rounds	(2-inch barrel) Barrel Length: 2" O.A. Length: 6.5" Height: 4.4" Width: 1.3" Weight: 20 oz. (unloaded); 24 oz.(loaded)

S&W SAFETY HAMMERLESS

When Horace Smith and Daniel B. Wesson established the Smith & Wesson company in 1854, their goal was to make quality firearms. Early Smith & Wesson rimfire revolvers were used in the Civil War; but in 1869 the company bought the patent for a top-break hinged revolver frame. By 1871, the company began receiving lucrative Russian military orders for large cavalry revolvers that had this new top-break configuration. The company worked on this windfall almost exclusively, eventually producing more than 200,000 weapons. The powerful .44 Russian round used in this model was the predecessor of the .38 S&W bullet used with the Safety Hammerless revolver (which later became the .44 Special).

In 1875, when the Russian contract was finally filled, Smith & Wesson discovered that Colt had managed to snap up much of the U.S. military revolver business, particularly with its Single Action Army Revolver (*see The Complete Guide to Service Handguns,* the companion guide to this). Realizing that its only chance of catching up with Colt lay in the civilian market, Daniel Wesson downsized the .44 Russian round into a .38-caliber configuration. This new cartridge, the .38 S&W, offered high performance in a small revolver that had great appeal for those who sought a concealed-carry handgun. With 14 grains of blackpowder, this early .38 S&W round contained a blunt-nosed lead bullet that weighed only 146 grains. Its muzzle velocity—579 feet per second—provided 108 foot-pounds of energy, which was remarkable for so small a cartridge in the blackpowder era. By the 1940s, ammunition makers who used smokeless powder had elevated these figures to 745 fps and 179 foot-pounds of energy at the muzzle with a round-nosed bullet. This performance was not too far behind many .38 Special loads fired from modern snub-nosed revolvers.

A year after unveiling its .38 S&W round, Smith & Wesson introduced the similar—but smaller and weaker—.32 S&W cartridge. For these new cartridges, S&W made in 1876 a single-action revolver; and four years later, its first double-action revolver appeared. Called the .38 Double Action, or Model 1880, it was well received by the public.

It was in February 1887 that Smith & Wesson introduced the Safety Hammerless, a small revolver that was to revolutionize the concept of safe concealed handgun carry. This revolver, officially called the "New Departure" or "Safety Hammerless," was the first modern concealable cartridge revolver. In terms of power, safety and operating convenience, this model was far ahead of the primitive derringers and cut-down holster revolvers that had preceded it. In fact, so inherently correct was the basic design of this weapon that it remained in production until 1940. Over 500,000 were made and sold in two calibers—.38 S&W and .32 S&W—with many still in use today.

The Safety Hammerless, like current Smith & Wesson "hammerless" designs, is not really a hammerless design at all. Instead, it has an invisible hammer, concealed wholly within the frame, where it can't snag clothing during a draw. With no exposed hammer surface for the shooter to thumb-cock, the only way to cock the hammer is by pulling the trigger. Consequently, the revolver can only be fired in the double-action mode.

The nickname for this cleverly-designed handgun—"Lemon Squeezer"—derives from its grip safety, which locks the hammer until the shooter's hand squeezes the grip hard enough to release it. This grip safety greatly lessens the chance of an accidental shooting while the revolver is carried in one's pocket. The Lemon Squeezer also has an inertia firing pin, which requires a solid blow from the falling hammer (thereby overcoming spring pressure) before it ignites the cartridge primer. This additional safety feature, which makes accidental firing still more unlikely even when the gun is dropped, has since been incorporated into a number of later handguns. These include the Colt M1911 series, Beretta's Model 1934, the Browning High Power, the CZ-75, and many others.

Another interesting feature of the Lemon Squeezer is its method of reloading. Once all rounds have been fired, a latch located behind the rear sight is released, opening the revolver from the top. By

This Smith & Wesson Safety Hammerless revolver is in well-worn but serviceable condition. Most guns of this type come in a blued finish with checkered hard-rubber stocks.

swinging the barrel and cylinder downward, all five empty cartridges are smoothly ejected simultaneously, allowing the shooter to insert fresh rounds. This simultaneous-ejection feature developed by Smith & Wesson unloads and reloads much faster than the gate-loading revolver that employs a cylinder crane. Unfortunately, this faster reloading comes at the cost of a weak frame at the hinge point, which limits the number of cartridges that can be safely used in such a weapon.

The centerfire cartridges used in S&W's Safety Hammerless were of the .38 and .32 caliber types. The .38 round, called the .38 S&W, is not to be confused with the later .38 Special round developed by Smith & Wesson in 1899 for the Model 10 (*see Complete Guide to Service Handguns*). The gun's hinged frame proved to be a basic design flaw, its continued firing causing excessive wear. This weakness also limited caliber selection and interfered with S&W's original plans to offer three different Safety Hammerless models in .32, .38, and .44 Russian calibers. Unfortunately, only a single prototype of the powerful .44 Russian version was ever made. Production of a big-bore Safety Hammerless revolver would have anticipated Charter Arms' Bulldog by nearly a century.

Variations. Still, Smith & Wesson enjoyed great success with the Safety Hammerless revolvers in the two smaller calibers. Production of the .38 version started in the summer of 1886 after a four-year development period. But with only 28 Safety Hammerless revolvers produced that summer, the gun was set aside for six months; full production resumed in early 1887. As time went on, the company introduced refinements to the Safety Hammerless revolver, resulting in five major variations in the .38 S&W version. These revolvers were referred to as the First Model through the Fifth Model.

The Smith & Wesson Safety Hammerless revolver also appeared in this smaller and significantly less powerful .32 S&W caliber version.

First Model. The First Model Safety Hammerless offered barrel lengths of 3.25 inches, 4 inches, and 5 inches. Among its features was a barrel latch bar located on the upper frame in front of the rear sight. Once all shots were fired, this bar had to be thumb-depressed on the left side in order to open the barrel. Only about 5,000 of the First Model were built, marked with serial number 1 through 5150.

Second Model. Created in late 1887, the Second Model remained in production until 1890. The shape of its barrel latch was changed for more convenient operation, and a new checkered piece of steel located behind the rear sight enabled the shooter to open the gun with ease. To accommodate the new barrel latch, an additional relief cut was made on the rear of the frame, and the trigger was reshaped for better control against overtravel. Second Model serial numbers continued where the First

Model's left off, reaching 42483 (or a total of about 37,000 revolvers).

Third Model. The Third Model, built from 1890 until 1898, introduced a new 6-inch barrel. In addition, the barrel latch was now made in two pieces, with a separate checkered part mounted on top of the frame for shooters to push down, unlatching the barrel for reloading. For added protection against accidental discharge, a hammer stop blocked the hammer from moving forward whenever the mechanism was open for loading or reloading. This stop was deactivated only when the barrel was fully locked and the revolver ready to fire. Third Model serial numbers picked up where Second Model numbers left off at 42483, running to 116002 for a total of about 73,519 revolvers.

Fourth Model. This model's major innovation was an even better barrel latch. Shaped like a "T," it featured checkered or knurled buttons on each side to assure a good grip for the thumb and forefinger to lift the barrel latch, unhinge the frame and open the action. The Fourth Model was made from 1898 until 1907, with serial numbers reaching 220000 for a total of about 75,000 revolvers.

Fifth Model. This last variation, which came in all existing barrel lengths, added an extremely concealable and desirable 2-inch barrel. Another major change was its front sight, which had been pinned to the barrel in earlier guns but was now forged as part of the barrel itself. To simplify construction and thus lower manufacturing costs, the extractor base pin was pinned into place, rather than being attached with a screw as in previous models. Checkered walnut stocks were also added, previous grip plates having been made of checkered black hard rubber or sometimes pearl. Smith & Wesson made more than 40,000 Fifth Model revolvers from 1907 on. It continued until Safety Hammerless production ceased altogether in 1940, with the top serial number of 261493.

With Smith & Wesson selling its .38 S&W "Lemon Squeezers" by the thousands, the even more compact .32 S&W revolver was also doing quite well, despite a woefully underpowered cartridge. From early 1888 to 1902, S&W made 91,417 of the First Model .32, whose barrel latch was similar to the Third Model .38 described above. The .32 Safety Second Model which followed had a barrel latch similar in design and operation to the Fourth and Fifth Model .38's. Second Models in .32 S&W caliber reached serial number 169999. The Third Model .32, with its integral front sight, was made from 1909 until production was discontinued in 1937. Its serial-number range began at 170000 and ended at 242981. The .32-caliber First Model Safety revolvers were available in 3 and 3 1/2-inch barrel styles, while the Second and Third Models came in 2-inch and 3-inch configurations.

But it was the .38-caliber version that rightly received the most attention. Despite its primary purpose as a civilian carry weapon, the Safety Hammerless featured in U.S. Army tests during 1889 competed against a Colt revolver with a cylinder mounted on a crane that opened to the left for reloading. For these tests, the Army ordered 100 Safety Hammerless revolvers with 6-inch barrels in .38 S&W caliber and 100 Colt Navy Model 1889 revolvers, also with 6-inch barrels but firing the slightly more powerful .38 Long Colt cartridge. While the Colt gun had better bullet penetration, the Smith & Wesson revolver proved more accurate and was faster to reload. After Smith & Wesson had bested the Colt in a dust test, both guns were allowed to rust. As a result, the Safety Hammerless suffered a broken mainspring and would not function at all.

The Army then sent the surviving Colt and Smith & Wesson guns to cavalry units for comparative troop trials. Reports from the field favored the Colt over the Smith & Wesson, in part because the Colt's exposed hammer spur could be thumb-cocked for a light single-action trigger pull. Thus did the Colt revolver win the 1892 Army revolver contract; and later, in 1905, it won a Marine contract as well.

Despite the loss of a lucrative military contract, the Safety Hammerless prospered in the civilian handgun market. Its production life drew to a close, however, in the late 1930s and early 1940s in favor of stronger revolvers with solid frames and side-opening cranes. In 1936, Smith & Wesson introduced a newly designed revolver, the "Terrier," which was a smaller .32-caliber version of the standard Military & Police Model with round butt and 2-inch barrel and an empty weight of only 17 ounces. The introduction of the Terrier (Model 32) was a clear sign that the days of the Safety Hammerless were numbered.

While several U.S. and British companies made guns chambered in .38 S&W, most of the new Smith & Wesson revolvers used the improved .38 Special round introduced in 1902. This round was too long to fit into the cylinder of the Safety Hammerless and other revolvers chambered for .38 S&W ammunition; but by the same token, the .38 S&W round was too large in diameter to fit into revolver cylinders made for the .38 Special. And so the Chiefs Special—Smith & Wesson's heir to the pocket revolver tradition—has used the .38 Special round since its introduction in 1950. The end of Terrier production in 1974 marked the demise of all Smith & Wesson-made firearms chambering the .38 S&W round.

A number of factors combined to finish the Safety Hammerless as a production handgun. Mechanically, its barrel latch was fragile and prone to failure after prolonged

Despite its age, this Safety Hammerless revolver placed five rapid-fire offhand shots into a 2.7-inch group from a distance of 25 feet.

firing and use, even with the weak cartridges it used. When ammunition manufacturers began moving to faster bullets with larger powder charges—including the .38 Special, .45 ACP, .38 Super Automatic and .357 Magnum—it proved too difficult to reinforce top-break revolvers so that they would accept these new rounds. By the 1920s, these stronger cartridges and the guns made to accommodate them were in great demand among police and civilians alike.

In addition, despite taking measures to lower the cost of the Fifth Model, the top-break design was always costlier to make than the newer hand ejector revolvers. Stoeger's 1940 catalog listed the retail price of the Safety Hammerless at $28 in .32 caliber and $31 in .38 caliber. By comparison, the more modern and stronger Terrier cost only $30, and the .38 Special Military & Police Model sold for $32.50. Colt's competing Pocket Model Automatic was listed at $24.25; and even Walther's fine Model PPK, a notoriously expensive pistol, cost only $34.

Despite its weak bullets and high price, the carrying and shooting properties of the "Lemon Squeezer" were so popular that it wasn't until World War II that Smith & Wesson was forced to concentrate on making military firearm models at the expense of civilian handguns. Only then did manufacture of the Safety Hammerless finally come to an end.

Nevertheless, the influence of the old Safety Hammerless was felt long after it ceased to be a production item. In fact, when Smith & Wesson introduced its Centennial Model in 1952, it revived the same grip safety and concealed hammer once used in the old Safety Hammerless. The Centennial remained in production until 1972 and is today considered one of the most highly desired guns on the used revolver market. As recently as 1990, Smith & Wesson revived and slightly modified the "hammerless" Centennial in its new stainless steel Model 640, currently in production.

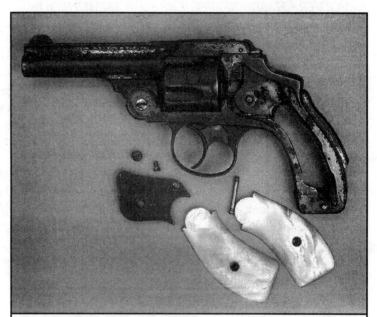

A disassembled S&W Safety Hammerless revolver is shown with its removable sideplate removed, exposing the internal hammer, leaf mainspring, and grip safety (from which the gun's nickname "Lemon Squeezer" derives).

Taking into account its age and primary mission as a concealed carry weapon, the Third Model Safety Hammerless is not a bad shooter. Its trigger pull, in which the initial movement of the trigger takes up the slack and the second movement fires the weapon, is similar to the two-stage pulls found in military firearms. If the shooter is patient and does not pull the trigger hurriedly, but hesitates slightly at the second stage before pulling the trigger all the way back, it's possible to get a decent trigger pull, thus improving accuracy. Thanks to the low pressure and slow speed of the .32 and .38 cartridges, recoil is not excessive either, despite the light weight of this gun.

The sights on the Third Model Safety Hammerless revolver are small and thin, particularly the V-notch rear sight, but at close ranges they are acceptable. With practice, a shooter can easily get used to this well-engineered revolver and do reasonably accurate shooting out to 25 feet or more. The biggest problem with it is finding suitable ammunition. Because so many Safety Hammerless revolvers were made and thousands still exist, both Winchester and Remington continue to make .38 S&W cartridges in 145- and 146-grain bullet weights. The smaller .32 S&W round also remains in production and reloading components for it are available as well. Strict cautions are in order, though, when loading ammunition into these old handguns. Whereas the .38 Special round is too long to fit the Safety Hammerless, 9mm Parabellum rounds made for automatic pistols and Federal's 9mmR (a rimmed revolver round built for Charter Arms's Pit Bull) both fit into the cylinders of S&W's old top-break revolver. But this hot modern ammunition develops far higher chamber pressures than the Safety Hammerless can handle. If used, it would quickly destroy the gun, injuring or even killing the shooter in the process. For example, the top allowable pressure listed by SAAMI for the .38 S&W round is 14,900 c.u.p. (copper units of pressure); but SAAMI's maximum allowable pressure for the 9mm round is a much higher 37,500 c.u.p. Worse still, the diameter of the .38 S&W bullet is .360 inches, while the 9mm bullet measures only .355 inches. Firing a 9mm bullet in a .38 S&W barrel would stress the old gun even more than these pressure figures would indicate. *DO NOT EVER, UNDER ANY CIRCUMSTANCES, USE ANY TYPE OF 9mm AUTOMATIC PISTOL ROUND IN A REVOLVER CHAMBERED FOR .38 S&W AMMUNITION.*

For the cautious reloader, some possibilities do exist. Speer, for example, markets a 110-grain jacketed hollowpoint in .38 S&W, a potentially potent chambering. Reloaders should stick with pressures comparable to the mild factory loadings, however, and not overload these old revolvers. Even with the proper ammunition, whether .32 S&W or .38 S&W, the age of these revolvers raises questions concerning their safety. Smith & Wesson products may be well-designed and well-built firearms, but age takes its toll on even the best of us. Any weapon that old has had several owners, raising questions about maintenance and upkeep. It's especially important to check the barrel latch, which can eventually work loose after repeated firings. A gunsmith may have to tighten or repair this part, which represents the weakest link in the gun's design.

Today, more than 100 years after its first appearance—and over 50 years after production ceased—the Safety Hammerless revolver remains an excellent and popular collector's item, one that has greatly influenced the creation of the contemporary small revolver. A surprising number of this landmark handgun are still in use, though their owners are strongly advised to use them for recreational shooting only.

S&W SAFETY HAMMERLESS

Manufacturer	Years Produced	Caliber/Capacity	Dimensions
Smith & Wesson Springfield, MA	1887–1940	.32 S&W or .38 S&W/5 rounds	(.38 First Model) Barrel Length: 3.25" O.A. Length: 7.5" Height: 4.25" Width: 1.3" Weight: 18 oz. (unloaded); 23 oz. (loaded)

2. COMPACT REVOLVERS

CONTENTS

Charter Arms Off Duty 28
North American Arms Mini-Revolver 30
Rossi Model 68 33
  Model 88 34
  Model 518 35
  Model 720 Covert Special 37
  Model 971 Comp 38
Ruger SP101 40
Smith & Wesson Model 34 42
  Model 37 44

Smith & Wesson (cont.)
  Model 38 46
  Centennial Models 442, 640 and 940 . . . 47
  Model 651 52
Taurus Model 65 53
  Model 85 54
  Models 85CH and CHS 55
  Model 94 57
  Model 605 59
  Model 941 60

For purposes of simplicity and clarity, "compact" or "small" revolvers are defined here as having short barrels—in general, three inches or less—and other features intended to suit them primarily for concealment. Revolvers are perhaps the best bet for self-defense in the small handgun category, particularly the lightweight revolvers descended from the Smith & Wesson Model 36 Chiefs Special. A number of these, such as the Charter Arms Off Duty and the Taurus Model 85, are discussed in the following section. Simple, strong and extremely reliable, these guns offer considerable power for their weight. They fire a cartridge—usually a .38 Special—that is capable of superior stopping power compared to a .25, .32 or .380 Auto cartridge.

Compact revolvers offer other pluses. While not quite as small as the smallest automatic pistols in terms of width, they are frequently lighter. Moreover, they often feature double-action trigger mechanisms, which allow the gun to fire simply by pressing the trigger. Unlike most automatic pistols, the double-action revolver eliminates the need to draw back the slide to load; nor is it necessary to move the manual safety from the "safe" to "fire" setting. Also, the magazine spring of a small automatic pistol is under tremendous tension even when the weapon is only partially loaded. A revolver's parts, by contrast, are at rest even when the gun is fully loaded. With an auto pistol, a misfired or dud cartridge requires that its primer be hit again, or the dud cartridge must be ejected by cycling the action manually. With a revolver, one simply pulls the trigger, turning the cylinder to bring the next cartridge into place under the firing pin. For all of the above reasons, a small double-action revolver is nearly foolproof.

Small revolvers do have their shortcomings, however. Because of their cylinders, even a small one is not as flat as an automatic pistol, making it more difficult to conceal. Also, because of their heavy recoil, small revolvers can be painful to shoot. They also suffer from a limited ammunition capacity, and are neither as fast nor as easy to reload as most automatic pistols. Despite the compromise a shooter must make in terms of ammunition capacity and shooting comfort, the reliable performance that usually results far outweighs the drawbacks.

CHARTER ARMS OFF DUTY

Charter Arms's Off Duty revolver made its debut in 1984, although it's actually a variation of the company's original revolver, the Undercover, which dates from the mid-1960s. Early Off Duty revolvers featured an exposed ejector rod similar to early Colt revolvers; but by the late 1980s the Off Duty had switched to a shrouded pattern, with both spur and bobbed hammers available.

With over 200,000 units sold up to 1992 (when Charter Arms filed for bankruptcy), the Off Duty has obviously been quite successful. After the firm was reorganized in 1993 as Charco, Inc., and moved from Stratford, Connecticut, to nearby Ansonia, the Off Duty was not surprisingly among the first models to be brought back into production. An excellent revolver, it's made mostly of steel, except for its lightweight alloy trigger guard and grip area. It's slightly smaller and lighter than Smith & Wesson's all-steel J-frame revolvers, such as the Chiefs Special, and it weighs only about an ounce more than S&W's alloy-framed Model 38 Bodyguard (*see* separate listing). The Off Duty also has a beryllium-copper firing pin said to be highly resistant to breakage, even after repeated dry firings. It also has a transfer bar, by which the hammer can reach the firing pin only when the trigger is pulled all the way back. This simple device goes a long way toward preventing accidental discharges.

One advantage of a revolver such as Charter Arms's Off Duty is that a shooter knows at a glance if it's ready to fire. In this view, the uncocked hammer and cartridge case rims, which are clearly visible, indicate the gun is ready to fire with a long double-action shot.

Charter Arms's Off Duty is one of the most accurate small revolvers made. This five-shot group, fired offhand from 10 feet away, measures only one inch across.

The standard stock on the original Off Duty revolver was a small wooden one, although Charter Arms's larger neoprene grips (often seen on the Bulldog revolver) will also fit. Off Duty revolvers now in production feature a good neoprene pattern with finger grooves at the front edge of the grip.

For a small revolver, the Off Duty has excellent sights that help make this a very accurate handgun in its class. It's also significantly less expensive than most of its competitors—chiefly Smith & Wesson, Colt and Taurus—and is about the same price as the Rossi revolvers. Like most small revolvers, the Off Duty kicks hard. It also hits hard at the muzzle end, especially when loaded with a round like Federal's Chiefs Special Nyclad hollowpoint. The only areas in which the Off Duty might be slightly inferior lies in its fit, finish and durability. For its price range and quality of service, though, this is an outstanding small revolver.

CHARTER ARMS OFF DUTY

Manufacturer	Years Produced	Caliber/Capacity	Dimensions
Charco Ansonia, CT	1984–Present	.38 Special/5 rounds	Barrel Length: 1.9" O.A. Length: 6.25" Height: 4.1" Width: 1.3" Weight: 17 oz. (unloaded); 19 oz. (loaded)

NAA Mini-Revolver

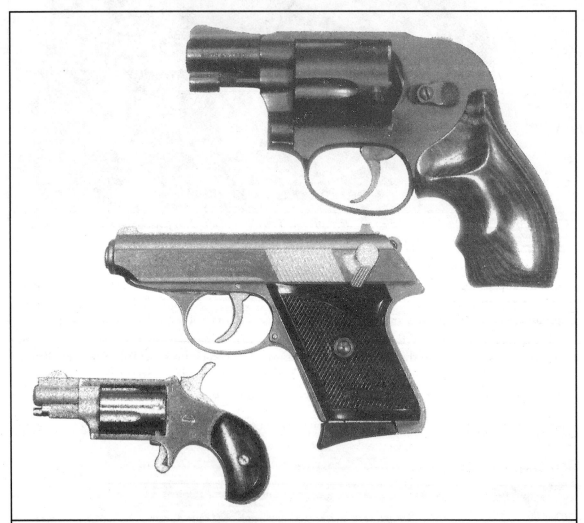

When North American Arms introduced its Mini-Revolver in .22 Short in 1974 (and a few years later in .22 LR), it succeeded in creating a well-made small firearm, albeit at the price of lower hitting power and accuracy. Its stainless steel barrel, cylinder and frame are beautifully fitted, and its smooth wooden grips fit the frame cleanly without gaps. A variation is available with a longer folding grip and longer barrel, and a .22 Magnum version is also offered (the .22 LR is recommended, however, for better control).

Safety features consist of an inertia firing pin, a sheath trigger and safety notches between the five

North American Arms's tiny Mini-Revolver (bottom) appears even more minute when compared with two other extremely portable handguns—the Smith & Wesson Model 38 (top) and the Walther TPH (center).

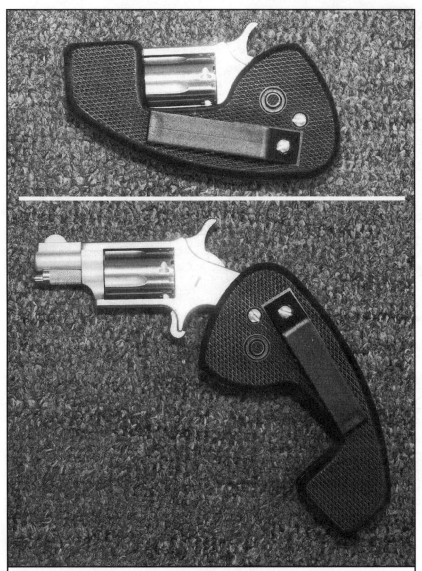

To improve the Mini-Revolver's handling, North American Arms offers an optional grip that folds into a pocket-size package (top). When deployed (bottom), it provides the shooter with a fairly substantial handle.

chambers. As an additional safety measure, most shooters opt to load only four of the five chambers, then lower the hammer onto the empty chamber. Reloading is slow because the cylinder must first be removed and the empty cartridge casings pushed out with a cylinder pin before the tiny .22 cartridges can be stuffed back into the charge holes one by one. To save space, the Mini-Revolver is equipped with a single-action hammer mechanism and a sheath-style trigger similar to that found on many 19th century revolvers and derringers. With the hammer cocked, as shown above in the I.D. photo, the trigger protrudes from its protective sheath just enough for the shooter's finger to apply pressure.

Like everything else on this gun, the Mini-Revolver's sights are tiny. Moreover, the small bird's-head grip prevents more than one finger on the firing hand from getting a firm grip on the gun. This makes it difficult to handle the recoil, even with the ordinarily mild-mannered .22 LR cartridge. Having to cock the hammer before each shot is a further hindrance to speed and accuracy, although the hammer itself is not hard to reach. As a result, the Mini-Revolver does not offer a great deal of accuracy much beyond arm's length. With some work, though, 3-to 4-inch groups at 25 feet are possible; and practice, while certainly not much fun, is at least not too expensive using .22 LR ammunition.

Several slightly larger versions of the gun—notably the Black Widow—are also in production.

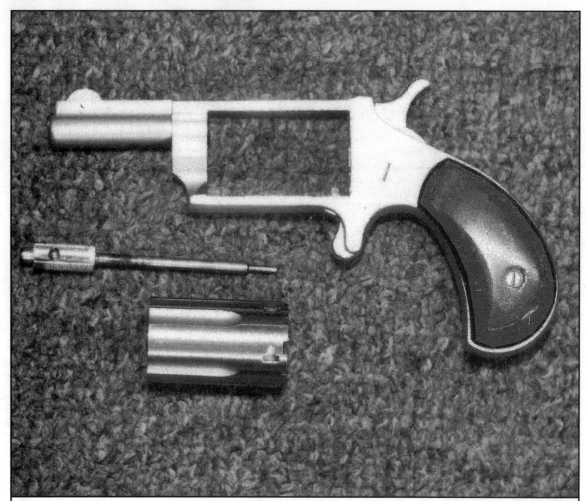

Reloading the Mini-Revolver is slow because the whole cylinder has to be removed. The cylinder retaining pin (shown here between the frame and cylinder) functions as an ejector rod.

These variations, with their larger grips and longer barrels, are sometimes chambered for the more powerful .22 Magnum cartridge. While they are more powerful than the original Mini-Revolver, these guns defeat the original purpose and inherent strength of the Mini-Revolver design. The true merit of this gun is simply this: it's the smallest revolver available. It may not be much of a gun in size, but it can defend its owner and, most important, it can go places where no other gun—not even the .25 caliber Baby Browning automatic pistol—can go.

NORTH AMERICAN ARMS MINI-REVOLVER

Manufacturer	Years Produced	Caliber/Capacity	Dimensions
North American Arms Company Spanish Fork, UT	1974–Present	.22 LR/ 5 rounds	Barrel Length: 1.1" O.A. Length: 4.0" Height: 2.9" Width: 0.8" Weight: 5 oz. (unloaded); 6 oz. (loaded)

ROSSI MODEL 68

Although Rossi ranks among the world's oldest gunmakers, having celebrated its 100th anniversary in 1988, it has been overshadowed, at least in the United States, by its fellow Brazilian competitor, Forjas Taurus. And yet, Rossi has long been a highly successful company, one that continues to make good, solid revolvers that are reasonably priced. They are well worth a close look by those who seek a small revolver for personal defense. Especially since the early 1990s, Rossi's quality has improved noticeably, making the company more competitive, even to the point of approaching Smith & Wesson's high standards. For example, Rossi's Model 68, like the Taurus Model 85 (*see* separate listing), is a close copy of Smith & Wesson's Model 36 Chiefs Special, discussed earlier.

In fact, Rossi's little handgun has been in continuous production since 1978 and has evolved into several variations to suit different needs. The standard gun comes with a 3-inch barrel (the minimum for an imported handgun barrel as mandated by the 1968 Gun Control Act); but for a small additional charge, Interarms, which markets the gun in the U.S., sells a 2-inch barrel that has been shortened in the U.S. Another variation involves grips, either a thin wooden type or a slightly larger finger-grooved neoprene one. Finally, a stainless steel version, called the Model 88 is offered (*see* next listing).

The factory neoprene grip on this Rossi Model 68 is among the fancier options available.

For reliable accuracy, the Rossi Model 68 is competitive with Smith & Wesson's Model 36, despite its slightly inferior finish and smoothness. On the other hand, the Rossi is much less expensive, running more than $100 below, on average, comparable Smith & Wesson guns.

The Model 68 performs acceptably accurate for this class of handgun. In test firing, the best five-shot, 25-foot offhand group measured 2.6 inches across. But when firing from 50 feet away, the gun's small sights and rough trigger produced groups of no better than 7.8 inches across (to be fair, though, all shots were fired in double action and offhand). When shooting at that distance, which is highly unlikely, any shooter would almost certainly have time to cock the hammer for more accurate single-

The Model 68 is quite capable of accurate fire. This five-shot, 25-foot off-hand group measures 2.6 inches. Note the two direct hits in the bull's-eye.

action firing and could even assume a braced position to improve accuracy.

The Rossi Model 68 may not be quite as smooth in operation as the revolvers produced by Smith & Wesson and Taurus, but it is well made and reliable, operates in a similar manner, accepts many of the same accessories, and is considerably less expensive. Indeed, it may not be long before Rossi overshadows Taurus, making it the "other gun made in Brazil."

ROSSI MODEL 68

Manufacturer	Years Produced	Caliber/Capacity	Dimensions
Amadeo Rossi S.A. Sáo Leopoldo, Brazil Imported by Interarms Alexandria, VA	1978–Present	.38 Special/5 rounds	Barrel Length: 2" or 3" O.A. Length: 6.5"or 7.5" Height: 4.6" Width: 1.3" Weight: 22-23 oz. (unloaded); 26-27 oz. (loaded)

ROSSI MODEL 88

The Model 88 made by Rossi beginning in 1983 is nothing more than a stainless steel version of the company's popular Model 68. All dimensions and features are the same, but early models, with their stiffer controls, were not as easy to operate as the blued version. But in two test firings, the Model 88 proved a pleasure to handle and shoot. Both smooth and accurate, it had a slick trigger pull, comfortable neoprene stocks, and a cylinder latch that operated without a hitch. On the negative side, the gun's trigger face is grooved, instead of smooth, and the sights are too small. As for concealment, the Model 88's now standard neoprene stocks can catch on clothing and cause the gun to "print" or reveal its position—something to keep in mind with any type of grip material, particularly with stocks that have checkering patterns.

Thanks to its easy trigger pull, the test Model 88 generally outperformed the blued Model 68 and, indeed, most of the small Smith & Wesson-type revolvers that were test-fired for this book. Our

ROSSI

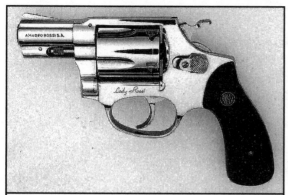

Rossi's stainless steel Model 88 "Lady Rossi" comes with a 2-inch barrel and slender rosewood grips.

With its easy trigger pull, the best five-shot 25-foot offhand group with the Model 88 measured 1.9 inches across.

best five-shot, 25-foot offhand group measured a well-centered 1.9 inches across, despite the gun's tiny sights and grooved trigger. Obviously, Rossi's Model 88 is a vastly improved gun over earlier models, and certainly its stainless steel is more durable than its blued steel counterpart. That, plus its accuracy, should help this model give stiff competition to Smith & Wesson and Taurus revolvers.

ROSSI MODEL 88

Manufacturer	Years Produced	Caliber/Capacity	Dimensions
Amadeo Rossi S.A. Sáo Leopoldo, Brazil Imported by Interarms Alexandria, VA	1983–Present	.38 Special/5 rounds	Barrel Length: 2" or 3" O.A. Length: 6.5" or 7.5" Height: 4.9" w/rubber stocks Width: 1.3" Weight: 22-23 oz. (unloaded); 26-27 oz. (loaded)

ROSSI MODEL 518

The Model 518 is the latest version of the .22 LR kit guns that Rossi has been making since the early 1980s, replacing the earlier Model 51. Rossi kit guns typically feature stainless steel finishes, 4-inch barrels and adjustable sights. The current Model 518 also comes with a choice of checkered wood or neoprene stocks.

As a multi-purpose concept, the kit gun is simple and intended primarily for carrying by campers or boaters. Self-defense is a secondary function of a kit gun. Because of this dual role, the kit gun should fire single-action shots with accuracy from a distance of up to 25 yards (for small game) as well as fire quick double-action shots at close ranges in defense against an attacking animal or human. Stainless steel or some other corrosion-resistant finish makes a great deal of sense in a gun meant primarily for outdoor use—which is no doubt why Rossi favors stainless steel for its kit guns.

This five-shot offhand group fired double-action from Rossi's Model 518 at a distance of 25 feet measures 1.7 inches across. A single-action group fired from a kit gun like Smith & Wesson's Model 34 would probably be much closer together.

Unfortunately, the Model 518 comes with a smooth-faced trigger, whereas a gun meant to be fired in the single-action mode should ideally have a grooved target-type trigger. Despite this minor complaint, the Model 518 is reasonably accurate, its trigger is smooth, and its sights are large and easy to align. Consequently, our best five-shot, 25-foot offhand group measured 1.7 inches across, with a follow-up 50-foot offhand group printing a 2.5-inch pattern. Recoil was negligible, even with CCI Stingers, one of the hottest rounds in .22 LR caliber. The only complaint concerned the gun's stiff cylinder latch, which complicated the reloading process.

Like other kit guns made by Smith & Wesson and Taurus, Rossi's Model 518 is a useful and versatile gun. And while it is not primarily intended for self-defense, it can serve that role, especially when used with high-velocity ammunition. The advantage of kit guns over more powerful revolvers and automatic pistols is their versatility. They're more likely to be around when needed, and they're easier to shoot fast and accurately than a more specialized handgun.

ROSSI MODEL 518

Manufacturer	Years Produced	Caliber/Capacity	Dimensions
Amadeo Rossi S.A. Sáo Leopoldo, Brazil Imported by Interarms Alexandria, VA	1993–Present	.22 LR/6 rounds	Barrel Length: 4" O.A. Length: 9" Height: 5.1" Width: 1.3" Weight: 30 oz. (unloaded); 31 oz.(loaded)

ROSSI 720 COVERT SPECIAL

Following its success with the Model 720 (in answer to Charter Arms's classic Bulldog), Rossi was encouraged to create a more specialized version with a specific intent: concealed carry. The result was the Model 720 Covert Special.

The chief differences between it and Rossi's standard Model 720 (*see Complete Guide to Service Handguns*, the companion volume) is the latter's bobbed hammer, making it fall flush with the rear of the frame and rendering it double-action only. Also, the Covert Special's sights are the low-profile, fixed style, and its barrel is a bit thinner. In other respects, the Covert Special is just like the standard Model 720: a five-shot, small-frame revolver in .44 Special with finger-grooved neoprene stocks and stainless steel finish.

Rossi's Model 720 Covert Special is an offbeat gun with lots of appeal. This five-shot offhand group fired from 25 feet measures just 1.2 inches across.

The Covert Special is a smooth-handling gun that could easily pass for a similar revolver made by Smith & Wesson, Colt or Ruger. Some Rossi-made revolvers are a trifle rough in fit and finish compared to more expensive revolvers—but not this one. Our best five-shot, 25-foot offhand group measured only 1.2 inches across, despite sights that are small and hard to see. This accuracy is clearly attributable to the trigger, which is extraordinarily smooth and pulls through smoothly without a hitch, making it easy in turn to place shots closer together. Despite the Covert Special's small frame, recoil was not unpleasant and the gun was easy to fire. Its added weight—half a pound or so heavier than a Charter Arms Bulldog—definitely improves its handling.

The Covert Special is a most impressive, easily concealable revolver that fires a cartridge widely respected for its stopping power. All it needs are improved sights and a smooth trigger face.

ROSSI 720 COVERT SPECIAL

Manufacturer	Years Produced	Caliber/Capacity	Dimensions
Amadeo Rossi S.A. Sáo Leopoldo, Brazil Imported by Interarms Alexandria, VA	1992–Present	.44 Special/5 rounds	Barrel Length: 3" O.A. Length: 9" Height: 5.1" Width: 1.35" Weight: 27 oz. (unloaded); 32 oz. (loaded)

ROSSI MODEL 971 COMP

Rossi's popular Model 971 comes in a number of variations. The compensated version discussed here is the one most suitable for concealment purposes, due to its thin, contoured rubber stocks and its relatively short barrel. First produced in 1993, the Model 971 Comp is available at this writing in stainless finish only, with a fluted cylinder holding up to six shots of .357 Magnum or .38 Special. The rear sight is adjustable and, in contrast with the gun's light-colored stainless frame, dark with a white outline that contrasts sharply with a red insert on the front sight. The front surface of the trigger is smooth, and trigger pull in both double action and single action is easy. Although the bolt cuts for the cylinder are placed right over the cylinder holes, there's no weakening of the cylinder so long as .357 Magnum ammunition made by a reputable manufacturer is used.

Despite its relatively small dimensions, the Model 971 Comp handles the .357 cartridge quite well. The compensator, consisting of two ports cut into the last half-inch of the barrel, does a fine job

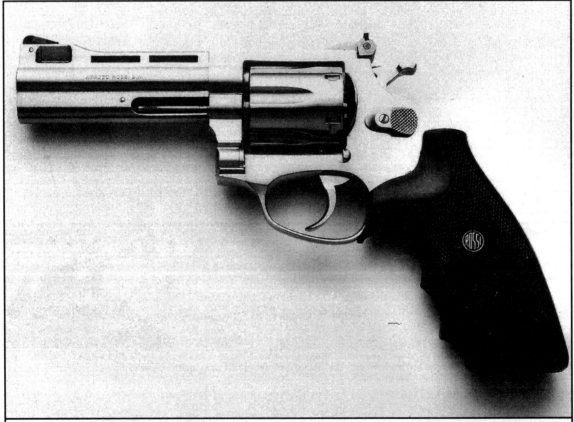

The Rossi .357 Magnum Model 971 now comes in a vent-rib version with 2.5-, 4- or 6-inch barrel.

The Rossi Model 971 Comp produced this five-shot offhand group fired from 25 feet and measuring 2.4 inches across.

of reducing muzzle climb and holding down recoil. Nevertheless, the powerful .357 Magnum cartridges still manage to create a large ball of flame at the muzzle. In testing, the best five-shot, rapid-fire offhand group fired from 25 feet measured 2.4 inches. All controls, including the trigger, cylinder latch and ejector rod, are smooth and easy to operate. In short, the Model 971 Comp is the best of the 971-type revolvers and, with its integral compensator, offers a different wrinkle.

ROSSI MODEL 971 COMP

Manufacturer	Years Produced	Caliber/Capacity	Dimensions
Amadeo Rossi S.A. Sáo Leopoldo, Brazil Imported by Interarms Alexandria, VA	1993–Present	.357 Magnum/ 6 rounds	Barrel Length: 3.25" O.A. Length: 9" Height: 5.4" Width: 1.45" Weight: 32 oz. (unloaded); 35 oz. (loaded)

RUGER SP101

When Ruger introduced the compact Model SP101 in 1988 (along with the service-sized GP100 revolver—*see Complete Guide to Service Handguns*), its most significant improvement over the popular, but older Model Speed-Six was its added strength. The SP101 was also quite versatile in that it was available in several calibers, including .22 LR, .32 H&R Magnum, 9mm, .38 Special and .357 Magnum. The .22 LR and .32 H&R Magnum caliber SP101s came with a 6-shot cylinder, while the other sported 5- shot cylinders. All are finished in stainless steel only.

As for accuracy, the SP101 in 9mm and .38 Special is a delight to shoot, although in .357 Magnum it's tough on the hands. The 9mm version comes with 10 "full moon" clips, each holding a complete cylinder of five rounds. The clips act as a speedloader and are easily dropped into the cylinder. Another advantage of a 9mm revolver over an automatic pistol in the same caliber is that revolvers will fire hollowpoints just as readily as FMJ bullets; whereas automatic pistols, particularly older ones, may not always feed hollowpoints with total reliability. In testing the Model SP101, our best five-shot, 25-foot offhand group using Winchester Silvertips measured 2.6 inches across; and at 50 feet, when fired under the same conditions, the group measured 3.7 inches across. These are quite acceptable results.

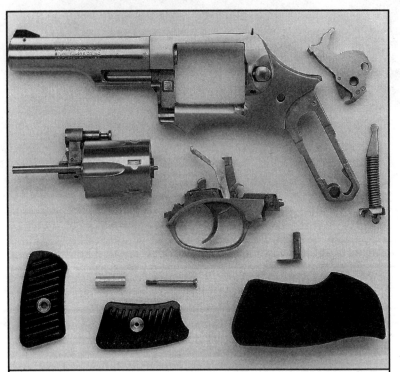

Ruger's SP101 can be fieldstripped in a matter of seconds without special tools. Available with 2-inch, 3¹/₁₆-inch or 4-inch barrel, this compact revolver comes in four different caliber offerings.

Like the similar Model GP100, the SP101 is easy to disassemble and reassemble, which is unusual for a revolver. This capability also becomes a very useful feature for weapons that need extensive cleaning. The SP101's only shortcomings, when compared to Smith & Wesson revolvers, are its larger size and slightly higher cost. Still, this excellent small revolver is readily concealable and stronger than most competing designs.

This five-shot offhand group, all double-action, was fired from the SP101 at 25 feet and measured 2.6 inches. At 50 feet, another 5-shot offhand group in double-action measured 3.7 inch.

RUGER SP101

Manufacturer	Years Produced	Caliber/Capacity	Dimensions
Sturm, Ruger and Co. Southport, CT	1988–Present	.22 LR or .32 H&R Magnum/6 rounds 9mm, .38 Special or .357 Magnum/5 rounds	Barrel Length: 2.25"-4" O.A. Length: 7.5"-9.75" Height: 5" Width: 1.33" Weight: 25-27 oz. (unloaded); 34 oz. max. (loaded, .22 LR)

S&W MODEL 34

Smith & Wesson introduced its first "modern"
.22-caliber revolver in 1911, but it was actually a
large, long-barreled target shooting model on a .32-caliber
frame, quite unlike the much smaller and handier Model 34
covered here. The concept of a "kit gun" in .22 Long Rifle caliber designed to accompany campers or fishermen came about
later, with production starting up in 1936. Manufacture stopped
several years later while Smith & Wesson turned its attention to World War II demand;
after the war, production of both the Target and Kit Gun models resumed.

The Model 34 Kit Gun dates from 1953. Mechanically, it resembles any S&W J-frame revolver, except for changes required to suit its original purpose as an outdoorsman's handgun. For example, a gun designed to kill small animals demands greater accuracy than is usually expected of a small revolver meant strictly for self-defense. For that reason, the Model 34 had an adjustable rear sight, a high ramped front sight, and a target-style hammer for easier thumb-cocking than other J-frame revolvers made by Smith & Wesson. And because the .22 LR charge holes in its cylinder are much narrower than those needed to fit .38 Special cartridges, this model can accommodate

With its adjustable sights and wide target trigger, Smith & Wesson's Model 34 J-frame kit gun is generally used for plinking, shooting small-game animals and personal defense. In .22 LR caliber, it offers the qualities of other Smith & Wesson J-frame revolvers with much less recoil and one extra shot.

up to six rounds (instead of only five). The Model 34 features an all-steel construction and has the same short 2-inch (actually 1.9-inch) barrel and rounded butt found on .38 Special J-frame guns; however, other barrel lengths and such options as square butts and lightweight alloy frames were also made available.

Despite its primary use as an outdoorsman's gun, the Model 34 should also be seriously considered as a defensive handgun. Along with its excellent reliability, it produces much less recoil than other S&W J-frame guns, and it has that one extra shot. Moreover, its adjustable rear sight can be dialed in the proper sight setting for whatever brand of ammunition is carried.

Most automatic pistols in .22 Long Rifle, when used for defensive purposes, too often seize up or misfire. But the Model 34 and the somewhat similar Taurus Model 94 (*see* separate listing) have addressed these shortcomings more than most other rimfire handguns. The reason is, of course, that they are revolv-

In test-firing a Model 34 in double-action mode at 25 feet, a 2.6-inch pattern emerged, with five of the six shots measuring only 1.9 inches.

ers. Should a dud round occur, one simply pulls the trigger again—an instinctive reaction that takes a minimum amount of time. The revolving cylinder automatically swings the malfunctioning cylinder charge hole out of the way and brings up another loaded with a more reliable round.

For shooting small game, a Model 34 in single-action mode offers a light single-action pull weight of less than five pounds and a large, clear sight picture. Out to 50 feet or so, the Model 34 is extremely accurate, but for defensive shooting at much closer ranges, and with less time to line up a shot, the Model 34 becomes a double-action weapon. As such, it test-fires an offhand group of 2.25 inches at 35 feet and 3.8 inches at 50 feet, respectively. For a small revolver in double-action mode, this is acceptable shooting. A .22-caliber automatic pistol may often produce better accuracy, but an automatic pistol using a rimfire cartridge is not a combination to inspire much confidence when reliable feeding and ignition are required.

As a training handgun, a kit gun or a defensive piece, the versatile Model 34, combined with S&W's outstanding reputation, is a viable choice.

S&W MODEL 34

Manufacturer	Years Produced	Caliber/Capacity	Dimensions
Smith & Wesson Springfield, MA	1953–1991	.22 LR/6 rounds	Barrel Length: 2" O.A. Length: 6.3" Height: 4.5" Width: 1.3" Weight: 21 oz.(unloaded); 22 oz.(loaded)

S&W MODEL 37

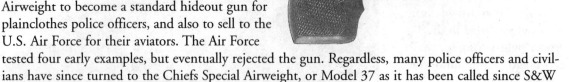

Smith & Wesson introduced its upgraded Chiefs Special Airweight on September 12, 1952, only two years after making the first Chiefs Special. The first model had reached serial number 1795 in the J-frame serial number range, beginning at "1" in 1950. Smith & Wesson had wanted the Chiefs Special Airweight to become a standard hideout gun for plainclothes police officers, and also to sell to the U.S. Air Force for their aviators. The Air Force tested four early examples, but eventually rejected the gun. Regardless, many police officers and civilians have since turned to the Chiefs Special Airweight, or Model 37 as it has been called since S&W began assigning model designations in 1957. Largely because it weighs a full ounce less than the Model 38 *(see* next listing), which until then had been the lightest production J-frame revolver, the Model 37 has enjoyed enduring popularity.

The first Chiefs Special Airweights—some 3,777—featured aluminum-alloy cylinders and frames. The only steel parts were the barrel, cylinder crane and lockwork. Following Air Force testing and complaints from police and civilian shooters, Smith & Wesson concluded that the lightweight aluminum cylinder was causing the gun to jam and simply wasn't strong enough. As a result, all Model 37s made since early 1954 have a steel barrel and cylinder (the aluminum-alloy frame was retained, however). At one time, S&W also offered the Model 37 in a larger, square-butt frame with a 3-inch barrel, but that type was discontinued. Two-inch barrels are now available, as are compact round-butt frames in blue or nickel finish. Oddly, Smith & Wesson has never offered the Model 37 in stainless steel, even though numerous other S&W revolvers, including small ones, have been available in that metal.

The Smith & Wesson Model 37 Airweight Chiefs Special has a lightweight aluminum-alloy frame that reduces its weight by nearly half a pound from the original all-steel version. The satin nickel finish shown above may be a better choice than blue for wear resistance, but it's much more conspicuous when concealment is important.

Because of its light weight, the Model 37 has a heavy recoil and can therefore be painful to shoot.

Shooters are advised to use Federal's Nyclad Chiefs Special load, featuring a 125-grain, nylon-coated soft lead hollowpoint. Expanding at slightly more than 700 feet per second, this low speed makes it unnecessary to increase the muzzle velocity to high levels, thereby increasing chamber pressure and the recoil impulse. Another advantage of Federal's Nyclad round is the low amount of pollution it produces, especially at indoor ranges.

Another useful tip for those planning to do some serious shooting with a Smith & Wesson J-frame revolver, especially such lightweight alloy-framed models as the Model 37, is to acquire a Spegel Boot Grip. By filling in the area just behind the trigger guard, the Boot Grip, which is available in smooth wood or checkered rubber, helps control recoil without adding bulk. Interestingly, Smith & Wesson began offering this grip in late 1993 on some of its J-framed revolvers.

Clearly, the Model 37 is a gun meant to be carried a lot but seldom used. Its trigger is not as smooth as a regular all-steel Chiefs Special, and it definitely transmits a strong kick into its tiny, narrow grips. Still, with practice and judicious ammunition selection, the Model 37 is capable of acceptable accuracy. In testing in the double-action trigger mode, our best five-shot, 25-foot offhand group measured 1.8 inches across; and at 50 feet the group measured 4.6 inches across using Federal's Nyclad load. One good feature of the Model 37 is how easy the exposed hammer can be cocked for more deliberate single-action shooting—time and circumstances permitting.

With practice, a Smith & Wesson Model 37 revolver can be reasonably accurate at close ranges. This five-shot, 25-foot offhand group measured 1.8 inches. At longer ranges to ensure greater accuracy, shooters can cock the exposed hammer for easier single-action trigger pulls.

For those who seek a gun light enough for carrying in a pocket or ankle holster, yet with the power of a .38 Special and the reliability and low maintenance of a revolver, the Model 37 is a top choice. Some may prefer the odd-looking Model 38 with its shrouded hammer, but the Model 37 weighs an ounce less and carries the more traditional styling of a Chiefs Special.

S&W MODEL 37

Manufacturer	Years Produced	Caliber/Capacity	Dimensions
Smith & Wesson Springfield, MA	1952–Present	.38 Special/5 rounds	Barrel Length: 2" O.A. Length: 6.5" Height: 4.4" Width: 1.3" Weight: 13.5 oz.(unloaded); 16 oz.(loaded)

S&W MODEL 38

Smith & Wesson first introduced the Model 38 as the "Bodyguard Airweight" in 1955 at serial number 66,000 (in the J-frame serial number range). The designation "Model 38" came about in 1957. The earlier Bodyguard's most distinctive feature was its humpbacked shape, which was created by extending the frame to cover all but the very tip of the hammer. This odd-looking effect had the significant advantage of making the revolver extremely smooth in shape and not likely to snag when drawn from a pocket. Unlike the Centennial series of guns, with their totally concealed hammers, the Bodyguard's hammer could still be thumb-cocked by shooters who preferred the single-action shot. The original Bodyguard also featured a lightweight aluminum-alloy frame, which Smith & Wesson still makes. But later on, the company added a steel-framed version—the Model 49—followed by an all-stainless steel version, called the Model 649. All three guns are still in production and remain S&W's most popular revolver types. Like the Model 37, the Model 38 is universally popular with police departments and civilian shooters as well as the U.S. military and other

S&W's Model 38 "Bodyguard" on the Chiefs Special J-frame features the characteristic hump shown at the rear of the frame. The steel shroud partially conceals the hammer and smooths the gun's contours. Although it is easy to carry, it is not smooth to fire. With practice, however, it is gratifyingly accurate, as demonstrated by this five-shot, 25-foot offhand group measuring 1.4 inches.

Replacing the standard factory wooden stocks with, say, Uncle Mike's neoprene "Boot Grip" (shown above) is an effective way to tame the fierce recoil of the J-frame revolvers like the Model 38 without spoiling their superb concealability. A host of holsters and other accessories have been made for these popular handguns.

government agencies.

Weighing only an ounce more than the Model 37, all cautions and recommendations about the Model 38 mirror those for the Model 37. In testing the former, our best five-shot, 25-foot offhand group measured 1.4 inches across, while a follow-up five-shot, 50-foot offhand group came in at 4.9 inches across, all using the Federal 125-grain Nyclad Chiefs Special load and fired exclusively in double-action mode.

The Model 38 is a prime choice for those who seek a .38 Special revolver light enough for pocket or ankle holster carry. The chief advantage of the Model 38 over the Model 37 is its integral hammer shroud, which adds only an ounce to its weight but makes it much easier to draw quickly when needed. Despite its age, the Model 38 remains the gun to beat for compact, portable power in a handgun.

S&W MODEL 38

Manufacturer	Years Produced	Caliber/Capacity	Dimensions
Smith & Wesson Springfield, MA	1955–Present	.38 Special/5 rounds	Barrel Length: 2" O.A. Length: 6.3" Height: 4.4" Width: 1.3" Weight: 14.5 oz. (unloaded); 17 oz. (loaded)

S&W MODELS 442, 640 & 940

Smith & Wesson's current Centennial series of revolvers is, for all practical purposes, a slightly modified reissue of the famous Model 40 Centennial revolver. First introduced in 1952, it was a logical update of the famous Smith & Wesson Safety Hammerless revolver (please see page 20). The Model 40 Centennial featured a concealed hammer completely enclosed within the frame, making it a kind of "hammerless" design. Like the Safety Hammerless, the Model 40 Centennial had a grip safety, but many shooters preferred to deactivate their safeties by attaching them to the frame with a roll pin provided by Smith & Wesson.

Although the Model 40 Centennial went out of production in 1974, its design was so popular and its discontinuance so lamented that Smith & Wesson reintroduced a modified stainless steel Centennial in 1990, called the Model 640. This sleek, compact gun has proven so popular that S&W has already placed four major variants in production:

1. The Model 442 Centennial "Airweight," a .38 Special version with blued finish and lightweight aluminum-alloy frame.

2. & 3. The Model 640, a stainless steel gun made from 1990 to 1994 in .38 Special caliber, later appearing in a .357 Magnum version (making it one of the smallest production .357 Magnum revolvers ever made).

4. The Model 940, introduced in 1991, fires the 9mm Parabellum cartridge usually associated with automatic pistols and submachine guns. The standard .38 Special Model 640 discontinued in 1994 has wooden grips. The current Model 640 in .357, the 1993-vintage Centennial Airweight and the current Model 940 all use Spegel's/Uncle Mike's neoprene boot grip to hold down the recoil created for small guns that fire powerful cartridges.

Let's turn now to a more complete look at each revolver in the Centennial series.

Model 442. The Model 442 Centennial Airweight ranks without a doubt among the most appealing small revolvers ever made. It differs from earlier Smith & Wesson J-frame airweight revolvers mainly because of its totally concealed hammer. While this deprives the gun of a single-action capability, the smooth contours that result are a big advantage. There's simply nothing to catch or snag on this gun, whereas the otherwise similar Model 37 Chiefs Special Airweight has a large spur hammer that invariably hangs up in pocket lining. Unlike the Model 38 Bodyguard, which features a partially exposed hammer, the Centennial Airweight is virtually impervious to lint and other items that can gum up the workings of a revolver. As a further advantage of the Centennial's enclosed hammer design, the rear portion of the frame enables the shooter to hold the gun lower in the hand, thus reducing recoil.

Accuracy is good, especially for a gun that can be fired only double action. Moreover, S&W has done a good job of lightening and shortening the trigger pull—not an easy thing to do in a small handgun. In testing the Model 442 at a range of 10 feet, we placed all five shots in a 1.3-inch group;

Smith & Wesson's Model 442 Centennial Airweight in satin nickel makes a good choice for corrosion resistance in humid or salty climates.

This five-shot offhand group fired from the Model 442 Centennial Airweight from a distance of 10 feet measures 1.3 inches across. At 25 feet, another group measured 2.3 inches across.

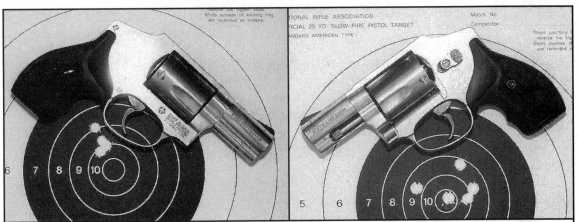

In .357 Magnum, S&W's Centennial Model 640 (the earlier version could fire only .38 Special) was a brilliant marketing move and is a formidable weapon for personal protection at close ranges. Although the gun is a handful to shoot, the five-shot group (left) fired from a distance of 10 feet measures .7 inch across. Another group (right), fired from a distance of 25 feet, measures 1.8 inches across.

and at 25 feet, our shots went into a 2.3-inch pattern. Ammunition used in these test firings was Federal Nyclad Chiefs Special 125-grain bullets in both standard pressure and P+. All in all, the Model 442 Centennial Airweight is an appealing compact handgun, made all the more so by its smooth contours compared to Smith & Wesson's Models 37 and 38.

Model 640. Smith & Wesson's decision to chamber the Model 640 in .357 Magnum, the most powerful defensive handgun cartridge, was a clever idea. To make this diminutive J-frame gun so that it could accommodate the big cartridge, Smith & Wesson changed the heat treatment of the metals used and also slightly lengthened both cylinder and barrel. The great power afforded by the .357 Magnum cartridge comes at a price, however. Recoil is impressive, even with a boot grip and lengthened barrel. Testing this gun resulted in the following responses: "Attention-getting . . . stinging recoil . . . lots of noise and muzzle flash . . . poor extraction. But still, it's an accurate and powerful gun." For some, though, the improvement in ballistic performance made possible by using the .357 Magnum cartridge will undoubtedly be worth the additional noise and recoil. Most likely, as with the similar Taurus Model 605 (*see* separate listing), the Model 640 will probably be fired most often with .38 Special and P+ rounds.

To give this gun in .357 its due, we found it extremely accurate up close. One five-shot offhand group fired from a distance of 10 feet measured a mere 3/4-inch across. Many revolvers chambered for the .357 Magnum cartridge suffer reduced accuracy when fired with shorter .38 Special rounds, however, and the Model 640 may be one of them. In firing .38 Special P+ rounds from a distance of 25 feet, our best five-shot offhand group measured 2.8 inches across. When using .38 (as opposed to .357) ammunition, one trades reduced power and accuracy for much less recoil and better extraction of spent cartridge casings. The decision whether to use .357 or .38 in a contemporary Model 640 comes down to each shooter's desires. A good compromise, if needed, is Remington's 125 grain Medium Velocity .357 round. Developed for Ruger's Model SP-101—the first of the small .357 Magnum revolvers to be mass-produced by a major manufacturer—Remington's Medium Velocity .357 round offers a useful compromise between power and recoil.

Model 940. Chambering a revolver for the 9mm cartridge—which is usually reserved for automatic pistols—may not seem very wise, but in the case of the Model 940 it actually makes a lot of sense, for several reasons. First, the 9mm cartridge is quite popular. Second, it's very compact for the power level it offers, making it a natural choice for a small J-frame revolver like S&W's 940. Third, the 9mm, though rimless, is easily carried in a 5-shot "full moon" clip. Since all five rounds are easily loaded at once, the Model 940 boasts nearly the same ease of reloading as the magazine-fed automatic pistol. Fourth, because the 9mm Parabellum's 19mm case length is considerably shorter than that of the .38 Special (29mm), the 940's ejector rod is long enough to extract all fired cases in one swift motion. And last, since many law enforcers are accustomed to J-frame revolvers, they've switched to 9mm.

Like other Centennial-type revolvers, the Model 940 is tough to shoot. Its workmanship, trigger pull and other attributes may be up to Smith & Wesson's high standards, but this revolver has a sharp, stinging recoil despite its well-designed rubber stocks. Also, because of the clips it uses, a "tactical reload" is impossible. Furthermore, the empties are difficult to remove. A pencil, cleaning rod or stick must be used to eject the fired cases from each cylinder. On the positive side, though, this five-cartridge clip is a handy, compact speedloader-type apparatus.

As with any Smith & Wesson snub-nosed J-frame revolver, accuracy is possible, but only after a

Chambering the Model 940 in 9mm Parabellum caliber makes this powerful little revolver an excellent backup gun for 9mm pistol owners.

A five-shot offhand group fired from the Model 940 measures 2.2 inches across. The four shots directly beneath the gun form a 1.4-inch pattern (the fifth shot went wide).

lot of work. Our best five-shot 50-foot offhand group, using Winchester Silvertip 115-grain hollow-points, measured 1.9 inches across. At 25 feet, the group measured 3.6 inches across, this time using P+ Cor-Bons 115-grain jacketed hollowpoints. P+ Cor-Bons are particularly unpleasant to shoot in this revolver, and even the standard pressure Silvertips kicked hard. Despite its heavy recoil and the need for carrying clipped ammunition, however, the Model 940 does make sense for shooters who like the reliability of a revolver along with the concealability of the 940's J-frame size, and who prefer the 9mm cartridge.

Overall, the modern Smith & Wesson Centennial revolver series offers superb workmanship and an impressive level of power considering its size. In fact, these small revolvers have so many appealing features that their lack of a single-action trigger capability is hardly missed.

S&W CENTENNIAL MODELS 442, 640 AND 940

Manufacturer	Years Produced	Caliber/Capacity	Dimensions
Smith & Wesson Springfield, MA	1990–Present	.38 Spec. (442), .357 (640), 9mm (940)/ 5 rounds (all)	(Model 940 except as noted) Barrel Length: 2" (2⅛" 640) O.A. Length: 6.3" Height: 4.5" Width: 1.3" Weight (unloaded): 16 oz. (442), 20 oz. (640), 23 oz. (940); 25.5 oz. (loaded)

S&W MODEL 651

Smith & Wesson first introduced its Model 651 in 1983. The gun went out of production in 1987 and was reintroduced in 1991 in .22 Magnum, the company's intention being to offer a small, J-frame rimfire revolver with slightly more power than its famous .22 LR Kit guns. The addition of stainless steel metallurgy was designed to make the Model 651 still more attractive to shooters who

This five-shot, 25-foot offhand group fired from a Model 651 revolver measures 1.8 inches. Loaded with six .22 Magnum rounds, this gun is both accurate and powerful.

worked, lived and traveled outdoors. Among its quality touches is the use of counterbored cylinders, thereby enclosing the head of rimfire cartridges in metal in case of a head separation. The newer version also offers finger-grooved synthetic round-butt grips as opposed to the original thin wooden J-frame stocks. Another nice touch is the Model 651's smooth combat trigger; conversely, its wide hammer and adjustable sights are more suited to a target gun than a defensive handgun.

It should come as no surprise, then, that the Model 651 is accurate and easy to shoot and has almost no recoil. Moreover, its wide adjustable rear notch sight and orange-insert ramp front sight combine to produce a large, clear sight picture. Its action is not quite as smooth as that found on most Smith & Wesson revolvers, but it is good enough. Our best five-shot, 25-foot offhand group measured 1.8 inches across, while at 50 feet another group measured 3.4 inches. CCI Maxi Mag ammunition was used for all groups fired.

For someone who needs a versatile outdoor gun for hunting small animals, while retaining a viable self-defense capability, the Model 651 could be a wise choice. Less powerful than a .38 Special revolver, it still offers adequate stopping power, one extra shot, and next to no recoil.

S&W MODEL 651

Manufacturer	Years Produced	Caliber/Capacity	Dimensions
Smith & Wesson Springfield, MA	1983–1987 1991–Present	.22 Magnum/ 6 rounds	Barrel Length: 4.0" O.A. Length: 8.7" Height: 4.8" Width: 1.3" Weight: 24.5 oz. (unloaded); 27 oz. (loaded)

TAURUS

TAURUS MODEL 65

The Model 65 made by Forjas Taurus of Brazil has been in production since 1978, but until 1993 it was available only as a service revolver for open-holster carry. It also featured a square butt and a 3- or 4-inch barrel. Taurus now offers a variation of the Model 65, which includes a rounded butt and shortened 2.5-inch barrel. These changes, among others, including a stainless steel version (shown above), have made the Model 65 a better revolver for concealment purposes. Based closely on Smith & Wesson's excellent Model 13/65 series, the Taurus Model 65 has been updated with coil springs and a transfer-bar safety mechanism that allows the gun to fire only when the trigger is all the way to the rear.

The Smith & Wesson Military & Police can chamber and fire .357 Magnum ammunition, but the Models 13 and 65 are at their best with .38 Special ammunition. That's how the FBI and many local police departments, which once used the Model 13 and Model 19 Combat Magnum exclusively with .38 +P

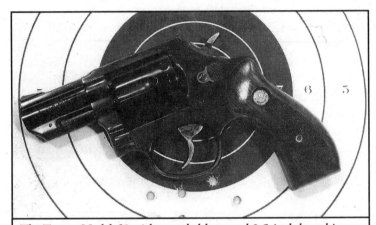

The Taurus Model 65 with rounded butt and 2.5-inch barrel is a viable concealment revolver, similar to smaller versions of the Smith & Wesson Model 13/65 series. The Taurus Model 65 proved better when fired with .38 than with .357 ammunition, as demonstrated by this 2.4-inch group at 25 feet using Cor-Bon +P+.

ammunition, feed them. After firing the Taurus Model 65 with both .38 Special +P+ and full-power .357 Magnum loads, it became obvious to us that this revolver is at its best with .38 Special. Our best five-shot offhand group fired from 25 feet measured 2.4 inches using Cor-Bon .38 Special +P+. Under the same conditions, the .357 Magnum load went into 3.2 inches. The recoil and muzzle flash with the .357 were also much more pronounced. Still, having a gun with this flexibility is most desirable.

Taurus offers excellent quality in its Model 65—combined with the easy concealability offered by the 2.5-inch barrel and rounded butt—at a very competitive price.

TAURUS MODEL 65

Manufacturer	Years Produced	Caliber/Capacity	Dimensions
Forjas Taurus S.A. Porto Alegre, Brazil Imported by Taurus Int'l. Miami, FL	1978–Present	.357 Magnum/ 6 rounds	Barrel Lengths: 2.5", 4" O.A. Length: 8.0" (2.5" bbl.) Height: 5.3" Width: 1.45" Weight: 34 oz. (unloaded); 37.5 oz. (loaded)

TAURUS MODEL 85

When Taurus introduced its Model 85 in 1980, the aim was to compete with Smith & Wesson's Model 36 Chiefs Special and the like. The Model 85 has since become one of the company's best-selling revolvers ever. Highly popular with police (and also civilians) as a backup handgun, it compares favorably with Smith & Wesson's similar—and sensationally successful—J-frame revolvers.

Taurus offers the Model 85 in blued, nickel (discontinued in 1993) and stainless steel finishes, with either 2-inch or 3-inch barrels. For concealment purposes, the 2-inch barrel makes more sense; but the 3-inch barrel has a longer ejection rod, making the removal of fired cartridge casings almost foolproof. In addition, the Model 85 retains the compact size and fine performance of the Chiefs Special. Its quality of workmanship is also comparable despite a price difference of more than $125 (blued).

In some respects, the Model 85 actually improves on its competition. For example, it includes a shrouded ejector rod and frame-mounted firing pin, neither of which is found in Smith & Wesson's J-frame revolvers. It can also fire +P ammunition, albeit on a limited basis, something not recommended for most small Smith & Wesson revolvers. The Model 85's sturdy grips are also preferred by many shooters to the skinny ones found on S&W's smallest revolvers. The Taurus grips give the shooter more to hold onto, an important consideration in a small revolver when firing the .38 Special cartridge.

The stainless steel Taurus Model 85 tested for this book was not especially accurate, however. Our

One feature of the Taurus Model 85 (above right) that sets it apart from a Smith & Wesson J-frame like the Model 37 (left) is the former's slightly larger and fuller stock (inset).

best 25-foot offhand group placed five shots in a broad 3.1-inch pattern, using Winchester Silvertip 125-grain +P hollowpoints. Two other groups at the same distance measured 3.5 inches across with Federal's 125-grain Nyclad Chief's Special. At 50 feet, using the same Federal ammunition, the group measured about 6 inches across.

Recoil with the Model 85 is not excessive, even with +P ammunition, but it lacks the smoothness of operation characteristic of a Smith & Wesson. The Taurus trigger, cylinder latch and ejection rod are all rougher and less fluid in their motion. This model sacrifices a little in handling in exchange for a lower price.

The Taurus Model 85 (top) features a coil mainspring exactly like Smith & Wesson J-frame revolvers. Even the shape of the butt portion of the frame is nearly identical.

TAURUS MODEL 85

Manufacturer	Years Produced	Caliber/Capacity	Dimensions
Forjas Taurus S.A. Porto Alegre, Brazil Imported by Taurus Int'l. Miami, FL	1980–Present	.38 Special/5 rounds	Barrel Lengths: 2" and 3" O.A. Length: 7.1" (2" bbl.) Height: 4.8" Width: 1.3" Weight: 21 oz. (unloaded); 23.5 oz. (loaded)

TAURUS MODELS 85CH & 85CHS

The Model 85CH was introduced by Taurus in 1991 to compete with Smith & Wesson's Model 38 Bodyguard, the S&W Centennial series and other revolvers featuring frames that are concealed or "hammerless." As its designation indicates, the Model 85CH has a concealed hammer. In Smith & Wesson's concealed-hammer designs, a frame extension conceals the hammer at all times, whereas the concealed hammer on the Model 85CH is bobbed. It sits flush in the frame until the trigger is pulled, at which point the hammer becomes visible for an instant before slamming forward and firing the gun. Unlike the standard Model 85 and most other revolvers based on Smith & Wesson's J-frame line, the hammer on the Model 85CH is double-action only and cannot be cocked at all for single-action firing. Several firearms experts maintain that having the trigger operate only in a single mode of operation is an advantage from both legal and tactical standpoints, although some disagree, preferring the single-action option (for example, when a long-range shot is necessary to prevent a crime from occurring).

Unlike the standard Model 85 with its large, checkered wooden stocks, the Model 85CH has a slimmer, banana-shaped grip made of smooth wood. Two examples of the Model 85CH were tested for this book: one blued and the other stainless steel (shown above). Based on that experience, we feel the standard Model 85 handles somewhat better and is easier to hold. Its larger, checkered grips give the shooter a better handle on the gun when firing, and their smooth, curved shape lessens recoil. When deciding between the Model 85 and the Model 85CH, it's advisable to test-fire both guns first.

The hammer spur on the Taurus Model 85CH has been cut away to make it flush with the rear of the frame (inset). Thus, the hammer can be cocked only by pulling the trigger.

Buying a gun is like buying a pair of shoes—what fits one individual may not work at all for another.

In testing accuracy, our best 25-foot offhand group, using the standard blued Model 85CH, placed five shots in a 1.4-inch pattern, with the stainless steel variation producing a 1.25-inch group at that distance. Our best 50-foot group fired from the blued gun was 3.4 inches across, while the stainless gun gave us a 2.4-inch group. The triggers on both guns were heavy and not as smooth as a standard Model 85 (which took Taurus several years longer to develop). For all Model 85 variants and other J-frame revolvers, Federal's 125-grain Nyclad Chief's Special is the preferred defensive load. Its efficient bullet design allows it to expand at the modest velocities that this model's short barrels can impart to a bullet. Save that high-powered +P ammunition for the medium-frame, longer-barreled revolvers that can make better use of it.

The design of the Model 85CH enabled Taurus to develop a concealed-hammer variant quickly and at minimal cost. Its one disadvantage—compared to the Smith & Wesson revolvers that feature fully concealed hammers—occurs in a quick-draw situation. Unlike the S&W Models 38/49/649 Bodyguard series and the Centennial-type revolvers, firing right out of a pocket with the Taurus revolver will almost certainly cause a malfunction, because the hammer is sure to get caught in the pocket lining. For this reason, and because of S&W's smoother concealed-hammer revolvers, the Model 85CH is not recommended. On the

This well-centered five-shot offhand group, measuring 2.25 inches, was fired with a Taurus Model 85CH from a distance of 25 feet.

other hand, the Model 85CH does offer equally reliable functioning at a lower price. Should Taurus ever decide to add an alloy-framed lightweight version of its Models 85 and 85CH, then it will certainly have a J-frame line designed to take on Smith & Wesson.

TAURUS MODELS 85CH AND 85CHS

Manufacturer	Years Produced	Caliber/Capacity	Dimensions
Forjas Taurus S.A. Porto Alegre, Brazil Imported by Taurus Int'l. Miami, FL	1991–Present	.38 Special/5 rounds	Barrel Length: 2" O.A. Length: 6.5" Height: 4.75" Width: 1.3" Weight: 21 oz. (unloaded); 23.5 oz. (loaded)

TAURUS MODEL 94

The Model 94, which made its debut in 1989, is an extremely interesting multi-shot revolver. With the .22 Long Rifle round being so much smaller than a .38 Special round, it's obvious that many more rounds can be placed in the Model 94's cylinder without sacrificing its reasonable size. Rather than limiting the rimfire revolver to six rounds, as if it were a larger centerfire cartridge, Taurus has produced an accurate, reliable nine-shot revolver. In essence, it's a kit gun with the firepower of an automatic pistol.

The Model 94 features the same basic action of the Model 85 from which it was devel-

The Taurus Model 94 is not a target shooter, at least not in double-action trigger mode; but this five-shot, 1.3-inch group at 25 feet is certainly acceptable for defensive shooting. A rapid-fire cylinder full of nine rounds from a Taurus Model 94 also produced an impressive group; thus it would make a powerful deterrent even in the small .22 LR caliber.

oped; in fact, some of the parts are interchangeable. Its smooth trigger and adjustable sights help accuracy, and recoil is negligible, making rapid-fire easy. Our best five-shot group at 25 feet measured 1.3 inches, and at 50 feet it covered 2.8 inches.

With nine casings to eject, the ejector rod on the Model 94 does not always remove the empties with a single stroke. But nine rounds, even of the relatively low-powered .22 LR, offer a lot of shooting before one has to reload. Moreover, its low recoil, accuracy, simplicity and large cylinder capacity make this model a serious possibility as a defensive handgun. It is available blued or in stainless steel.

TAURUS MODEL 94

Manufacturer	Years Produced	Caliber/Capacity	Dimensions
Forjas Taurus S.A. Porto Alegre, Brazil Imported by Taurus Int'l. Miami, FL	1989–Present	.22 LR/9 rounds	Barrel Lengths: 3", 4", 5" O.A. Length: 7.1" (3" bbl.) Height: 4.8" Width: 1.3" Weight: 25 oz. (unloaded); 27 oz. (loaded)

TAURUS MODEL 605

In its ongoing competition with Smith & Wesson, Taurus decided in 1995 to upgrade its Model 85 to handle .357 Magnum ammunition, just as Smith & Wesson brought forth its Model 640 Centennial in the same caliber. The Taurus revolver that resulted is called the Model 605.

Like any small-frame revolver in .357 Magnum caliber, it's difficult to shoot. Taurus has supplied finger-groove Santoprene stocks, however, with barrel porting offered on the Model 605 Custom. As with any .357 Magnum revolver, the shorter .38 Special rounds will also fit, so shooters will undoubtedly opt for this caliber choice, especially in its stouter +P and +P+ loadings. The Remington 125-grain Medium Velocity round, already popular in small .357 Magnum revolvers (*see* Ruger Model SP101 on page 40) will undoubtedly be used in the Model 605s as well. For those who are up to handling full-power .357 Magnum rounds in this small revolver with its fierce recoil, at least they can be confident the gun will survive. (Taurus once fired more than 11,000 rounds in a Model 605 without damage to the gun).

Taurus's compact Model 605 revolver is made with 2 1/4-inch or 3-inch barrel and finger-grooved Santoprene grips, in blued or stainless steel finish (shown above). In .357 Magnum caliber, this little gun has plenty of kick.

TAURUS MODEL 605

Manufacturer	Years Produced	Caliber/Capacity	Dimensions
Forjas Taurus S.A. Porto Alegre, Brazil Imported by Taurus Int'l. Miami, FL	1995–Present	.357 Magnum, .38 Special/5 rounds	Barrel Lengths: 2.25", 3" O.A. Length: 7.3" (2.25" bbl.) Height: 4.8" Width: 1.3" Weight: 24.5 oz. (unloaded); 27.5 oz. (loaded)

TAURUS MODEL 941

In 1992, Taurus upgraded its Model 94 concept *(see* page 57) and created the Model 941. Whereas the Model 94 offered nine shots of .22 Long Rifle on a small frame, the Model 941 can fire eight shots of the more potent .22 Magnum. As a self-defense handgun round, the .22 Magnum is worth serious consideration. Its advantages over .38 Special, .357 Magnum, .44 Special and other more traditional revolver rounds include reduced recoil and lower cost. Although .22 Magnum is considerably more expensive than .22 LR, the former is still appreciably less costly than any centerfire rounds. Therefore, more ammunition can be bought for a given amount of money than is possible with revolvers using centerfire cartridges.

Because the kit gun concept stresses accuracy out in the field, Taurus makes the Model 941 in

The Taurus Model 941 produced this all-double-action five-shot, 2.2-inch group at 25 feet. A single-action off-hand group fired from twice that distance opened up the group by only .3 inch.

The Taurus Model 941 is an upgraded version of the model 94 shown above (top). Despite their long barrels, adjustable rear sights, enlarged grip and target-style hammer, they clearly owe a debt to S&W J-frame revolvers, such as the Model 36 Chiefs Special (bottom).

blued and stainless steel versions, along with a choice of 3-inch and 4-inch barrel lengths. The 3-inch stainless model tested for this book showed good workmanship overall, although its operating controls—trigger, cylinder latch and ejector rod—are not as smooth and easy to operate as Smith & Wesson's Model 651. The full-checkered wooden stock on the Model 941 is excellent, though, and helps keep the gun in balance and makes recoil recovery easier.

Like the Model 94, the 941 has a smooth-surfaced trigger and adjustable sights, both of which help accuracy. Although the .22 Magnum is loud and produces a great deal of muzzle flash in a short 3-inch barrel, the gun's substantial weight produces very little recoil. Despite its heavy double-action trigger pull, the Model 941 delivered good accuracy in our tests. A five-shot offhand group of 2.2 inches was fired at 25 feet; and at 50 feet the group measured only 2.5 inches (the result of a very smooth and easy single-action trigger).

Chambering eight rounds of .22 Magnum in a single cylinder makes the Model 941 a serious defensive handgun at close ranges as well as a useful trail gun. Its nearest competition—Smith & Wesson's Model 651—is smoother to operate, but it costs more and holds only six shots. Taurus's own .22 LR Model 94 is also lower in cost and a little smoother in operation as well, while holding one extra shot of a slightly less powerful cartridge.

TAURUS MODEL 941

Manufacturer	Years Produced	Caliber/Capacity	Dimensions
Forjas Taurus S.A. Porto Alegre, Brazil Imported by Taurus Int'l. Miami, FL	1992–Present	.22 Magnum/ 8 rounds	Barrel Lengths: 3", 4" O.A. Length: 7.9" (3" bbl.) Height: 4.9" Width: 1.3" Weight: 27 oz. (unloaded); 29 oz. (loaded)

3. CLASSIC COMPACT PISTOLS

CONTENTS

Astra Model 2000 Cub	64	
Model 5000 Constable	65	
Beretta Model 1934	67	
Bersa Model 844	69	
Colt 1903 Pocket Model M	71	
CZ Model 27	73	
FN Browning		
Model 1900	75	
Model 1910/1922	76	

Makarov Model PM. 79
Mauser Model HSc 82
Ortgies Pistol. 85
Ruby Pistols 89
Smith & Wesson Model 469 92
Walther Model 4 93
  Model 8 94
  Model 9 96
  Model PPK 97

For the most part, the best-selling handguns are the small-caliber compact pistols in .22, .25, .32, .38 and .380 calibers. It's easy to figure out why. Most automatics in these relatively low-powered calibers feature a simple unlocked breech, or "blowback" construction. It is less complex, and therefore less costly, than the locked-breech mechanisms found in most larger automatic pistols. Moreover, these guns are mostly small in overall length and height; they are light in weight, and they are flat, making them relatively easy to carry in reasonable comfort. Since the .32 ACP cartridge appeared in 1899, with the smaller .25 ACP following in 1905, hundreds of these small .25 - and .32-caliber automatic pistols have been produced. So too have pistols firing the .380-caliber cartridge since it first appeared in 1908. All three of these cartridges were the creations of John M. Browning and helped him gain tremendous success as

a designer of handguns and ammunition.

Arranged in A-to-Z order by manufacturer or trade name, the pistols described in the following section have stood the test of time and serve as the basis for a number of later, popular designs. Because many of them were produced in large quantities, spare parts are readily available for maintenance purposes. However, as with the older revolvers, a strong caution is urged in the use and reliance upon some of these vintage models. Before using any old gun, no matter how advanced its design or impeccable its reputation, it is absolutely essential that the owner and/or prospective buyer take the weapon to a qualified gunsmith— one who is familiar with that gun design— for inspection, testing (if necessary) and clearance. Even after the gun is given the OK, it's a good idea to limit the older guns to standard factory ammo, especially the milder loadings.

ASTRA MODEL 2000 CUB

The Model 2000 "Cub," which first appeared in
.22 Short (1954) and in .25 ACP (1956), was an
update by Astra of the Browning-inspired Model 200
"Firecat" introduced in 1920. Both pistols remained in
production until 1966, when Astra dropped the 200. The
2000 remains in production but, because of its size, can no
longer be imported legally into the U.S. (under the provisions of the Gun
Control Act of 1968). Nevertheless, the gun is not at all uncommon in this
country, Astra having made several hundred thousand of them. Also, the Colt
Junior, manufactured between 1957 and 1968 in Spain and from 1970 to
1972 in the U.S., was identical to the Model 2000 except for its markings. In

The Model 2000 is a beautiful, sleek pistol, which despite its small size and light weight, produced virtually no recoil when test-fired. This five-shot offhand group fired from 15 feet away measures a mere 1.1 inches across.

all, some 25,000 .22 Short Colt Juniors and about twice that many .25-caliber models were manufactured. A longer-barreled sporting model, the "Camper," and some caliber conversion kits were also made in limited quantities.

Whereas the Model 200 featured three safeties (thumb, magazine and grip), the Model 2000 sports a sleeker frame, eliminating the grip safety. It also has an exposed, rounded hammer instead of the internal striker found on the Model 200, which Astra offered in a variety of finishes, including blued, chromed and deluxe engraved versions plated in chrome, silver and even gold.

The controls on the single-action Model 2000 are typical of an Eibar-style pistol, which American shooters have difficulty getting used to. The safety, located just above the trigger at the midpoint of the frame, pushes down so that the pistol can be fired once the hammer has been cocked. When the safety is pushed up, it locks the trigger; and with the slide retracted fully to the rear, it also locks into a notch on the left side of the slide, holding the slide open. The exposed portion of the barrel can then be turned, allowing it to unlock from the frame. In that way, it's possible to separate the barrel and slide from the frame when servicing the pistol. The magazine release is a push-button type located at the bottom left of the frame, similar to some Beretta pistols.

The pistol tested for this book proved sensationally accurate at distances appropriate for self-defensive use. For instance, one five-shot group, fired at 15 feet, measured only 1.1 inches across. Reliability proved flawless with several ammunition brands tested.

Typical of Astra products, the Model 2000 is a well-made and reliable pistol whose extraordinarily compact size makes it a viable pocket pistol. While the .22 Short and .25 ACP rounds it uses are quite weak, the development of modern .25-caliber ammunition has improved the odds. It should be remembered, though, that these are last-ditch weapons to be used at close range—the very essence of civilian self-defense.

ASTRA MODEL 2000 CUB

Manufacturer	Years Produced	Caliber/Capacity	Dimensions
Astra Unceta y Cia. Guernica, Spain	1954–Present	.22 Short/7 rounds .25 ACP/6 rounds	Barrel Length: 2.25" O.A. Length: 4.4" Height: 3.3" Width: 0.8" Weight: 13 oz. (unloaded); 14 oz. (loaded)

ASTRA MODEL 5000 CONSTABLE

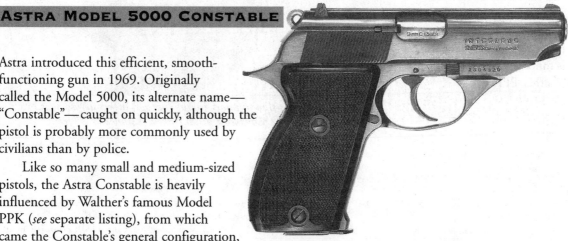

Astra introduced this efficient, smooth-functioning gun in 1969. Originally called the Model 5000, its alternate name—"Constable"—caught on quickly, although the pistol is probably more commonly used by civilians than by police.

Like so many small and medium-sized pistols, the Astra Constable is heavily influenced by Walther's famous Model PPK (*see* separate listing), from which came the Constable's general configuration, dimensions and double-action trigger mechanism. The Constable differs, however, in numerous details. For example, its grip is slightly larger, allowing an extra round to be carried, and its disassembly is different. The Constable's slightly larger frame makes it a more pleasing gun to fire than the PPK, particularly for large-handed shooters. On the minus side, however, is the Constable's concealability, which is slightly compromised compared to the PPK. As for controls, the Constable has added a slide release lever, a useful feature that, among other things, makes it possible to reload one-handed and also makes it easier to clear a jam. Astra cleverly designed this useful feature so that it adds little to the gun's bulk.

The Constable remained a mainstay of the Astra line for more than 20 years, appearing in .22 LR, .32 and .380 calibers. Different barrel lengths and sight options have been offered, as well as a choice of a standard blued finish or other extras, including deluxe engraving. All options offered serve to demonstrate the impressive versatility and reliability of this pistol.

Although Astra discontinued the standard Constable in the early 1990s, it remains an excellent small pistol and is much less expensive than the Walther PPK.

Astra's Constable is one of many Walther PPK clones. Unlike most of the copies, this Spanish-made gun is an improvement over the German original. The Constable (left) has a longer grip tang than the PPK (right), an improvement that helps protect the shooter's hand. The Constable also has a bigger grip that is more suited to the needs of large-handed shooters.

This five-shot offhand group, only 1.2 inches across, was produced by a Constable pistol from a distance of 25 feet.

ASTRA CONSTABLE

Manufacturer	Years Produced	Caliber/Capacity	Dimensions
Astra Unceta y Cia. Guernica, Spain	1969–1992	.380 ACP/8 rounds (also .22 LR, .32 ACP)	Barrel Length: 3.5" O.A. Length: 6.5" Height: 4.6" Width: 1.1" Weight: 25 oz. (unloaded); 28 oz. (loaded)

BERETTA

BERETTA MODEL 1934

In 1915, the Italian arms firm of Pietro Beretta, the
world's oldest continuously operating industrial concern, introduced its first automatic pistol for Italy's armed forces.
Several pistols followed, with each design improving slightly on the
preceding one and the gun's popularity becoming more and more
widespread. The gun that really put Beretta on the map as a serious pistol manufacturer, however, was the Model 1934. The Italian Army adopted this gun in
.380 ACP in 1934, and the Italian Navy and Air Force followed by ordering a .32
ACP version, called the Model 1935. First used in the invasion of Ethiopia in
1936, and later in the Spanish Civil War (1936–1939), the Model 1934 was used
extensively during World War II by Italian, German, Finnish and Romanian
troops. It also became a favored war trophy and souvenir among Allied troops.

The rugged, straightforward design of the Model 1934 was the key element
in its construction. A simple, single-action pistol, it used the absolute minimum number of parts,
each one made stronger than required. The result was a sturdy and reliable little pistol that was much

*Beretta's Model 1934 is a long-lived design that remains in service in several countries. A single-action pistol,
it is shown ready to fire. The hammer is cocked; safety rotated fully forward to expose a red dot and the letter
F on the frame; and the shooter's trigger finger has moved from its safe position outside of the trigger guard
onto the trigger.*

more durable than its compact dimensions suggested.

The Model 1934 did have some shortcomings, though. In order to release the thumb safety, the shooter had to rotate it a full 180 degrees forward. Also, the slide locked open on an empty magazine; but upon removal of the magazine, the slide moved forward. There being no separate slide stop, the empty magazine wedged the slide open only as long as it remained in the gun. The Model 1934 also had a very stiff recoil spring, making it difficult to draw the slide back. The trigger pull was also excessively heavy, as was the magazine release. Accuracy was sometimes poor, and feeding reliability with anything but military-style, full-metal-jacketed (FMJ or "ball") ammunition was not a sure thing. Finally, a prominent finger extension along the bottom of the magazine caused snags on clothing.

Despite these shortcomings, Beretta sold over a million Model 1934 and 1935 pistols. They remain in military and police service in several countries and are still popular among civilian shooters throughout the world.

BERETTA MODEL 1934

Manufacturer	Years Produced	Caliber/Capacity	Dimensions
Pietro Beretta S.p.A., Gardone, V.T., Italy	1934–1974	.380 ACP/7 rounds .32 ACP /8 rounds (Model 1935)	Barrel Length: 3.5" O.A. Length: 5.9" Height: 4.7" Width: 1.1" Weight: 26 oz. (unloaded), 29 oz. (loaded)

BERSA MODEL 844

When Bersa introduced its Model 844 in 1964, it was considered an "upgunned" version of the company's ancestral .22 LR handgun, the Model 644, with some added Beretta, Bernardelli and Walther influences. Mechanically, it's a blowback-operated (unlocked breech) automatic pistol with a single-action trigger (Bersa didn't introduce its double-action model until 1984). A well-made pistol constructed of steel forgings, the Model 844 features checkered plastic grips and a magazine with a finger rest at the bottom small enough for even a large-handed shooter to get a firm grip. Operating controls include a magazine

Bersa's Model 844 offers good practical accuracy. This five-shot offhand group fired from a distance of 25 feet measures 1.8 inches across.

release on the lower portion of the left grip. The pistol has two manual safety devices: a frame-mounted cross-bolt button to lock the trigger, and a slide-mounted safety that acts on the hammer without decocking it.

Tests conducted on the Model 844 indicated good accuracy, especially considering the small sights. The pistol is rather heavy for a .32 caliber, making it quite stable and quick to recover from recoil. The trigger pull is smooth and easy, which is unusual for a single-action pistol right out of the box. Using four test loads—a brand each of French and German FMJ, Winchester Silvertip hollow-points and Glaser Safety Slugs—reliability was flawless.

The only negative traits were the pistol's overlapping safety devices. In an emergency, a shooter could easily forget which safety was on and which was off, leaving him unable to fire the pistol at all. When looking for a small defensive handgun—a class into which the Model 844 seems to fit—a double-action pistol or revolver makes a better choice. Still, for its modest price, this pistol offers acceptable accuracy and good reliability.

BERSA MODEL 844

Manufacturer	Years Produced	Caliber/Capacity	Dimensions
Fabrica de Armas Bersa SA, Ramos Meija, Argentina	1964–1983	.32 ACP/8 rounds	Barrel Length: 3.2" O.A. Length: 6.4" Height: 4.5" Width: 1.1" Weight: 24 oz. (unloaded); 28 oz. (loaded)

COLT 1903 POCKET MODEL M

In 1903, Colt introduced its now-famous Pocket
Model in .32 ACP caliber, designed by the legendary John Browning. At the same time, Fabrique Nationale (FN)
of Belgium began marketing a slightly larger version in 9mm
Browning Long caliber for military use. A few years later, Colt brought out a
.380 ACP ("Automatic Colt Pistol") version identical to the .32 model, except its
magazine capacity was reduced by one round.

Colt's highly successful Pocket Model introduced the American shooting public to both .32 and .380 calibers, which have since achieved worldwide popularity in
a host of pistols. Far and away the more popular, the .32 caliber was chambered by
Colt in more than 700,000 Pocket Models. During the course of a 42-year production run, in contrast, the company made "only" 138,000 in .380 caliber, which was still a tremendously successful run
by almost any standard.

Among the Pocket Model's largest buyers were the U.S. armed forces, which brought many thousands into service in both calibers as a General Officer's handgun and for use by aviators, detectives
and others for whom the standard M1911A1 pistol was later considered to be too bulky or too heavy.
It also saw service among Allied troops and was widely distributed among police forces, many of
whom still use it as a backup pistol. Thousands of these guns remain in service in civilian hands, pro-
tecting homes and businesses the world over.

A gun will do its owner no good if it is inaccessible when needed. Fortunately, the Pocket Model
is well designed with comfortable carry in mind. Its enclosed hammer, surrounded completely by a
smoothly contoured slide, cannot snag on clothing during a draw. And its grip safety is a useful supplement to the manual safety lever, especially when the gun is carried loosely in a large overcoat pocket. The sights are also well-rounded to avoid snagging.

Like most pistols of its vintage, the Pocket Model is capable of single-action firing only. The
hammer, therefore, must be cocked by drawing the slide back for the first shot; for subsequent shots,
the recoiling slide cocks the hammer. This need to cock the hammer, combined with its invisibility
when the gun is fully assembled, may cause some confusion concerning the Pocket Model's safety and
readiness to fire. Despite the concealed hammer, though, shooters can easily determine the gun's readiness to fire simply by checking the manual safety; only when the hammer is cocked can it be pushed
up into its safe position. A further safety feature (added after serial number 468,097) is a magazine
disconnect safety.

Colt's Pocket Model and the similar but slightly larger FN Model 1903 inspired numerous competitors and imitators, notably Spain's "Ruby," made by Gabilondo (*see* separate listing). These copies,
produced from 1909 on, found wide use in World Wars I and II, especially among the French, Italian
and Finnish armed forces. Despite their widespread production and use, however, the Spanish copies
usually omitted certain desirable features, such as the grip safety, and suffered from inferior workmanship compared to the Colt and FN versions.

The main drawback to the Pocket Model, from the modern standpoint, occurs during reloading.
The magazine release, which in the popular European fashion is located at the "heel" of the grip,
must be held secure to its rear position with one hand; meanwhile, with his oher hand, the shooter

must draw out the empty magazine.

Despite the above and other minor objections that might be raised from the vantage point of nearly a century of automatic pistol design, the Pocket Model remains an impressive pistol. Sleek and easy to carry, it fits the hand well and is ruggedly built, like all Browning-designed firearms. Pocket Models can be quite accurate, too, as well as reliable. In short, they rank high when it comes to personal protection, particularly for right-handed shooters.

COLT 1903 POCKET MODEL M

Manufacturer	Years Produced	Caliber/Capacity	Dimensions
Colt Industries, Firearms Division Hartford, CT	1903–1945	.32 ACP/8 rounds .380 ACP/7 rounds	Barrel length: 3.25" O.A. Length: 7.01" Height: 4.8" Width: 1.0" Weight: 20 oz. (unloaded); 23 oz. (loaded)

CZ

CZ MODEL 27

Soon after Czechoslovakia was created as an independent country out of the ashes of the Austro-Hungarian Empire in 1918, it began producing its own military small arms. (Czechoslovakia has now become the independent countries of the Czech Republic and Slovakia.) All through the pre-World War II period, Czech guns were sold to military and police firearms markets worldwide, earning an excellent reputation for solid workmanship and superb design. During World War II, the Germans eagerly appropriated Czech-produced firearms for use by their armed forces, notably the SS; and after the war, the Communist movement adopted Czech-made weapons to a great extent. The CZ 27, often called the vz 27 (vz meaning "vzor," or model), was the most popular Czech pistol, with over 400,000 produced during the war years alone for use by Germany. By the time production ended in 1951, total CZ 27 production exceeded 600,000 pistols.

Development of the CZ 27 began in 1926, with series production commencing a year later. Simplified considerably from the earlier, moderately successful vz 22/24 series, the CZ 27 was a rugged blowback design chambered for the then-popular .32 ACP (7.65mm Browning) pistol cartridge. Initially, these guns went to Czech police and border guards, but following their occupation of Czechoslovakia in 1939, the Germans took large quantities of CZ 27s, which they designated the *Pistole Modell 27* for use by the Army, SS, Gestapo and Luftwaffe.

Guns manufactured during the prewar period were of excellent quality and are immediately recognizable by the slide markings *Ceska Zbrojovka A.S. Praze.* Those made for the Nazis during the per-

The German slide markings on this CZ Model 27 pistol indicate that it was made during the Nazi occupation of Czechoslovakia in the 1940s.

iod 1939–1945 fall into two distinct groups. Guns made up to June 1941 were marked *BOHMIS-CHE WAFFENFABRIK A.G. IN PRAG* along the slide top and *Pistole Modell 27 Kal. 7,65* on the left side of the frame. On guns made from June 1941 to war's end in 1945, the slide-top markings were eliminated altogether, while the slide designation now read *fnh Pistole Modell 27 Kal. 7,65*. Production quality fell off markedly during the war years, with later examples being especially crude and unsafe due to several new manufacturing shortcuts that would be considered unacceptable by peacetime standards.

In 1946, CZ 27 production resumed, using mostly wartime parts. Two years later with the Communist takeover of Czechoslovakia, the left-side slide markings were changed to *CESKA ZBRO-JOVKA-NORODNI PODNIK* on the top line, with *STRAKONICE* on the second line. The caliber designation — 7,65 — appeared within a circle that followed the slide inscription.

Like Beretta's Model 1934 pistol (*see* page 67), the primary emphasis of the CZ 27 was on its simple, rugged design. Like the Beretta, it featured a single-action trigger mechanism, with the magazine follower holding the slide open when the last shot was fired. When the magazine was removed for reloading, the slide snapped shut. The CZ 27's .32-caliber cartridge is not to be taken lightly, even though it is small and has largely disappeared from military and police use. With good bullet placement, the .32 ACP cartridge can be a serious wounder — or even a killer.

While its performance may not be especially impressive, the basic design of the CZ 27 is good and sturdy. During the World War II and Vietnam war eras, it established an excellent reputation and is still frequently encountered at gun shows, its military use having largely ended. Warning: shooters should handle such pieces with extreme caution, particularly the late-war models detailed above.

CZ MODEL 27

Manufacturer	Years Produced	Caliber/Capacity	Dimensions
Ceska Zbrojovka Strakonice, Czechoslovakia	1927–1951	.32 ACP (7.65mm)/ 8 rounds	Barrel length: 3.8" O.A. Length: 6.5" Height: 4.8" Width: 1.1" Weight: 25 oz. (unloaded); 28 oz. (loaded)

FN BROWNING MODEL 1900

Fabrique Nationale's highly successful Model 1900 was a creation of John M. Browning's inventive mind. Fabrique Nationale owes much of its success to Browning-designed pistols and other firearms; in fact, the company once named him, "The Father of Automatic Pistols." Developed between 1897 and 1899, the Model 1900 acquired several "firsts" to its credit; for example, it was the first pistol to use the .32 ACP cartridge, which now enjoys worldwide distribution. It was also Browning's first joint venture with FN, the start of a long and extraordinarily fruitful partnership that led not only to a number of excellent pistol designs but also to repeating shotguns, automatic rifles and even machine guns. The Model 1900 was also the first automatic pistol to be adopted by various armed forces, including the Belgian, Russian and Dutch armies plus numerous European and Asian police forces. On the other hand, many others, notably Great Britain, tested the gun without adopting it, stating that its small caliber was the problem, not its reliability, which was considered excellent by the standards of the day.

Unfortunately, the Model 1900 was also a favorite among the lawless, most notably the terrorist Gavrilo Princip, who used a Model 1900 on June 28, 1914, to kill the Archduke Francis Ferdinand, heir apparent to the Austro-Hungarian throne, and his wife Sophie, a shocking assassination that ignited World War I. A close copy of the Model 1900, called the Type 64, one version of which can be equipped with a silencer for assassination purposes, still serves in the North Korean armed forces.

The Model 1900 remained in production from 1899 to 1912, when FN stopped its manufacture to concentrate efforts on the superior Model 1910 pistol (*see* following listing). Total Model 1900 production by FN alone was over 700,000, with additional tens of thousands of copies, mostly of questionable metallurgy, coming out of Afghanistan, China, Korea, Pakistan and other parts of the world.

From a mechanical standpoint, the Model 1900 is interesting because its recoil spring is located above, rather than below, the barrel. This serves to lower the bore axis and so reduce recoil, which contributes greatly to the fine accuracy of this pistol. A few modern guns, notably several of Smith & Wesson's rimfire pistols, also use this configuration.

Today, the Model 1900 would not rank as anyone's top choice among automatic pistols; but since so many were produced, they may emerge anywhere, and they do work. If you have one, though, make sure it's a genuine Model 1900 made by FN before firing it—and be sure to take it to a gunsmith for a thorough examination. Pirated copies are usually dreadfully poor in quality and are simply not safe to shoot. Fortunately, the unintelligible slide markings on these copies are frequently dead giveaways.

FN BROWNING MODEL 1900

Manufacturer	Years Produced	Caliber/Capacity	Dimensions
Fabrique Nationale (FN) Herstal, Belgium	1899–1912	.32 ACP (7.62mm)/ 7 rounds	Barrel Length: 4.0" O.A. Length: 6.7" Height: 4.8" Width: 1.1" Weight: 23 oz. (unloaded); 26 oz. (loaded)

FN BROWNING MODEL 1910/1922

Like Colt's 1903 Pocket Model, FN's Model 1910
is still another of John Browning's designs. One of the sleekest
pistols ever made, it sustained its popularity for decades and was
widely distributed among military, police and civilian populations.
Even now, the Model 1910 (and the slightly larger Model 1922) remain in military and police service in a few countries, a tribute to their outstanding design
and workmanship.

The chief inspiration for the Model 1910's design is clearly the Colt Pocket
Model, which Browning had designed several years earlier. Among the features carried over from the Pocket Model into the Model 1910 include its grip, magazine and thumb safeties,
along with the pistol's overall compactness and smoothness. In other respects, though, the Model
1910 represents several innovations, chief among them the placement of the recoil spring around the
barrel, rather than above or below it. This feature gives the Model 1910 an exceptionally sleek and

*The FN Model 1922 was similar to the earlier Model 1910 (shown above), but longer and taller. Note the slide
extension, kept in place by a small spring-loaded catch.*

compact slide assembly, one that's been widely copied ever since. The use of an internal striker—
instead of an exposed hammer—has eliminated yet another possible snagging problem. In general, the
Model 1910 is a small pistol, one that feels even smaller than it really is, which is a good characteristic
to have in a concealed-carry gun.

Unlike earlier Browning-designed guns, the Model 1910 offers easy caliber interchangeability

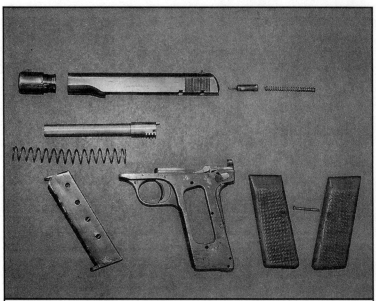

The FN Model 1922 disassembles into the following components (top to bottom): muzzle bushing followed by slide, firing pin and spring; barrel with recoil spring underneath; magazine, frame and grips.

between .32 ACP and .380 ACP, simply by switching barrels. Some Model 1910s were even sold with twin barrels, although most came in .32 caliber. When used as a .32 ACP pistol, the Model 1910's magazine held seven rounds (six rounds in .380). Although Browning and Fabrique Nationale patented the Model 1910 in 1909, its manufacture did not actually begin until 1912. Most likely, FN wanted to get as much mileage out of the old Model 1900 as possible before switching over to the Model 1910. In any case, once FN began making the Model 1910, it proved extremely successful for them. Although prewar military sales were disappointing, several large European police forces and many civilians took to it quickly. The occupation of Fabrique Nationale's factory by the Germans in World Wars I and II halted production of the Model 1910, but otherwise it was kept in production until 1980, accumulating the total production of an impressive 701,266 units. Even though official military sales were limited, the Model 1910 saw considerable action as a substitute standard pistol. It was also popular among military men as a personal item because of its small size; this made it an ideal concealed backup arm in the event of capture. Eventually, police forces in Denmark, Holland, Japan, Sweden and numerous other countries bought Model 1910s, as did military forces in Burundi, Canada, the Netherlands and Peru.

Like the Models 1900 and 1903 before it, the Model 1910 inspired numerous copies. Gunmakers in Belgium, Czechoslovakia, Finland, Germany, Italy, Japan and Spain all made more or less exact copies of the Model 1910. Astra's remarkably successful Model 300, Model 400 and Model 600 series also owe a lot to FN's pistol as well. In fact, FN made its own improved version in 1922, after Yugoslavia's armed forces had requested a slightly enlarged Model 1910 without reducing its performance specifications. In response, FN created the "Modele 1910/22," which featured a longer barrel, an attachment to lengthen the slide, and a deeper grip (allowing an 8-shot .380 caliber or 9-shot .32 ACP magazine).

Although civilians understandably preferred the smaller model, the Model 1910/22 proved more successful in military sales than had the Model 1910. Yugoslavia's original order called for 60,000 pistols, and within a few years Greece, the Netherlands, Turkey, France and Belgium had also ordered this larger model for their own armed forces. The Model 1922 was also one of the FN-made pistols kept in production by the Nazis (mostly in .32 caliber) after they took over FN's plant in May of 1940. Suspended after the war, Model 1910/22 production resumed in 1950 and continued until 1959.

The FN Model 1922's reputation for accuracy was well-deserved, as this 5-shot offhand group fired from a distance of 25 feet indicates. The pistol shown served in Yugoslavia's armed forces.

Despite its small size, the Model 1910 is a strong, solid gun that points and balances well in the hand. The thumb safety, although undersized, is well-shaped and easy to move down into its fire position. The Model 1910's recoil is surprisingly low (considering its size), even when using .380-caliber bullets; its trigger, moreover, is exceptionally light and crisp in its release.

Among its few weak spots, due mostly to John Browning's need to miniaturize the gun as much as possible, are the Model 1910's sights, which are not much more than a narrow channel cut into the top of the slide. The grip safety requires strong pressure to keep it depressed into the rear of the frame long enough to fire the gun, a characteristic that could make the Model 1910 (and the Model 1922) difficult for some shooters to hold properly. As in Colt's Pocket Model, the slide on the Model 1910 does not remain open following the last shot. Also, the magazine is a very tight fit, and its release is located inconveniently on the bottom rear of the frame.

The Model 1910 remains a fine pistol for casual shooting and is still a viable choice for self-defense. Its exceptionally smooth, clean lines are a real plus, as is its capability for instant caliber interchangeability between .32 and .380 with a simple barrel change.

FN BROWNING MODEL 1910/MODEL 1922

Manufacturer	Years Produced	Caliber/Capacity	Dimensions
Fabrique Nationale Herstal, Belgium	1912–1980	.32 ACP/7 rounds .380 ACP/6 rounds	Barrel length: 3.5" O.A. Length: 6" Height: 3.9" Width: 1.1" Weight: 21 oz. (unloaded); 25 oz. (loaded)

MAKAROV

MAKAROV MODEL PM

In the years immediately following World War II, the influence of the Walther double-action pistols—Models PP, PPK and P.38—spread far and wide. Among the oddest results of this influence was the *Pistolet Makarova*, or PM—usually referred to simply as "Makarov" in the U.S. Produced in the former Soviet Union and first appearing in Soviet service around 1952, the handy Makarov was originally intended as a limited-issue pistol for use by aircrewmen, high-ranking officers and armored vehicle operators. (The Makarov replaced the larger Tokarev pistol, discussed in *Complete Guide to Service Handguns*, in the Soviet Union and most other European communist countries.) The Makarov has gone on to become one of the world's most widely produced and issued military and police handguns. In those countries where it serves, it fills the tactical niches occupied elsewhere by such disparate guns as the FN High Power, Smith & Wesson Models 10 and 36, and the Walther PPK. The Makarov is especially popular in communist, ex-communist and Third World nations throughout Europe, Asia, Central America, Africa and the Middle East. Factories in Russia, East Germany, China, Bulgaria and Poland have all produced Makarovs.

Similar to the PPK, though not an exact copy by any means, the Makarov features a sturdier and simpler design, with only about half as many parts, and fires a more powerful cartridge. While slightly larger than the PPK, the Makarov is still small enough for a person to carry at all times, giving it a significant advantage over such service pistols as the M1911A1, FN High Power, or P.38—all of which are holster guns, not pocket guns.

In addition, the Makarov has a better trigger pull than the PPK, is more ruggedly built for arduous military service, and even has an enlarged trigger guard for easier handling while wearing heavy winter gloves. To help counteract the corrosive effects of hydroscopic salts used in the primers of ammunition commonly used by communist armies, the Makarov features a chrome-lined barrel. In fact, wherever the Makarov is made, its overall workmanship, fit and finish are rated good to excellent.

The 9x18mm Makarov round used in this pistol is probably based on the 9mm Ultra round created in wartime Germany. The 18mm case length is midway between that of

The Makarov (bottom) is considerably smaller than either the Beretta Model 92F (M9) or the Tokarev (top), which it supplanted. To Russians, the Makarov is considered primarily a last resort, hence it is made small and handy. U.S. and other Western armed

the .380 ACP (17mm) and the 9mm Parabellum (9mm), thus lending the 9x18mm Makarov round a power level that falls between the two "westernized" pistol rounds. A similar round—the 9mm Police—was created in the early 1970s in West Germany for possible use in the Walther PP Super and SIG-Sauer P230 pistols, but the German police opted instead for a 9mm Parabellum pistol.

The 9x18mm Makarov round uses a 94-grain, full-metal-jacketed bullet with a muzzle velocity of about 1100 feet per second. Its diameter is .363 inches, whereas .380, 9mm Police and 9mm Parabellum bullets all measure about .355 in diameter. This slight difference in dimension means that guns designed for the .380 or 9mm Police round cannot chamber Makarov ammunition; but in a pinch the Makarov pistol can—with some loss of accuracy and reliability— use .380 or 9mm Police ammunition.

Although for many years the Makarov was an extremely rare collector's item in the U.S., its importation in recent years has soared. Beginning in 1989, the Chinese exported their version, called the Type 59, to the U.S., followed in 1992 by a former East German pistol, called the PM, and in 1993 by Makarovs made in Russia and Bulgaria (the Russian pistol, now called the Baikal IJ-70, is covered separately in the backup pistol section that follows).

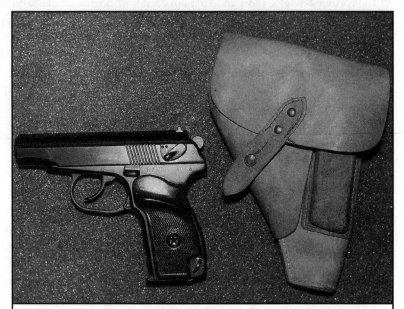

This East German version of the Makarov—the Pistole M—has a target-style grip with prominent thumbrest to satisfy U.S. importation requirements. The full-flap leather military holster with spare magazine pouch was also used for the Luger, P.38, FN High Power, Beretta Model 1934, and numerous other European military handguns.

As the availabilty of Makarov-type pistols has increased, so has the proliferation of Makarov ammunition. During the early 1980s, genuine Makarov ammo cost almost a dollar a round; but later in that decade, the Chinese began exploring the same type of Makarov-caliber ammunition used by their military. This early product was both Berdan-primed and corrosive, making it difficult, if not impossible, for reloaders—but at least it was a beginning. Today Makarov ammunition made by Norinco is still Berdan-primed, but the primers are now noncorrosive. Czech and Yugoslav 9x18mm Makarov ammunition is also available in the United States. Beginning in 1993, several U.S. ammunition manufacturers responded to the increasing availability and soaring popularity of the Makarov pistol by offering their own ammunition. Lee now offers reloading dies and bullet molds for this caliber; and CCI has introduced a Blazer round in 9x18mm Makarov using a Berdan primer, a non-reloadable aluminum case, and a 95-grain FMJ bullet. Then, in late 1993, Hornady introduced a 9x18mm Makarov round with Boxer priming and a reloadable brass case. It fires a 95-grain XTP jacketed hol-

This five-shot 25-foot offhand group, measuring 1.7 inches, was fired with a Chinese-made Makarov, showing that the pistol is quite accurate.

lowpoint bullet, making it the best 9x18mm Makarov round yet offered for defensive shooting purposes. The Cor-Bon and MagSafe ammunition companies offer even higher-performing Makarov ammo.

The Makarov is an excellent automatic pistol, one that's built for rugged service and can take a lot of abuse—unlike many small automatic pistols that look and feel like toys and frequently break like toys. Tactically, it's the equivalent of such small .38 Special revolvers as the Smith & Wesson J frames, Charter Arms's Off Duty, and Colt's Detective Special. The Makarov is more pleasant to fire, though, than those small revolvers and it holds more shots (8 as opposed to 5 or 6). On the other hand, it's slightly heavier than the lightest revolvers, making it a little more difficult to conceal. It's a better shooter at extended ranges—50 feet and beyond—than the PPK or most of the snubby revolvers. But some small revolvers whose hammers can be cocked for single-action shooting may be equally accurate.

The Makarov's only weak point is its magazine, which is difficult to load. Aside from that, it's an excellent, sturdy, reliable gun that offers good power for its small size.

MAKAROV MODEL PM

Manufacturer	Years Produced	Caliber/Capacity	Dimensions
Former Soviet State Factories and Others	1948(c.)–Present	9mm x 18 (9mm Makarov)/8 rounds	Barrel Length: 3.5" O.A. Length: 6.3" Height: 4.9" Width: 1.1" Weight: 25 oz. (unloaded); 29 oz. (loaded)

MAUSER MODEL HSc

Walther's introduction of the Models PP and PPK in the late 1920s and early 1930s cut heavily into the sale of Mauser-Werke's line of pocket pistols. Although the Mauser pistols were well made, they looked dated compared to the new Walthers, and they also lacked a double-action trigger mechanism. Even as it introduced the Model 1934 pistol—it was nothing more than the Model 1914 pistol with a new rounded grip—Mauser began developing a modern double-action pistol that could compete on equal terms with the PP and PPK.

The first Mauser double-action pistol reached the prototype stage in 1937. Called the HSa, this pistol showed promise but required some minor changes—particularly in the double-action trigger mechanism—in order to avoid infringing on Walther patents. The third prototype—the HSc—served as the basis for the production model, which finally entered service in 1940.

The HSc represented in many ways a mechanical improvement over the Walther pistols. It required fewer parts, was easier to manufacture, and has become a reliable weapon capable of withstanding arduous military and police service. Its extraordinarily sleek contours made it well suited to pocket carry. In fact, everything on the gun was designed for ease of concealment; for example, its controls and sights were kept low in profile to avoid catching on the shooter's clothing. The magazine release is located on the lower rear, or heel, of the grip, making the gun's contours even slimmer and less prone to accidental release. Another welcome feature of a heel-mounted magazine release is its ambidexterity in operation (as opposed to a conventional button). Conversely, guns equipped with the heel-mounted magazine release have two shortcomings: they are slower to reload compared to pistols equipped with a magazine release button; and they require both hands to reload.

Although the HSc may at first appear to be a hammerless or concealed-hammer design, the small tip of the hammer does, in fact, protrude far enough for the pistol to be thumb-cocked for a single-action first shot. Most encounters with a handgun occur at extremely short distances—rarely more than 21 feet and often as close as an arm's length—so it makes sense to practice at close ranges in the double-action mode. Thumb-cocking is a good feature to have, though, in a defensive handgun because it makes for a much lighter and shorter trigger pull in a single-action mode than one finds in a double-action pistol. It also makes the single-action shot more accurate, particularly at distances beyond 50 feet or so. Conversely, a hammer with a large exposed spur can get hung up in one's clothing or caught in a holster. A rounded hammer, as on the Walther PPK, or the vestigial spur found on the HSc or Smith & Wesson's Model 38 Bodyguard revolver, may offer the best compromise: a single-action capability with little or no risk of snagging.

The HSc appeared too late for significant commercial sales, but its wartime record was excellent, thanks in large part to Germany's Army which contracted for about 75,000, and the German Navy which ordered another 14,000. The German police bought about 22,500 HSc's during the war years too. Immediately after the war, France put the captured Mauser factory in Oberndorf back into production, assembling about 20,000 HSc pistols from parts stockpiled by the Germans during the war. France's wartime allies then pressured the French into halting production and destroying the Oberndorf plant. Nonetheless, those HSc pistols served the French police well for many years thereafter.

In 1949, several ex-Mauser employees founded the Heckler & Koch company in Oberndorf. Their first small-arms project—the HK-4 pistol—borrowed heavily from the HSc design. Among its features was easy interchangeability of ammunition, including conversion kits enabling an HK-4 pistol to fire any one of four different calibers: .22 LR, .25 ACP, .32 ACP and .380 ACP. The HK-4 remained in production until about 1985, despite disappointing sales compared to other contemporary H&K projects.

In addition to Heckler & Koch manufacturing postwar HSc-type pistols, a reconstituted Mauser-Werke factory resumed HSc production in 1970 in both .32 and .380 caliber. Compared to the wartime model, this postwar German-made HSc had wooden grips of a slightly different design and a magazine with a small plastic extension at the bottom to help support the pinky finger. Interarms imported these guns to the U.S. until Mauser ceased production in 1979 (*see* photo on previous page).

During the mid-1970s, Mauser licensed HSc manufacture to the Italian gunmaker Renato Gamba SpA. Aside from its markings, Gamba's initial production was a faithful copy of the HSc. But from 1979 on, the Italian company reworked the HSc design, adding a high-capacity magazine that held up to 15 rounds in .32 caliber and a recurved trigger guard. The magazine release button was

This HSc is one of the earliest produced. Note its wooden grip and high-polish blued finish.

The Mauser HSc is accurate for a medium-frame automatic pistol of prewar design. This five-shot, 25-foot off-hand group measures 1.6 inches across.

also repositioned slightly behind the trigger guard. These changes produced a noticeably larger and heavier gun, practically destroying Mauser's original concept of an easily concealed pocket pistol.

Reliability, accuracy and a good trigger—along with its smooth contours and light weight—have made the HSc an excellent choice for concealed carry. Among its shortcomings are its cartridges (.32 and .380 caliber), which are rarely as reliable or effective as the larger 9mm, .38 Special or .45 ACP. While one can hardly fault the HSc's design, its underpowered cartridge is a legitimate drawback. But that can be said about many small automatic pistols.

MAUSER MODEL HSC

Manufacturer	Years Produced	Caliber/Capacity	Dimensions
Mauser-Werke Oberndorf, Germany; Renato Gamba, SpA., Italy	1938–1945 1970–Present	.32 ACP/8 rounds .380 ACP/7 rounds	Barrel Length: 3.4" O.A. Length: 6.4" Height: 4.25" Width: 1.1" Weight: 23 oz. (unloaded); 26 oz. (loaded)

ORTGIES PISTOL

The Ortgies pistol, largely overlooked in recent years, is nevertheless an interesting, well-made gun with good handling and shooting characteristics. Very popular in its heyday, it still has potential as a working handgun and a comparatively inexpensive collector's item.

The history of the Ortgies pistol dates back to 1916, when Heinrich Ortgies, a German citizen, was living in Liege, Belgium, home of the FN factory and other prominent Belgian gun-manufacturing concerns. Whether Ortgies was inspired by Belgian designs or not, he did file three patents during the period from 1916 to 1918 for a new automatic pistol. In 1919, after moving back to Germany, Ortgies established in Erfurt a firm called Ortgies & Compagnie to manufacture his pistol. Offered originally in 7.65mm (.32 ACP) caliber, it became highly popular with civilians who wanted, for self-defense purposes, a pistol that was both compact and powerful. With its smooth shape, small size and light weight, the Ortgies pistol was easy to carry in a pocket and ready for a rapid, snag-free draw. Its fit and finish were superior to most of today's guns; it was extremely well-made, highly accurate by pistol standards and was reasonably priced.

The right-side view of the Ortgies pistol reveals its bottom-mounted magazine release and the "CAL.7,65m/m" marking on the barrel exposed by the ejection port. The grip safety has been pushed into the frame in its "fire" position and will remain that way until it's released.

Between 1920 and 1922, Ortgies & Compagnie made over 10,000 of these impressive pistols, most of them ordered by German civilians. But during that same period, Ortgies also received an order for several thousand pistols from the Czechoslovakian army. The Ortgies was primarily a civilian weapon, however, lacking such military refinements as a lanyard loop and slide hold-open device; nonetheless, the Czech military was obviously impressed with the Ortgies pistol. Not only did the Czechs keep these sidearms in service (after withdrawing a large order for Dreyse pistols), they placed a large follow-up order several years later for more Ortgies pistols from the Erfurt firm of Deutsche-Werke AG, which had bought the rights to the Ortgies pistol in 1921.

Using the Ortgies pistol, this off-hand five-shot group fired from a distance of 50 feet measures a spectacular 1.6 inches across.

Deutsche-Werke's manufacturing run lasted almost ten years, with the 7.65mm version remaining by far the most popular. But the 6.35mm (.25 ACP) and 9mm Kurz (.380 ACP) models, which Ortgies had developed earlier, also went into series production. By 1922, the changeover from Ortgies & Compagnie to Deutsche-Werke was complete. Heinrich Ortgies, by now doubtless a wealthy man, apparently dropped out of the pistol-making business altogether.

The Ortgies pistols made by Deutsche-Werke enjoyed a much longer and larger production run than had the original guns made by Ortgies & Co. The Deutsche-Werke version became especially popular throughout central Europe, Central and South America and the U.S. While most sales were commercial, the Czech army continued to order the pistol, including 6,510 units in December 1923 and 5,000 more in April 1924. Sometime between 1929 and 1932, Deutsche-Werke halted manufacture of the Ortgies pistol. Not only did it look dated compared to Walther's fancy new Model PP, introduced in 1929, but the ensuing Great Depression of the 1930s seriously hurt the German economy. Still, by the time production stopped, over 250,000 Ortgies pistols had been produced.

During the post-World War II period, the Ortgies pistol inspired several descendants, including Italy's Vincenzo Bernardelli SpA, which made pistols strongly resembling the Ortgies, of virtually the same size. In addition, the German firm, Erma, introduced a slightly modified version of the .25-caliber Ortgies, called E.P. 25.

Like most automatic pistols of its day, the Ortgies model featured a single-action trigger. Its controls included a magazine release mounted on the bottom rear or heel of the frame, the kind so often disliked by American shooters but which remains popular in Europe. Like many older small-caliber automatics, its slide did not stay open after the final shot. It also had tiny sights, which displeases modern shooters who are accustomed to the ergonomic sights found on today's pistols. Still, the low-profile sights imparted exceptionally sleek, smooth contours to the gun, making it unlikely to catch during a rapid draw.

The .32 ACP version of the Ortgies pistol tested for this book preferred ammunition featuring full-metal-jacketed bullets, as opposed to Winchester Silvertips or Fiocchi hollowpoints. The lack of a slide hold-open latch made clearing jams difficult, but for a vintage design the test pistol proved extremely reliable, jamming only twice in the midst of an extensive course of fire. The Ortgies was impressively accurate, too. A typical five-shot group in rapid fire from a distance of 25 feet spanned 1.7 inches, while another spectacular group fired from 50 feet measured a mere 1.6 inches across.

As for safety arrangements, most Ortgies pistols are the .25- and .32-caliber versions, which have only a grip safety located at the rear of the frame. When the striker is cocked (by pulling back the slide), the grip safety protrudes until it's depressed by the shooter. This allows the pistol to fire once the trigger is pulled. In most other grip safeties, including those found on John Browning-designed Colt and FN pistols, the grip safety automatically springs back once the shooter has relaxed his hold on the grip, thus rendering the pistol safe again. The grip safety found on the Ortgies pistol, however, remains in the depressed or firing position until a small button—located on the left side of the frame just beneath the slide—is pushed, causing the grip safety to pop back. The .380 Ortgies model also has an active manual safety catch to supplement the grip safety/release button arrangement.

The safety system on the Ortgies pistol is actually faster to operate than the grip safety found on

The Ortgies pistol easily disassembles into the parts shown (top to bottom): slide, recoil spring, firing-pin assembly, frame (with barrel attached) and magazine. All Ortgies magazines made by Deutsche-Werke were nickel-plated and bear a "7,65m/m" marking on one side and a "9m/m" marking on the other, the same magazine feeding either round.

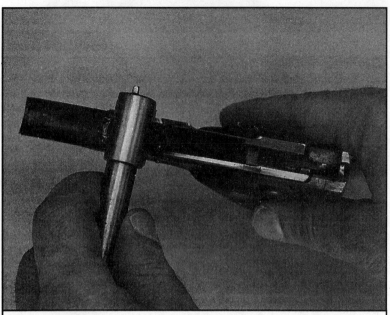

The barrel of the Ortgies pistol is easily detached from the frame by turning it left through 90 degrees, then lifting it off its seat in the frame (a method originally patented by Heinrich Ortgies).

Browning-designed pistols, because its release, similar to the modern Heckler & Koch P7, is completely instinctive. Another similarity is that both pistols will fire should the shooter, while pressing the trigger, suddenly depress the grip safety, usually causing an errant shot to be fired by mistake. While the Ortgies pistol may be fast to fire, it requires extreme caution, because once a shooter has taken a cocked-and-loaded Ortgies pistol firmly in hand, he's working with a weapon that's ready to fire instantly. With all its speed and efficiency, and in the interests of safe gun handling and responsibl ownership, the safety arrangements of the Ortgies pistol demand extensive familiarization.

Interestingly, the grip-safety release button on the Ortgies pistol also doubles as a disassembly latch. To field-strip an Ortgies pistol, the first step is to remove the magazine from the grip, then pull back the slide (to make sure the firing chamber is unloaded). Next, the slide is drawn back and held, with the front of its slide serrations even with the rear of the grip-safety button. At this point, the grip-safety button is depressed while at the same time the rear end of the slide is lifted out of the frame. The tubular firing pin, guide rod and spring are then removed and the recoil spring pulled off the front of the barrel (the barrel can be cleaned while still on the frame or it can be easily removed by turning it 90 degrees to the left and lifting it off the frame).

The Ortgies is a well-designed, well-made pistol that is at once unusually smooth, sleek and graceful. Moreover, it carries, handles and shoots well. Fortunately, these pistols remain on the market and spare parts are readily available. As German handguns go, it was never an expensive gun and is still a low-priced item, making it popular with entry-level handgun collectors.

ORTGIES PISTOL

Manufacturers	Years Produced	Caliber/Capacity	Dimensions
Ortgies & Compagnie, Deutsche-Werke both of Erfurt, Germany	1920–22 1922–c. 1928	.32 ACP (7.65mm)/ 8 rounds .380 ACP (9mmKurz)/ 7 rounds (also .25 ACP)	Barrel Length: 3.5" O.A. Length: 6.4" Height: 4.3" Width: 1.1" Weight: 23 oz. (unloaded); 27 oz. (loaded)

RUBY PISTOLS

The first Eibar-type pistol was introduced in Spain around 1907. The most famous version, the Ruby, was created by the Gabilondo Company of Spain in 1914. Based on the John Browning-designed FN Model 1903, the Eibar-type Ruby lacked much of the FN's refinement, but they were more than adequate for low-pressure .32-caliber cartridges. When World War I erupted in August of 1914, Gabilondo offered the Ruby to neighboring France, whose army, desperate for a small personal defense weapon, saw merit in the Ruby design.

The Ruby pistol issued to French and Italian armed forces during World War I featured a lengthened grip for holding a nine-round magazine (top). The prewar commercial seven-shot model (bottom) also found its way to the front, albeit in much smaller numbers. The top pistol was made by Gabilondos y Urresti, forerunner of today's Llama Gabilondo y Cia and creator of the original Ruby pistol in 1914. The smaller gun was made by Alkartasuna, a company made up of former Gabilondo employees who supplied handguns to the French.

Thus, in the spring of 1915, France awarded Gabilondo an open-ended contract for 10,000 pistols per month, later increasing its order to 30,000 per month. And when the Italians joined the Allies in 1915, they too ordered Ruby pistols from Gabilondo, though in smaller quantities than the French.

Since Gabilondo could not meet this enormous demand on its own, the company subcontracted the pistol to various other Spanish gunmaking firms. Of the four major Spanish handgun manufacturers still in business, three of the four made their own variations of the Ruby design for the French (Star made a Ruby-style pistol of its own design but with similar characteristics for the French market).

Eventually dozens of companies in and around the Basque town of Eibar supplied arms of this pattern to the French and Italian armed forces. By war's end, an estimated one million Ruby-type pistols had gone to France and by all accounts performed adequately.

Gabilondo discontinued its own Ruby design shortly after the war, but other manufacturers, particularly in Spain and France, continued to manufacture weapons of the same type, although mostly in the smaller six- and seven-shot prewar pocket versions. The resulting flood of cheaply made automatic pistols gave the Spanish gunmaking industry a largely unjustified reputation for shoddy work-manship. Pistols of this type served in huge numbers during the Spanish Civil War (1936–1939), after which the Spanish government forced all but four Spanish handgun manufacturers to cease business. Ruby-type pistols also served widely in World War II in the Finnish, French, German, Italian and Yugoslav armed forces. Although it has been decades since any official agencies used a Ruby-type pistol, many of these guns remain extant.

The Ruby is a blowback-operated automatic pistol with a single-action trigger. Its grips are made of black, checkered hard rubber or wood, often with interesting company logos pressed into them. The magazine capacity on French-contract guns was most commonly nine rounds, but concealment models with six or seven rounds were available. Much rarer were high-capacity models containing 12- or 20-round magazines, some including a selector switch on the slide to allow for fully automatic fire.

The operating controls include a magazine release in the bottom rear of the frame and an unusual manual safety that doubles as an aid in disassembly. After locking the slide open with the manual safety, one simply grabs the barrel and rotates it, disengaging the locking lugs from the slide. The barrel then comes out through the front of the slide, after which the safety is released, allowing the slide to

The Alkartasuna Ruby pistol is about the same size as the modern Colt Mustang shown below it.

be removed from the frame as well.

The Ruby-type pistol tested was an Alkartasuna seven-shot compact model probably made shortly after World War I. Despite its age, the gun performed surprisingly well. Five-shot off-hand groups fired from a distance of 25 feet measured as little as 1½ inches across, which is good shooting for a small pistol. Trigger pulls vary in their ease of operation, but the Alkartasuna's seemed better than most pistols of this type. Its reliability was flawless using both FMJ and Winchester Silvertip hollowpoint ammunition.

Because magazine interchangeability was limited among the Ruby-type pistols, the French marked their pistol frames with the manufacturer's initials. "GU" on this model stands for Gabilondos y Urresti, forerunner of Llama Gabilondo y Cia.

The main arguments against Ruby-type pistols are their advanced age and the wide variations in their quality of manufacture. One should never carry one of these pistols cocked. Instead, carry it in "Condition Three"—loaded magazine, empty firing chamber—cocking and loading it at the first sign of danger. Ruby pistols are not usually hard to find, often showing up in gun stores as trade-ins and at gun shows. As always, take it to a reliable gunsmith for a safety check before firing the weapon.

RUBY PISTOLS

Manufacturer	Years Produced	Caliber/Capacity	Dimensions	(Alkartasuna 6-shot)
Various Spanish/ European Firms	1914 –late 1940s	.32 ACP/6, 7, 9, 12 or 20 rounds	Barrel Length: 3.1" O.A. Length: 5.8" Height: 4.1" Width: 1.1" Weight: 25 oz. (unloaded); 28 oz. (loaded)	

SMITH & WESSON MODEL 469

When Smith & Wesson first introduced the Model 469 in 1983, it hoped the U.S. armed forces would be interested in such a concealable 9mm pistol with its high-capacity magazine. Although military interest failed to develop, the gun became an instant success with civilians and police forces. In fact, it quickly became the company's best-selling automatic pistol and is still available as the Model 6904 with only slight modifications.

Mechanically, the Model 469 is typical of the automatic pistol design begun by Smith & Wesson's Model 39, produced in the mid-1950s. It features a modified Browning short-recoil mechanism, double-action trigger and a Walther-type, hammer-dropping manual safety. Subsequently, the Model 469 eliminated the removable bushing found on earlier Model 39- and 59-series guns, and also included a passive firing-pin safety.

Considerably smaller than any previous Smith & Wesson automatic pistol, the Model 469 offered excellent quality of manufacture, including grips made of stippled black plastic (known as Delrin) and good sights.

The Model 469 proves its accuracy with this five-shot offhand group using Federal's 9BP jacketed hollowpoint ammunition. Fired from 25 feet, the group measured 1.2 inches across.

In testing the Model 469, accuracy, handling and reliability were excellent. The double-action trigger pull for the first shot was not good, but it can be mastered with practice. Its only serious drawback is a pronounced finger-rest magazine extension which, while it certainly makes the gun easier to handle, adds more than 1½ inches to the height of the pistol. Some owners of this model have actually sanded down the finger rest. Still, even without any modifications the Model 469 is a top choice for a powerful concealable weapon—even by today's high standards.

SMITH & WESSON MODEL 469

Manufacturer	Years Produced	Caliber/Capacity	Dimensions
Smith & Wesson Springfield, MA	1983–1988	9mm/12 rounds	Barrel Length: 3.5" O.A. Length: 6.9" Height: 5.3" Width: 1.2" Weight: 26 oz. (unloaded); 32 oz. (loaded)

WALTHER MODEL 4

The Waffenfabrik Walther, the German manufacturing firm founded by Carl Walther in the late 1880s, introduced its fourth major pistol design around 1910. An enlarged version of the Model 3 pocket pistol, it was intended to be a police pistol; but the onset of World War I changed that when the German armed forces ordered 250,000 of these pistols to serve as a substitute standard handgun for their P08 Luger.

In any event, the Model 4 firmly established Walther in the handgun business, and soon the factory had to be moved into a new, larger facility in Zella-Mehlis, with many additional workers hired to meet the large military orders. At the end of World War I, the factory was closed down briefly, with operations resuming in early 1920. Though Model 4 production tapered off significantly in the 1920s, it was still being made until 1929, when it was replaced by the advanced double-action Model PP. The Model 4 saw considerable service

The Walther Model 4 proved quite accurate in tests. This five-shot offhand group fired from a distance of 25 feet measures only 1.5 inches across.

among German police forces between the World Wars: in fact, many were still being used by German military and police forces as late as 1945.

The Model 4 is a blowback-operated automatic pistol with a single-action trigger. Its grips are usually made of hard rubber, with caliber markings on early pistols of 7,65 on their top portion (as a reminder to use only 7,65mm (.32 ACP) ammunition). Later guns use the company logo—CW (for Carl Walther)—in the same spot. In any event, the overall impression is of a much more refined gun than the contemporary Spanish-made "Ruby" pistols (*see* page 89).

Walther made several variations of the Model 4, but after the first few hundred guns (which Walther adapted from leftover Model 3 slides) all were the same size and were similar mechanically as well. The operating controls on the Model 4 included a magazine release in the heel, and a recoil spring wrapped around the barrel and kept in place by an elongated bushing. Sleek and handy, it is comparable in size and performance to the Ruby pistol currently used by the French. The two Model 4s tested produced fine accuracy for such small pistols. Reliability was flawless using military ball (FMJ) ammunition; the only jam, which occurred at the onset of testing with hollowpoint ammunition, was easily corrected. Like the Ruby-type pistols, however, the Model 4 suffers somewhat from advanced age. Its manufacturing quality, though, has never been in doubt.

WALTHER MODEL 4

Manufacturer	Years Produced	Caliber/Capacity	Dimensions
Waffenfabrik Walther Zella-Mehlis, Germany	1910–1918	.32 ACP (7.65mm)/ 8 rounds	Barrel Length: 3.5" O.A. Length:6" Height:4.2" Width: 1.1" Weight: 19 oz. (unloaded); 22 oz. (loaded)

WALTHER MODEL 8

The Model 8, which the Walther company introduced in 1920, was a great success, with over 250,000 built by the time production stopped midway through World War II. It was extremely popular among civilians and also served in a number of police forces and armies, especially Germany's armed forces.

A blowback-operated automatic pistol with a single-action trigger, the Model 8 is built of the best materials and boasts excellent workmanship. Most have a deep blued finish, with grips made of plastic or exotic material (although most customers opted for the basic model). In all, the Model 8 is a beautiful gun, with clean, sleek lines—definitely one of the most appealing handguns ever made. Its high standards of fit and finish only add to the overall effect of a classy and refined product. Indeed, it has become somewhat of a collector's item and rarely comes cheap.

One of the Model 8's most appealing features is its easy disassembly. One simply removes the magazine and draws back the slide to clear the weapon of ammunition. Next, the trigger guard is pulled down at the front and, while the front of the guard is held down, the slide is drawn back, up and clear of the frame. This same takedown system was used later with great success in Walther's

The Walther Model 8 disassembles into the following components (top to bottom): slide, frame and magazine. The removable recoil spring surrounds the barrel, which is pinned to the frame.

PP/PPK series. Operating controls include a magazine release in the heel of the frame and a manual safety located on the left side of the frame slightly ahead of the grip.

The Model 8 is a bit larger than most .25-caliber pistols, which may account for its popularity as a service pistol. And yet, while it is extremely accurate, its .25-caliber cartridge is quite weak. All of the cautions about old single-action automatic pistols apply to this one as well.

WALTHER MODEL 8

Manufacturer	Years Produced	Caliber/Capacity	Dimensions
Waffenfabrik Walther Zella-Mehlis, Germany	1920–1943(c.)	.25 ACP (6.35mm)/ 8 rounds	Barrel Length: 2.8" O.A. Length: 5.1" Height: 3.6" Width: 0.8" Weight: 13 oz. (unloaded); 15 oz. (loaded)

WALTHER MODEL 9

In 1921, the Waffenfabrik Walther firm of Germany introduced its Model 9, one of the smallest and most clever automatic pistols ever invented. Like several of Walther's later pistols, including the PP/PPK series and the P.38, the Model 9's design is so good that it has been copied by a number of manufacturers of small auto pistols.

The 6,35 marking on the grip of this Model 9 refers to the 6.35mm Browning cartridge, popularly known in the U.S. as the .25 ACP.

A cocked-striker indicator on the Model 9 alerts the shooter that the pistol is ready for firing. Note how the indicator protrudes slightly from the slide, indicating the striker is cocked and, assuming the gun is loaded, the gun will fire when the trigger is pulled. This is not a loader-chamber indicator as that found on later Walther PP series and P.38 pistols.

Oddly enough, the Model 9 is actually a revised version of Walther's very first pistol, the Model 1, which the company had introduced in 1908. The Model 9 was built to a higher standard, however, with many beautifully embellished models still existing, including those plated in gold and silver and engraved to a greater or lesser degree.

Mechanically, the Model 9 features an open-slide design that exposes the entire upper portion of the barrel. The recoil spring, which lies underneath the barrel, is held in place by a small piece fitted into the rear of the slide and frame. The rear portion of the striker protrudes from the rear of this piece, indicating the gun is ready to fire. This assumes, of course, that the shooter has loaded the firing chamber. Unlike some later Walther designs, the cocked-striker indicator on the Model 9 does not indicate whether a round has been loaded into the firing chamber. And, like many pocket pistols of its era, the Model 9 uses a bottom magazine release, with a manual safety lever (located along the left side of the frame just behind the trigger) that must be pushed down to fire.

Like the slightly larger Walther

Model 8, the Model 9 proved extremely popular in pre-World War II Europe and elsewhere. The A.F. Stoeger Company imported Model 9s into the U.S. throughout the prewar years, and they were also sold widely in Africa by the Charles Heyer Company of Nairobi, Kenya (then a British colony).

During World War II the Model 9, thanks to its small size and light weight, became a popular hideout pistol among German armed forces personnel. Despite carrying only six rounds of the weak .25-ACP cartridge, it provided enough fire power when needed. After war's end and the capture of the Walther factory in 1945, the Model 9 went out of production. Later, in 1961, Walther revived the design in modified form, and it became known as the Model TP. Walther's current Model TPH is similar in concept, though not in design, to the Model 9, as are several other highly successful modern vest-pocket pistols, notably the Raven and the Jennings.

The Model 9 is extraordinarily trim and light, hence easily carried. Its sighting equipment—consisting of a simple hemispherical front sight blade and a groove along the rear of the slide for a rear sight—may be tiny and primitive, but adequate for its purpose as a defensive weapon. Recoil is virtually nonexistent. Actually, aside from the weakness of its .25-caliber cartridge and striker spring, the Model 9 has no real shortcomings. Still, anyone who uses this pistol as a defensive handgun should have a competent gunsmith look it over before firing it.

WALTHER MODEL 9

Manufacturer	Years Produced	Caliber/Capacity	Dimensions
Waffenfabrik Walther Zella-Mehlis, Germany	1921–1945	.25 ACP/ 6 rounds	Barrel Length: 2.0" O.A. Length: 4.0" Height: 2.4" Width: 0.8" Weight: 9 oz. (unloaded); 11 oz. (loaded)

WALTHER PPK

Between 1908 and 1929, the German firm of Waffenfabrik Walther made a series of pistols of high quality but unimaginative design. Walther was committed to pistols, however, and sought a larger share of the ever-growing police and civilian handgun market. Thus, in 1929, Walther introduced the *Polizei Pistole* or PP, a pistol of such advanced design that it has been copied by literally scores of manufacturers. The PP's rugged construction, its fixed barrel pinned to the frame, its recoil spring surrounding the barrel, and its double-action trigger mechanism, all have for more than 60 years stood as the standard against which medium-frame automatic pistols have been judged.

Among the Model PP's features is a manual safety that is easily accessible to the right thumb. It can be left down in the safe position and pushed up to the fire position before shooting, although many shooters leave it in the fire setting all the time, relying upon the stiff double-action trigger pull for safe carrying. That way, the shooter has only to pull the trigger to fire the gun.

Sensing that a more concealable version of the PP would sell well, Walther unveiled a shortened version later in 1929 called the PPK, which caught on immediately. Its advanced features, combined with a wide choice of calibers (.22 LR, .25 ACP, .32 ACP and .380 ACP), its rugged construction and

Walther's PP (right) remains in production, but its later Model PPK (left), which is slightly smaller, has become a more popular gun for concealed-carry applications. Note the PPK's shorter barrel, slide and grip.

the famous Walther quality all contributed to its immediate and enduring success. This was especially true in European police and military circles prior to World War II. Its appearance coincided with the rise to power of the Nazis in Germany, becoming one of their top pistols, dubbed *Ehrenwaffe*, or "Honor Weapon."

During wartime, Germany's armed forces used both the PP and the PPK in large quantities, making them highly desired captured items among Allied troops. By 1945, the German government and Nazi Party had purchased more than 200,000 PPs and more than 150,000 PPKs. After the war, when the Allies halted German armaments production, manufacture of these pistols continued in other countries, notably France, Turkey, the U.S. and possibly China. The PP remains a top police pistol through much of Western Europe, Asia and Africa, although it has been largely supplanted in its native Germany by 9mm handguns. The PPK is still widely used as a concealable police pistol, especially in Europe, while both guns serve in several military establishments as aircrew pistols and as armament for off-duty officers.

Variants of the PP/PPK series include the rare KPK, a slightly modified PPK from the late wartime years. The KPK had a lightweight aluminum alloy frame and a lengthened slide that almost completely enclosed the hammer. The PPK/S was introduced in 1969 to appeal to the U.S. market, which had just been closed to the PPK by the Gun Control Act of 1968. The PPK/S combined the short barrel and slide of the PPK with the PP's slightly taller frame (to meet the U.S. government requirement that imported handguns must be at least 4.0 inches high). The PPK/S is still extremely popular in the U.S. Combining the short barrel of the PPK with the longer, handier grip of the PP make the PPK/S, in the opinion of many knowledgeable shooters, the finest pistol of the entire PP series.

One of the major problems with the PP series pistols, and with Walther pistols in general, is that they are more expensive than many competing handguns. Walther quality has never come cheap. Because of this, Interarms wisely negotiated manufacturing licenses with Walther for several of the company's more popular guns. Manufacture of the models PPK/S (introduced 1979), PPK (introduced 1986) and TPH (introduced 1987) now takes place at Ranger Manufacturing in Gadsden, AL. Since these three models are being made domestically, Interarms can sell them for far less than similar guns imported from Germany. And the PPK and TPH are too small (under provisions of the Gun Control Act of 1968) to be imported in any case. Not only are the American-made guns far less expensive than their German counterparts, but their quality is fully competitive with that of pistols made in Walther's own factory. Interarms also offers these pistols in a stainless steel finish option not available from Walther.

The PPK, along with the PP and P.38, features a loaded-chamber indicator. When a round is in the firing chamber, the pin protrudes slightly (shown just above the hammer), providing a more advanced feature than the cocked-striker indicator on Walther's earlier Model 9.

A PPK is shown ready to fire a double-action first shot. Its slide-mounted safety has been moved forward and up, exposing a red dot. The loaded-chamber signal pin protrudes from the rear of the slide. The trigger finger of this woman's shooting hand is in the act of moving from its safe position outside the trigger guard onto the trigger. Note the size of the gun in relation to the woman's small hand.

The PPK, despite the age of its basic design, remains a good, compact handgun by modern standards. It competes primarily with such small, short-barreled .38 Special revolvers as Colt's Detective Special and Smith & Wesson's J-frame series. Using a modern .380 cartridge of advanced design, a PP or PPK offers a level of stopping power competitive with that of a .38 Special cartridge fired from a short barrel (such as the 1.9-inch barrel of Smith & Wesson's Chiefs Special). In addition, a PPK pistol is more comfortable to shoot than a .38 Special revolver, because its recoil levels are milder than the .38 Special's and therefore more easily mastered. Moreover, the sleek, smooth lines and compact dimensions of the PPK also suited it to

The PPK/S introduced in 1969, combined the slightly taller frame of the PP with the short barrel/slide of the PPK. These features have made the PPK/S extremely popular in the U.S.; it is considered by many to be the finest pistol in the PP series.

concealed carry.

There remains room for improvement, however. Double-action pistols made by Walther are notorious for a heavy double-action trigger pull, and the PP/PPK series is no exception. The double-action trigger pull of a typical PPK, for example, may run from 18 to 20 rounds, making first-round hits difficult. Single-action follow-up shots, though, have a much lighter trigger. With practice, a skilled shooter with a PPK can achieve good accuracy up to 50 feet. As for reliability, a small .38 revolver is, given certain gun/ammunition combinations, considerably better than a small automatic pistol.

The PP/PPK series also has a propensity for hammer bite, a painful condition that results when the hammer or slide pinches the shooter's hand (especially left-handers) with the slide in full recoil. Early PPKs made until the early 1940s have an especially short grip tang and are equally notorious for their hammer bite propensities. Even later PPKs, with their slightly longer grip tang, and the still larger PP and PPK/S, have been known to injure unwary shooters.

Despite these shortcomings, the tremendously successful PP/PPK series pistols are well designed and beautifully made, sparking a revolution in compact pistol design that continues to this day. The PP's double-action feature, its method of construction, even its attractive appearance, all have inspired numerous imitators over the years and remain the standard by which knowledgeable shooters judge compact automatic pistols.

WALTHER PPK

Manufacturer	Years Produced	Caliber/Capacity	Dimensions (current PPK)
*Originally Waffenfabrik Walther Zella-Mehlis, Germany	1931-1945 (Orig.); 1953-Present	.22 LR, .25 ACP, .32 ACP, .380 ACP/ 6-7 rounds	Barrel Length: 3.5" O.A. Length: 6.1" Height: 3.9" Width: 1.1" Weight: 21 oz. (unloaded); 24 oz. (loaded)

*Currently Carl Walther Waffenfabrik, Ulm (Donau), Germany; also postwar production under license by Manurhin (France), Interarms (U.S.), and others.

4. SMALL CALIBER/ BACKUP PISTOLS

CONTENTS

Accu-Tek AT-380 .103
American Arms PK 22 105
  PX 22 107
Baikal IJ-70 111
Beretta Model 21 113
  Model 70 114
  Models 84F/85F 116
  Model 86 120
Bersa Models 83, 85 and 86 121
Browning Model BDA-380 124
  Buck Mark 125
Colt
  .380 Government Model/Mustang Series . .128
  Woodsman Series 132
CZ Model 83 134
Davis D38 Derringer 136
  P-380 137
European American Armory .380 European .139
FÉG Model B9R 141
  Model PA-63 (AP-9, PMK-380) 142
  Model SMC-380 (SMC-918) 145
Grendel P-12 148

Heckler & Koch P7K3 150
Hi-Point Model CF 152
Intratec Protec 25 154
Jennings/Bryco Model 38 157
Jennings J-22 158
Iver Johnson (AMAC) Pony 160
Mitchell Arms Trophy II 161
Navy Arms TT-Olympia 165
PSP-25 168
Raven 172
Remington Model 51 174
Ruger Mark II Government Target Model . .175
Russian PSM 179
Seecamp LWS-32 181
Semmerling LM-4 183
SIG-Sauer P230 185
Smith & Wesson Model 41 187
  Model 2213/2214 188
  Sigma .380 Compact 192
Taurus Model PT-22/PT-25 194
  Model PT-58 197
Walther Model TPH 200

This section details more than 50 popular low-powered pistols. Relatively small in size and chambered in .22, .25, .32 and .380 caliber, these are the handguns most often chosen as "backups" for emergency use. You will also find listings of a few larger guns chambered in the same light-weight calibers as the true backups. These are usually target pistols or outdoorsmen's guns, which can, in an emergency, be pressed into defensive use. Many such guns—notably pistols made by Beretta, Walther, Ruger and High Standard—are widely used by armed forces around the world and are quite capable of defensive duties.

Carrying a small, backup pistol requires compromise; that is, you must be prepared to give up hitting power, shooting comfort, accuracy and sometimes even reliability. But if your choice is a good one, and your small defensive handgun is close at hand when needed, the compromise can literally be a lifesaver. As an old saying goes, "A .25 in the pocket beats a .45 in the briefcase every time."

Good concealability involves not only overall length, but width and height as well. The best concealable handguns should be no more than 6.5 inches long and one pound (16 ounces) in weight. Light weight is obviously an important asset to any gun used for backup purposes, especially for those who plan not to use a holster. Thickness is a critical dimension for concealability, so much so that width specifications are given for each gun. Most backups hover around the one-inch mark, but innovative engineering — witness the S&W Sigma with its .8 inch width — has resulted in remarkably thin designs. The small gun must also have snag-free contours to prevent it from catching on clothing or a holster at critical moments. And last, but certainly not least, the small gun must be totally reliable. When firing weak cartridges, you need the assurance that your small defensive handgun will fire every time.

As for ammunition, the best choice for a small gun of this kind is not necessarily the best choice for a larger gun, even when it uses the same caliber. Your ammunition priorities should be as follows: reliability, power and accuracy.

Within the small pistol category, you have the choice among derringers and automatics. The derringer is the poorer choice because of its limited ammunition capacity, which is usually only one or two rounds (although as many as four shots are possible with some models). Derringers also come in awkward shapes, which make them difficult to hold and shoot accurately. They do have a good power-to-size ratio, however, and they usually are available for a relatively low cost.

Automatic pistols provide smooth, flat contours and are quicker and easier to reload than either derringers or revolvers. Manufacturers continue to work hard in developing superior small automatic pistols, and most of those in the low-powered calibers feature a simple unlocked breech or " blowback" construction. This is less complex, therefore less costly, than the locked-breeched mechanisms found on most larger automatics. Still, small automatics are generally more complicated than revolvers. The magazine spring, for example is under tremendous tension even when the gun is only partially loaded; so it is always necessary to move the manual safety from the "safe" to "fire" position. Also with an automatic, a misfired or dud cartridge requires that its primer be hit again, or the "dud" must be ejected by cycling the action manually. Manufacturers still have a way to go in providing foolproof reliability.

Here, however, are the best of those available on the market today.

ACCU-TEK AT-380

In 1990, Accu-Tek introduced the AT-380 to join its other pistols in .32 ACP, .22 LR and .25 ACP calibers (9mm and .40 S&W pistols have also been developed). The AT-380, in particular, has gained respect and a growing reputation as a useful concealable pistol for law-enforcement personnel and civilians alike.

Available in stainless or blued finishes, the AT-380's profile, construction and disassembly method are generally similar to those found in Walther's Model PPK (*see* separate listing). There are some important differences, however. The trigger mechanism on the AT-380 is single-action only; unlike the Walther pistol, its trigger guard must first be unfastened by an Allen-head wrench before the slide can be removed from the frame. The manual safety does resemble the Walther pistol's and moves in the same directions—up to fire and down to safe. But when the AT-380's safety lever is lowered, it does not automatically decock the hammer in Walther fashion. With its manual safety on, the AT-380 simply interposes a piece of steel between the hammer and firing pin. As a result, the AT-380 can be carried cocked and locked if desired; or if you elect to carry the pistol with its hammer down (uncocked), you must cock it before shooting.

The Accu-Tek AT-380 uses a pivoting trigger guard for disassembly much like the Walther PP-series pistols. Its trigger guard must first be detached by loosening the allen-head screw barely visible in this photo.

Another useful safety feature on the AT-380 is its firing-pin block, which can be disconnected only by pulling the trigger through its complete stroke before firing. With no magazine disconnect safety, the Accu-Tek gun will still fire with the magazine removed from the grip. While some prefer a magazine safety as an aid against careless handling, others prefer the ability to fire the pistol even while reloading or when the magazine is lost or damaged. In order to appeal to both sides, some automatic pistols are available with or without the magazine safety feature. The magazine release on the AT-380 is located on the left side of the frame, just underneath the slide, in PP/PPK style. The plastic finger extension on the magazine bottom also resembles the Walther model; but unlike the PPK, the slide on the AT-380 does not remain open after the shooter has fired the last round.

For a small pistol, the AT-380 has commendable accuracy. The author's five-shot offhand group, using Winchester 85-grain Silvertip hollowpoints, measures 1.6 inches across at a distance of 25 feet. At 50 feet, it measures 4.6 inches. By small pistol standards, the AT-380's sights are very good. Its trigger pull is stiff, though, with a great deal of creep in it, but that shortcoming does not seem to mar the gun's accuracy. Recoil, thanks to the pistol's shape, is not at all objectionable, nor is its overall handling in its class. Obviously, one

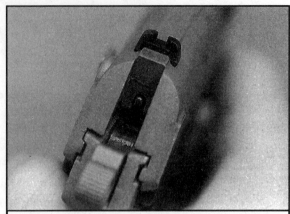

The AT-380's sights are excellent for such a small pistol. Well-rounded, the rear sight, shown here, is large enough for a generous sight picture.

Despite its size, the Accu-Tek AT-380 is surprisingly accurate, as shown in this 1.6-inch offhand group fired from 25 feet.

cannot expect to find the same performance and features of a full-sized pistol in such a diminutive gun. The chief consideration in using a gun like the AT-380 is to attain the highest degree of miniaturization possible. Overall, Accu-Tek has done a fine job with this gun.

ACCU-TEK AT-380

Manufacturer	Years Produced	Caliber/Capacity	Dimensions
Accu-Tek, Chino, CA	1990–Present	.380 ACP/5 rounds	Barrel Length: 2.75" O.A. Length: 5.7" Height: 4.0" Width: 1.0" Weight: 16 oz. (unloaded); 18.5 oz. (loaded)

AMERICAN ARMS PK 22

Originally made in the 1980s by Erma-Werke (Dachau, Germany) and imported into the U.S. by Charter Arms, the PK 22 was available in slightly larger .380 ACP and .32 ACP versions (Model 79K) and in .22 LR (Model 40). Shortly before it went out of business in 1991, Charter Arms gave up importation of this line of automatic pistols, which was picked up by American Arms. Because of unfavorable exchange rates, though, prices on imported pistols rose quickly to the point where they were no longer competitive with U.S.-made guns. As a result, American Arms astutely decided to manufacture the .22-caliber pistol locally, dropping the imported centerfire version. Called the PK 22, the small .22-LR version now costs only about half of what it did as an import.

Today the PK 22 is part of American Arms's "Classic Series," consisting of four pistols: the P-98, CX 22, PX 22 and PK 22—all styled to resemble their older, established ancestors, i.e., the P-98 resembles the Walther P. 38, the CX 22 is a full-sized PPK twin, the PX 22 looks like a downsized PPK, and the PK 22 resembles a small version of the Colt M1911A1. Despite their external similarity to older pistols, these Classic Series models are all based on Walther's PP/PPK series *(see* separate listing). All four have a recoil spring placed around the barrel, with dismantling controlled by pulling down the trigger guard, thereby separating the slide from the frame. Any resemblance of the P-98 and PK 22 to non-Walther designs is strictly external. What appears to be an M1911-type recoil spring plug and muzzle bushing at the front of the slide on the PK 22 are strictly cosmetic and nonfunctional, having been molded into the slide.

The manual safety on the PK 22 is located on the slide, PPK-style, and operates like the Walther pistols: "Down to safe and up to fire." Unlike the PPK, however, lowering the PK 22's safety lever to

The American Arms PK 22 (right) is similar in concept to the Walther PPK (left).

the safe position does not decock the hammer; it simply blocks the hammer's access to the firing pin by shielding the latter with a piece of steel (similar to the Accu-Tek AT-380 discussed earlier). This makes it possible to carry the pistol cocked and locked, which is the way many will choose to carry the pistol: ready for immediate firing.

The PK 22's similarity to the Walther PPK becomes obvious when shown disassembled for cleaning.

The PK 22 shoots with considerable accuracy and flawless reliability, which is no mean feat with rimmed .22 LR cartridges in an automatic pistol. Its one design problem is an incredibly heavy double-action trigger pull, which seems to be a flaw endemic to Erma-Werke designs. In contrast, the single-action trigger pull is light and easy to manage. Testing this gun for accuracy in double-action shooting, however, proved impossible, its pull being so heavy that by the time the pistol fired, the shot almost went off the target completely. When fired with the first shot single-action at 25 feet (using CCI Stingers) from the offhand position, five shots measured 1.6 inches; using Imperial ammunition from Canada, the group expanded to 1.7 inches; 1.9 inches with CCI Mini Mag; 2.7 inches using Federal Hi-Power; and 29 inches with RWS subsonics. Most groups were well-centered and looked better than these numbers indicate; for example, the TWS group placed three of the five shots in the 10-ring in a touching pattern only 1/3 inch across. A five-shot offhand group at 50 feet, using CCI Stingers, went into 3.6 inches.

Aside from its nearly impossible double-action trigger, the PK 22's overall handling is good. Unlike the Walther pistols, its slide does not remain open after the final shot is fired, a common fault of small, low-cost pistols. In its favor are the PK 22's flat, smooth contours, its reliability and more than acceptable accuracy. So for those who consider a .22-caliber automatic pistol adequate for personal defense, the PK 22 is a good buy.

The PK 22 is extremely accurate in single action, as this photo indicates. But the double-action trigger was so heavy that all five shots had to be fired single action.

AMERICAN ARMS PK 22

Manufacturer	Years Produced	Caliber/Capacity	Dimensions
American Arms, Inc. North Kansas City, MO	1991–Present	.22 LR/8 rounds	Barrel Length: 3.3" O.A. Length: 6.3" Height: 4.7" Width: 1.0" Weight: 22 oz. (unloaded); 23 oz. (loaded)

AMERICAN ARMS PX 22

Like the PK 22, the PX 22's design was the creation of Erma-Werke of Germany. Because this pistol is less than four inches high, it cannot be imported into the United States, so it became necessary to find a U.S.-based manufacturer to assemble or build the pistols locally. Iver Johnson initially took on the project, selling the Erma-designed pistol throughout the 1980s as the Model TP-22 in .22 LR caliber and Model TP-25 in .25 ACP. American Arms acquired these guns in 1989, calling them the PX 22 and PX 25.

Although the PX 22 may be a downsized Walther PPK *(see* separate listing) both in appearance and in function, it uses a bottom magazine release, which is only occasionally found on genuine PP/PPK pistols. Also, the slide on the PX 22 does not remain open after firing the last shot, as it does in the Walther pistols. The PX 22 features a slide-mounted safety lever which, in Walther-style, goes down to safe and up to fire; but in its safe position the hammer

The American Arms PX 22 (bottom) is essentially a slightly downsized PPK (top).

does not decock. Instead, the manual safety lever on the PX 22 merely blocks the hammer's access to the firing pin (same as the PK 22). This makes it possible to carry the pistol cocked and locked, an option not available on Walther pistols. Since the double-action trigger pull on the PX 22 is not nearly as heavy as that of the PK 22, carrying the former with the hammer down—in readiness for a double-action first shot—becomes a realistic alternative to cocked-and-locked carry.

The PX 22 proves accurate and reliable with a variety of cartridges. The double-action trigger pull, while heavy, is nowhere near as bad as the PK 22's. In recent tests, the double-action first shot typically widened the groups only by an inch or two. At 25 feet, when shooting from the offhand position, five shots placed inside 2.1 inches using Winchester's T22 Target brand. Other groups measured 3.1 inches with CCI Mini Mag, 3.8 inches using Imperial ammunition, and 4.0 inches with Winchester Super-X. A five-shot offhand group fired at 50 feet with Winchester Super-X ammo went into 5.3 inches.

To disassemble the PX 22, remove the magazine (1) and draw back the slide to clear the firing chamber. Then lower the trigger guard and prop it open (2). Finally, remove the slide backwards and upwards as shown (3). Completely disassembled, the PX 22 pistol (4) reveals (from top to bottom): slide, recoil spring, frame/receiver and magazine.

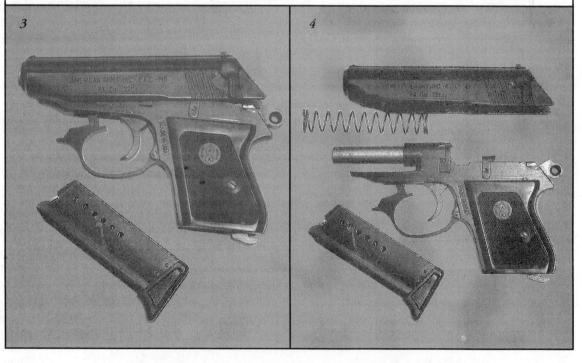

Despite its difficult double-action trigger pull, the PX 22 is reasonably accurate. This five-shot group, fired off-hand from a distance of 25 feet, measures 2.1 inches across.

A .25-caliber version of this gun is also available, and while centerfire .25 ACP ammunition is much more expensive than .22 rimfire, the former is less likely to malfunction. Rimfire primers occasionally refuse to ignite the powder charge in a cartridge, causing a hangfire (delayed ignition) or a misfire (no ignition). Also, the rimfire cartridge, with its widened rim around the rear of the cartridge, does not always feed reliably into the firing chamber of a small automatic pistol. Finally, .22-rimfire ammunition, being quite dirty, tends to gum up the inside of a gun more than most centerfire cartridges. This condition is easy to fix, of course, if one takes the time to clean the gun after every firing—good advice for any gun, whatever the caliber. Because rimfire ammunition is comparatively inexpensive, it does encourage more frequent practice than centerfire ammunition. The key to this light handgun, with its smooth contours, is simple: learn to shoot it as accurately as you possibly can, and of course practice, practice, practice.

AMERICAN ARMS PX 22

Manufacturer	Years Produced	Caliber/Capacity	Dimensions
American Arms, Inc. No. Kansas City, MO	1989–Present	.22 LR/7 rounds	Barrel Length: 2.9" O.A. Length: 5.4" Height: 3.8" Width: 1.0" Weight: 15 oz. (unloaded); 16 oz. (loaded)

BAIKAL

BAIKAL IJ-70

The Baikal IJ-70 is nothing more than a Russian-made Makarov PM pistol (*see* page 79) slightly altered so that it can be imported into the United States. As the exclusive manufacturer of this pistol for nearly a decade, the Russian gunmaker did, as one may have assumed, build an improved version of this classic. And so, to enable its importation into the U.S., Baikal and K.B.I., its importer, have modified the slide on the IJ-70 to include an adjustable rear sight. While it looks shoddy compared to the sleek unaltered Makarov, this rear sight is reasonably efficient without adding excess bulk. The Baikal's height— 4 inches— satifies the minimum size for an importable handgun.

Baikal also makes an IJ-70-01 version with the standard fixed rear sight, but this is for sale only in Europe and Asia. Other Makarov pistol manufacturers have had to modify their guns as well. Norinco has added an adjustable rear sight—fortunately with a less obtrusive pattern than the Baikal's. Sometimes it includes target-style grips with a prominent thumbrest on the left side. Other Makarovs made in eastern Germany and imported to the U.S. by Century Arms also have a sporting-type grip, equipped with a nonessential thumbrest.

Although the Baikal IJ-70 is one of the least accurate Makarov variations available, it fired this very respectable 2.4-inch, five-shot offhand group at 25 feet.

The Makarov's well-deserved reputation as a reliable and accurate pistol is certainly upheld by the IJ-70. Its minimum service life of 4,000 rounds, together with a stated reliability rate of 99.8 percent, works out to eight failures or fewer using 9x18mm Makarov ammuniton. Those who fire .380 ACP or 9x18mm Ultra or Police ammunition from a Makarov pistol are unwise to do so. Besides, an improved 9x18mm Makarov round is now widely available from several different manufacturers, including an excellent lightweight high-velocity hollowpoint round by Hornady; it is also reasonably priced.

In testing the Model IJ-70, a five-shot offhand group fired from a distance of 25 feet (using Norinco 94-grain FMJ) measured 2.4 inches cross. From 50 feet, it measured 4.7 inches. The pistol's adjustable sights work well, although the IJ-70 is hardly what one would call a target pistol. The trigger pull in double action is fairly heavy but smooth, while in single action it delivers a pronounced creep before releasing the sear. Overall, it's a good military trigger that's conducive to accurate shooting. Recoil is negligible and the gun is well suited to rapid fire.

The only shortcoming of the Model IJ-70 (aside from its rear sight) is a blued finish that lacks durability. Built more ruggedly than a Walther PP-series pistol, and much less expensive, the Baikal IJ-70 is an excellent choice for deadly accurate, close-range rapid fire. Indeed, this high-quality defensive weapon ranks among the top choices for a small automatic pistol.

BAIKAL IJ-70

Manufacturer	Years Produced	Caliber/Capacity	Dimensions
Baikal Izhevsk, Russia	1994–Present	9x18mm Makarov/ up to 8 rounds	Barrel Length: 3.7" O.A. Length: 6.3" Height: 5.0" Width: 1.2" Weight: 26 oz. (unloaded); 32 oz. (loaded)

BERETTA MODEL 21

When Beretta began selling its Model 92F to the U.S. armed forces in 1985, two smaller double-action pocket pistols based on the tiny single-action Model 950 were already in production at the Beretta U.S.A. plant in Accokeek, MD. The Model 20 had been introduced in Italy in the late 1960s, but because it was less than four inches high, it could not be imported into the U.S. A revised version went into production in this country in 1983 to satisfy the requirements of the Gun Control Act of 1968. This excellent .25-caliber pistol received mostly favorable reviews but went out of production within a few years, to be replaced by the improved Model 21. Although Beretta developed this pistol in Italy, it never went into production there. Instead, the company's Brazilian subsidiary, now owned by Taurus, built the Model 21 in Brazil and later, under Taurus management, developed it into the Taurus PT-22 and PT-25 (*see* separate listing). In the meantime, Beretta U.S.A. took up mass production of the Model 21 design in 1984, and it has since become one of the firm's best pistols.

While the Model 21 shares many features of the Model 950 (*see Complete Guide to Service Handguns*), the former's double-action trigger mechanism makes it a little larger. Initial issues came in

This photo illustrates how small, hence how concealable the Model 21 is in the hand.

a beautifully polished blued or nickel finish with smooth walnut grips. Then, in 1993, a Model 21 with a matte Bruniton finish—similar to current production Models 92 and 84/85—also came on line. This new model featured checkered plastic grips instead of fancier walnut ones; and because it was less expensive to produce than the blued or nickel guns, the price was a little lower. Since the low-pressure .22- and .25-caliber cartridges do not require a locked breech, the Model 21 uses a blowback mechanism. It also has an open-topped slide, and a tipping barrel similar to the earlier Model 950 and the later Model 86 in .380 caliber. The Model 21 has the same type of low-profile sights as the Model 950 too.

The Model 21's manual safety systems are much the same as the current-production Model 950BS. A manual lever located on the left side of the frame blocks the sear when pushed up into its safe position, and there's a half-cock notch on the hammer. Shooters thus have the choice of carrying a Model 21 either cocked and locked for a single-action first shot, or with its hammer down for a double-action first shot. The safety does not decock the hammer mechanically, though, so when the hammer is cocked and you need to lower it by hand, great caution is advised. Alternatively, you can load the gun by filling up the magazine, inserting it into the grip, then releasing the barrel latch and loading the last round right into the barrel, leaving the hammer uncocked and safely down throughout the whole procedure.

The accuracy of the Model 21 is, again, similar to that of the Model 950. Its barrel latching system has all the advantages and weaknesses of the 950. Still, the Model 21 seems absolutely reliable, even in its .22 LR version (.22 rimfire rounds are difficult to operate reliably in an automatic pistol, which is why John Browning designed the .25 ACP round to begin with). Armed with reputable brands of ammunition, Beretta has virtually eliminated feeding and ignition problems with rimfire ammunition in its Model 950 and Model 21.

Within the limitations imposed by its low-powered cartridges, the Model 21 is overall an excellent gun. Its competitive price, its accuracy and reliability make it a good choice for self-defense.

BERETTA MODEL 21

Manufacturer	Years Produced	Caliber/Capacity	Dimensions (.22 LR)
Beretta U.S.A. Accokeek, MD	1984–Present	.22 LR/7 rounds .25 ACP/8 rounds	Barrel Length: 2.5" O.A. Length: 4.9" Height: 3.6" Width: 1.1" Weight: 11.8 oz. (unloaded); 13 oz. (loaded)

BERETTA MODEL 70

In the early post-World War II period, Beretta began to look for a successor to its fantastically successful but aging Model 1934. The long-awaited replacement—the Model 70—finally appeared in 1958. Eventually, it became a whole series of pistols that were available in .380 ACP, .32 ACP and .22 LR calibers.

Although all Model 70 pistols shared a common frame, with a choice of lightweight aluminum alloy or heavier, more durable steel, Beretta offered variations in several barrel lengths and sighting options. These included the standard

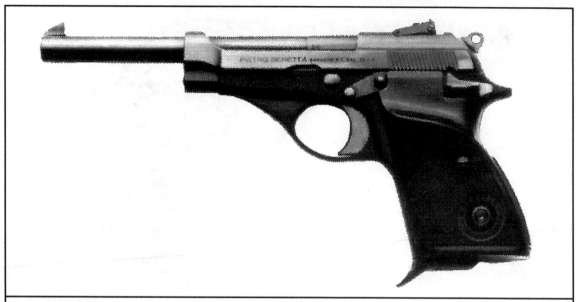

Beretta's Model 71 was a .22 LR version of the Model 70 that was equally accurate and reliable.

Model 70 in .380 ACP, .32 ACP and .22 LR calibers, and the later Model 70S, introduced around 1976, which included a magazine disconnect safety in all three calibers. Beretta sometimes sold the .22 version of the Model 70 as the Model 71, while the Models 72, 73, and 75 were .22 LR variants with longer barrels (just under 6 inches). The Model 74 also had a longer barrel and added an adjustable rear sight. While not a true target pistol, it was quite accurate, as most Model 70s are.

The Model 76 was Beretta's most deluxe version of the Model 70 series. Made in .22 LR, it had a lengthened slide assembly to stabilize the long barrel, anatomical wooden grips and specialized target sights. It was quite accurate and became one of the most popular versions of the Model 70. In all, the series sold extremely well and remained in production for 30 years, giving way finally in the late 1980s to more modern Beretta double-action pistols.

Despite its many similarities to the Model 1934, the Model 70 owed even more to the Model 951, from which came the Model 70's anatomical grips, external slide release lever and push-button, sear-blocking manual safety. Still, the Model 70 remained a medium-frame pistol meant to fill the tactical niche that had been so ably filled for decades by the Model 1934. Times changed, though, and .32- and .380-caliber pistols were no longer eagerly sought by military buyers. The lessons of World War II had taught, among other things, that large-caliber guns, particularly those chambered for the 9mm and .45 ACP, were the wave of the future.

For these and other reasons, the Model 70 was not adopted in any significant numbers by the world's armed forces. But it did become extremely popular in the civilian self-defense market and with the espionage community. The feature of the Model 70 which most appealed to these organizations was its extreme reliability. The pistol could also be fired rapidly and was devastatingly accurate at close ranges. It pointed well and was easy to carry. Its only weak spots—all of which compromised concealability—were its pointed front sights, prominent magazine extension and, on some models, bulky grips with a prominent left-side thumbrest. Fortunately, aftermarket accessories became available to correct

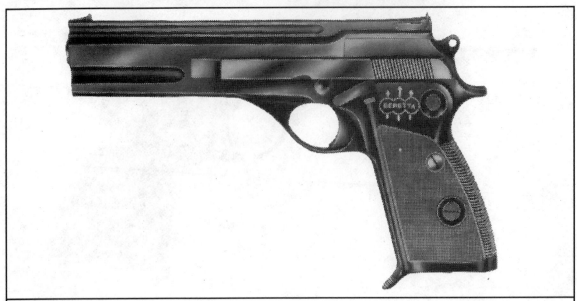

Beretta's most deluxe version of the Model 70 was the Model 76. In .22 LR, it had a lengthened slide assembly and specialized target sights. It was known for its accuracy and became one of the most popular versions of the Model 70.

most of these problems.

Overall, many consider the Model 70 to be the best small single-action automatic pistol for defensive purposes yet built. If you can find one of these handguns, it will not disappoint you.

BERETTA MODEL 70

Manufacturer	Years Produced	Caliber/Capacity	Dimensions (Model 70S)
Pietro Beretta, S.p.A. Gardone, Val Trompia, Italy	1958-Late 1980s	.380 ACP/ 7 rounds	Barrel Length: 3.5" O.A. Length: 6.5" Height: 4.8" Width: 1.4" Weight: 23 oz. (unloaded); 26 oz. (loaded)

BERETTA MODELS 84F AND 85F

When Beretta began selling its Model 92F to the U.S. armed forces in 1985, the demand for this new pistol skyrocketed. To take advantage of the celebrity status, Beretta wisely decided to revise its 1975-vintage Model 84/85 line, chambered in the .380 ACP cartridge, to more closely resemble the Model 92F. Thus in 1987 did the Models 84F and 85F come into being.

While the earlier Models 84 and 85 had a polished blued finish and rounded trigger guard, the updated 84F and 85F substituted the matte Bruniton finish and squared "combat" trigger guard of the Model 92F in 9mm. The modified .380s also added a chrome-lined barrel bore, which extended barrel life and simplified cleaning. Because of the low power of the .380 cartridge, the Models 84F and 85F retained the unlocked breech or blowback mechanism of the earlier Models 84 and 85, plus their frame-mounted ambidextrous safety levers (in preference to the slide-mounted decocking levers of the Model 92F).

The open-topped slide on Model 84F/85F pistols also followed the Beretta heritage. Their disassembly procedure is identical to that of the bigger Model 92, as are their double-action trigger mechanism and alloy frame. Although the Model 84F/85F pistols are slightly larger than a Walther PP, they are no heavier, thanks to their alloy frames.

Their slightly longer grips make them comfortable to hold in an adult-sized hand. The grips on the Model 84F, with its 13-shot, high-capacity magazine, are 5mm (about ¼ of an inch) wider than the 8-shot Model 85F grips (both models have the same maximum width as measured across the safety levers). The grips on both pistols are checkered black plastic, as on the Model 92F. Beretta also offers optional checkered walnut grips at a slightly higher price.

Similar to the Model 92F, the sights are well set up for instinctive shooting, featuring the two-dot system. The front sight on the 84F/85F pistol series has a white dot and is integral with the slide; the

The Model 85F is identical to the Model 84F, except for the slightly slimmer frame required to hold the smaller-capacity, eight-round magazine.

This right-side view of the Model 85 reveals its ambidextrous safety. The Model 84 series, introduced in 1975, was one of the first pistol designs offered by a major manufacturer to acknowledge the needs of left-handed shooters.

rear sight, which dovetails into the slide, is drift-adjustable for windage and is highlighted with a white hemisphere.

Like the full-sized military models, the Model 84F/85F pistols boast a variety of safety features. These include a firing-pin lock that is deactivated only by the trigger; an ambidextrous manual safety that operates with the hammer cocked or uncocked; and a loaded-chamber indicator. Beretta has eliminated the half-cock notch on the hammer found on earlier Model 84/85 types, but it has retained the useful decocking position to the safety levers: when pushed all the way up, the manual safety automatically lowers the hammer to its uncocked position.

Like most Beretta pistols, the trigger on the 84F/85F pistol leaves much to be desired. The single-action trigger has too much slack or creep, while the double-action trigger starts out rather spongy, then breaks sharply. Still, in tests conducted for this book, the Model 85F proved both accurate and reliable. One five-shot, 25-foot offhand group, using Winchester Silvertip 85-grain hollowpoints, measured just 2 inches across. Other 25-foot groups with a variety of hollowpoint and FMJ rounds measured in the 2.5-inch range. At 50 feet, a five-shot off-hand group measured 2.7 inches, using

CCI Blazer 88-grain jacketed hollowpoints.

Overall, the Beretta Models 84F/85F offer good performance. Some may prefer all-steel guns, but then an alloy frame is not so important on a medium-frame, small-caliber pistol like these .380s, especially compared to a larger 9mm, .40 or .45-caliber pistol. These Berettas are highly competitive and, in the author's opinion, come in a very strong second to the top-ranking CZ 83 discussed later.

This five-shot offhand group, fired from a distance of 50 feet and measuring just 2.7 inches, exemplifies the sensational accuracy of Beretta's Model 85F.

BERETTA MODELS 84F AND 85F

Manufacturer	Years Produced	Caliber/Capacity	Dimensions
Pietro Beretta, S.p.A. Gardone, Val Trompia, Italy	1987–Present	.380 ACP/ 13 rounds (84F)* .380 ACP/ 8 rounds (85F) *(10 rounds since 1995)	Barrel Length: 3.8" O.A. Length: 6.8" Height: 4.8" Width: 1.4" Weight: 84F—23 oz. (unloaded); 29 oz. loaded) 85F—21 oz. (unloaded); 24 oz. loaded)

BERETTA MODEL 86

When Beretta's Model 92F won the U.S. armed forces contract in 1985, still another Beretta pistol—the Model 86—was affected. Over a period of many years, Beretta had carefully developed this .380-caliber pistol, which was similar in size to the Model 85 but had the tipping barrel of the Models 950, 20 and 21. Because of the demand for the Model 92F, Beretta had to put the Model 86 on hold for more than five years. Despite tantalizing rumors of this new .380 tipping-barrel pistol, the Model 86 did not appear in quantity until 1992.

Although a lot of work went into developing this gun, the results were mixed at best. First, the good news: The Model 86 is beautifully made and quite accurate. Its construction, fit and finish are flawless. The trigger is crisp (though heavy in double action) and the ambidextrous safety levers operate with a short, positive motion far superior to that found on Beretta's 9mm pistols. The gun is slim and conceals well.

But the overshadowing bad news about the Model 86 is its barrel-latching system, which is far inferior to that of the Models 950, 20 and 21 and seriously compromises its value as a fighting handgun. In the smaller Beretta pistols, the barrel latch is located on the left side of the frame, slightly ahead of the leading edge of the grip, putting it directly under the thumb of a right-handed shooter. In the event of a misfire, it takes only a fraction of a second to pop open the barrel and eject the misfired round. Remember, in the Models 950, 20, 21 and 86 there is no extractor; the shooter cannot merely rack the slide in the event of a misfire, as with most automatic pistols.

Unfortunately, the designers of the Model 86 put the slide release lever on the left side of the frame, its traditional location, and moved the barrel latch over to the pistol's right side. Thus, in the event of a nonfiring round, the shooter must push the barrel latch fully forward with the right-hand trigger finger, eject the round from the barrel, lower the barrel, hold it down while rotating the barrel latch 180 degrees to the rear (to lock it), and then operate the slide to bring up a fresh—and hopefully functional—round. It may be argued that misfires are rare with modern factory-loaded ammunition—but they do happen!

With good, reliable ammunition, though, the Model 86 operates very efficiently. Its sights are similar to those found on Models 84, 85 and 92F. These, combined with the good trigger pull, contribute to high accuracy. In testing, the author fired a five-shot, 25-foot offhand group that measured 1.2 inches across, using IMI-made Samson 95-grain FMJ rounds. At 50 feet, a five-shot offhand group, using Winchester 85-grain Silvertip hollowpoints, measured 2.7 inches. Overall, though, the Model 86, while well-made, is probably best left to collectors of Beretta pistols in favor of the Models 84 and 85 discussed earlier.

BERETTA MODEL 86

Manufacturer	Years Produced	Caliber/Capacity	Dimensions
Pietro Beretta, S.p.A. Gardone, Val Trompia, Italy	1990–Present	.380 ACP/8 rounds	Barrel Length: 4.33" O.A. Length: 7.33" Height: 4.8" Width: 1.3" Weight: 23 oz. (unloaded); 27 oz. (loaded)

BERSA MODELS 83, 85 AND 86

The Bersa line began as an inexpensive group of .22 LR, .32 ACP and .380 ACP single-action pistols based loosely on the ever-popular Walther PP line. Its prices were significantly less than one would pay for a Walther, but handling and reliability were compromised to some extent. Then in 1989, Bersa introduced the much-improved Models 83 and 85 with double-action triggers. The Model 86—a combat version of the Model 85—followed in 1992 (a .22 LR version, the Model 23, is also available). All offered in a rich blue or satin nickel finish, the guns are attractive and well-made.

All Bersa pistols are Walther-style blowbacks featuring frame-mounted safety levers on the left side. The magazine release is located, Walther-style, high up on the left side of the frame slightly beneath the slide. These guns look like the Walthers, too, but they have fuller grips and feature non-hinged trigger guards. To disassemble them, a takedown lever located on the right side of the frame must be rotated.

Perhaps underrated, the Bersa line from Argentina is well worth a look. Chambered in .380 ACP, the Model 83 is available with eight-round magazine, while the Model 85 is available in high-capacity format.

The Models 83 and 85 are equipped with attractive, blond-colored walnut stocks, which are stippled for a comfortable yet secure hold. Bersa's wooden stocks are among the best available on a combat pistol. Unfortunately, not enough manufacturers offer them. Oddly, the grip on the seven-shot Model 83 feels about the same in width as the 13-shot Model 85 (limited to 10 rounds for U.S. civilian sale since 1995), the reason being that the wooden stocks (or grip plates) on the Model 83 are much thicker than the Model 85. It would seem to make more sense if the Model 83 were made as slim as possible, especially since it must give up six rounds of magazine capacity. The Model 86 stock is a textured rubber type that wraps around the

The latest Bersa .380-caliber, medium-frame pistol, the Model 86, sports a matte finish, squared trigger guard and rubber grips.

entire grip frame, not unlike those found on some modern Colt pistols.

All three guns have adequate sights, set low enough to minimize snagging on one's clothing or holster during a fast draw from concealment, and large enough to obtain a decent sight picture. The rear sights are adjustable for windage, with all three pistols' sights using the three-dot sighting system so popular on today's pistols. These up-to-date Bersas also feature a firing-pin safety in which the firing pin is blocked against any forward motion until the full rearward motion of the trigger unlocks it. They also include a magazine disconnect safety, which prevents firing whenever the magazine is removed from the grip—even when a round is left in the firing chamber. This particular safety feature should never be used as a substitute for common sense and courtesy, of course. A gun must always be handled as if it were loaded and could go off at any moment.

With their recurved, hooked trigger guards and lengthened grip tangs, these Bersa pistols suffer somewhat in looks. Still, the extended grip tang has a definite function; i.e., it protects the shooter's hand from being injured by a recoiling slide or cocking hammer. The recurved trigger guard, on the other hand, is an unfortunate affectation that some target shooters popularized a number of years ago.

We refer to the "finger-forward" two-handed grip, in which the first finger of the support hand holds the leading edge of the trigger guard. This finger-forward hold may have some limited value on the shooting range, particularly when used with a bench support, but it is at best only marginally useful as a defensive grip. Those who support this shooting style claim that the extended index finger of the support hand helps reduce recoil, thereby allowing faster follow-up shots. Unfortunately, any time saved this way is lost at the outset as the wandering index finger assumes a position that effectively isolates it from the other fingers of the support hand.

Another problem with this finger-forward hold is that the recurved trigger guards designed for it represent a potential source of snagging, either when the pistol is drawn or on reholstering. Accidental shootings while reholstering are, as we know, fairly common, so any feature of a gun that complicates reholstering—an operation often carried out under great stress—is certainly undesirable. The recurved-triggerguard argument is not solely an indictment of Bersa's otherwise fine pistols; it's a criticism of a gun style that should be made extinct. In general, one should look for a gun with smoothly contoured lines rather than lots of sharp, angular surfaces. Smooth guns are, after all, much easier to carry and shoot.

Based on the author's limited experience with Bersa pistols, they appear to be good if not exceptional performers. The double-action trigger pulls are long but not as heavy as Walther's PP or PPKs. Reliability is sometimes a weak point, and you may want to test-fire one of these guns before buying; if so, use a variety of ammunition types before making a decision. Automatic pistols—smaller ones in particular—can be fussy about what ammunition provides the best performance. In general, though, Bersa Models 83, 85 and 86 are solid, attractive, well-made guns. They may not have the market appeal or resale value of a Beretta or a Walther, but, like the Astra Constable, they offer good performance at a reasonable price.

BERSA MODELS 83, 85 AND 86

Manufacturer	Years Produced	Caliber/Capacity	Dimensions
Bersa S.A. Ramos Mejia, Argentina	1989–Present (Models 83/85) 1992–Present (Model 86)	.380 ACP/7 rounds (Model 83) .380 ACP/13 rounds (Models 85/86)	Barrel Length: 3.5" O.A. Length: 6.6" Height: 4.75" Width: 1.4" Weight: 22-26 oz. (unloaded); 33 oz. (loaded)

BROWNING BDA-380

In 1975, Beretta introduced its .380-ACP Model 84, an advanced pistol featuring a 13-round, double-column magazine, a reversible magazine release catch, and an ambidextrous safety. The last two features appealed to left-handed shooters, and in fact the Model 84—and the eight-shot Model 85 that followed soon after—were among the first automatic pistols made to suit left-handed as well as right-handed shooters.

In the late 1970s, Fabrique Nationale Herstal (FN) had a problem. Its pocket pistol—the outmoded Model 1910—had been an excellent gun for its time but held little appeal for modern shooters. And so, in 1978, FN (a major shareholder of Beretta stock) told the company to start designing a modified version of the Model 84. Known in Europe as the "FN 140DA" and in America as the "Browning BDA," this ranks high among the medium-frame automatic pistols now available.

The BDA-380, which debuted later than the initial BDA, differs from Beretta's Model 84 chiefly in its slide construction, which is a conventional closed pattern with a small ejection port. The BDA's safety arrangements are also different. After the hammer is lowered into a resting half-cock position, the manual safety can, if one so chooses, be left down in the safe position. Like the Model 84, the BDA features a loaded-chamber indicator built into its extractor.

Browning offers the BDA-380 in either blued or nickel finishes, with smooth wood grips. The sights, which are not quite up to Beretta standards, resemble the marginal sights offered on early FN Browning High Power pistols. Despite this, the BDA-380 shoots well and, considering its 13-round magazine capacity (reduced since 1995 to 10), is easy to carry and conceal. Not an inexpensive handgun, it is, however, worth looking into by those who seek a high-quality .380-caliber pistol.

BROWNING BDA-380

Manufacturer	Years Produced	Caliber/Capacity	Dimensions
Made in Italy for Fabrique Nationale/Browning Herstal, Belgium	1982–Present	.380 ACP/10 rounds	Barrel Length: 3.8" O.A. Length: 6.75" Height: 4.9" Width: 1.4" Weight: 23 oz. (unloaded); 27 oz. (loaded)

BROWNING

BROWNING BUCK MARK

Since Browning introduced its fine single-action rimfire Buck
Mark in 1985, it has grown into a series of automatic pistols designed
for a variety of shooting activities, including personal defense, plinking,
target shooting and competition. Its magazine holds 10 shots, which is the same
capacity as competing models made by Mitchell Arms (High Standard) and Ruger.
Like its competitors, the Buck Mark is large for a .22-caliber pistol, but its size contributes to the gun's excellent accuracy, handling and reliability. Another plus is the Buck
Mark's traditional all-steel construction. And, like its distant ancestor, the Colt Woodsman
(designed by John Browning in 1915), its internal hammer is concealed by the slide.

Not surprisingly for a target pistol, the Buck Mark boasts excellent sights, producing a sight picture that is large and clear. The front sight is an unmarked Patridge pattern, while the rear sight is
fully adjustable for windage and elevation.

The gun's fit, finish and workmanship are excellent. Standard finish is a functional matte blue
with attractive, highly polished slide flats. Its grips of checkered black plastic (wooden grips are also
available) are comfortable to hold. A manual safety is located on the left side of the frame. All operating controls are in the same places where owners of the Colt M1911 or Browning High Power pistols

*Browning's Buck Mark is a useful outdoorsman's pistol that can also be pressed into action as a defensive hand-
gun in an emergency. It is extremely accurate, as indicated by this 1.1-inch, 25-foot offhand group.*

The Micro Buck Mark, a recent addition to the target-type .22 LR Buck Mark series, has a reduced-length barrel of only 4 inches, which makes it quite concealable.

would expect to find them.

The Buck Mark shoots extremely well. Recoil is negligible in a gun this size shooting a .22 LR cartridge. The single-action trigger on the standard out-of-the-box model is light and crisp, but newer Buck Mark variants have adjustable triggers, which shooters can tune to suit their needs. Thanks to these superior aspects, the Buck Mark is impressively accurate. One five-shot, 25-foot offhand group measured 1.1 inches across, while at 50 feet it covered just 2.2 inches. With a rest, the Browning pistol is even more impressive, firing a five-shot group measuring less than half an inch across.

In addition to its accuracy, the Buck Mark has demonstrated flawless reliability, even when firing old and otherwise questionable ammunition. Rimfire ammunition, we know, is notoriously unstable and unreliable compared to centerfire ammo and is less likely to fire when needed. And when .22-rimfire rounds do misfire, they are less likely to fire when struck by the firing pin a second time, or even many times, whereas malfunctioning centerfire ammunition frequently will fire under the same conditions. For that reason the author prefers revolvers in .22 Long Rifle or .22 Magnum over automatic pistols. Revolvers turn their cylinders to bring a fresh, unfired round beneath the firing pin each time the trigger is pulled. But the Buck Mark's reliability when tested was impressive, firing perfectly every time.

Probably the best choice in the Buck Mark series for self defense is the Micro Buck Mark, which comes with a reduced-length barrel of only 4 inches long. For that reason, the Ruger Mark II, Smith & Wesson's 2214, Mitchell Arms' High Standard series, and the Colt Woodsman series, in addition to the Buck Mark itself, are not the best choices for personal defense. They are included in this volume, though, because so many people carry only this type of handgun. Moreover, these guns can and do work to protect one's life when no larger-caliber handgun is available. In the outdoors, for instance, a person may have nothing but one of these pistols to use in an emergency situation. But beware the light trigger pull of a .22-caliber pistol and plan your shots even more carefully than you might with a gun firing a larger round.

The Buck Mark is an excellent gun and one of the least expensive target-type pistols available in .22 Long Rifle caliber. Yet its performance is competitive with the most expensive models.

BROWNING BUCK MARK

Manufacturer	Years Produced	Caliber/Capacity	Dimensions
Browning Morgan, UT	1985–Present	.22 LR/10 rounds	Barrel Length: 5.5" O.A. Length: 9.5" Height: 5.5" Width: 1.3" Weight: 32 oz. (unloaded); 33.5 oz. (loaded)

COLT .380 GOVERNMENT MODEL/ MUSTANG SERIES

In 1983 Colt, one of the oldest and most respected names in the firearms industry, reentered the world of small-caliber pistols with its new .380 Government Model. Based on the time-tested and widely accepted M1911 design, the .380 became an instant success and is now widely used as a backup pistol by police and civilians alike.

Four years after unveiling its .380 Government Model, Colt brought out the little Mustang .380 line. Except for being shortened by half an inch, and with a shorter frame and a magazine capacity reduced from seven to five rounds, the Mustang is identical to the .380 Government. With the shortening of the barrel, the muzzle bushing (found on both the .380 Government Model and the original .45-caliber M1911 design) was eliminated. Not only did this simplify the manufacturing process and reduce the number

The Colt Mustang Plus II combines the full grip length of the .380 Government Model with the shorter compact barrel and slide of the Mustang.

A modern .380 Colt Mustang Pocketlite (bottom) is an excellent backup gun for the M1991A Commander (top) or any other Model 1911-series pistol.

of parts that could break or malfunction, it also made disassembly for cleaning and maintenance much easier.

The standard all-steel .380 Government weighs 21.75 ounces, but an alloy-framed Pocketlite version, weighing about a pound, is available. The steel-framed Mustang, by contrast, weighs 18.5 ounces unloaded, and the Mustang Pocketlite, with an aluminum-alloy frame, weighs 6 ounces less. An intermediate version, the Mustang Plus II, features the standard Mustang's shortened barrel and slide joined to the slightly larger frame of the .380 Government Model. This allows it to hold two rounds more than the Mustang, hence the "Plus II" designation.

Like the .380 Government, the Mustang is a medium-frame, locked-breech, single-action automatic pistol. The Pocketlite version tested for this book has a nickel finish, but Colt also offers it in a polished blued finish. Fit and finish are excellent throughout. The sights on these Colt pistols are low-profile, well-rounded and most unlikely to snag on clothing. However, in one area Colt has taken miniaturization a bit too far, as the sights are undersized for combat accuracy.

Although the Colt .380 Government Model and Mustang are in a class of small pistols that usually come with unlocked breech and a simple blowback action, Colt decided in favor of a breech-locking mechanism based on the John Browning-designed short recoil system used in the classic M1911 and M1911A1 pistols. In this system, recoil causes a link (located beneath the barrel) to pull the rear end of the barrel out of alignment with the slide. This locking system adds significantly to the cost of these guns, but it does serve to make the recoil soft and more manageable, even in the Mustang Pocketlite.

Colt has updated the safety mechanisms on all its pistols, the .380 series included. For example, a firing-pin lock is released only when the trigger is pulled all the way to the rear at the moment the pistol is fired. A half-cock notch on the hammer helps lower the risk of accidental firing should the shooter's thumb slip while cocking the hammer. A manual safety lever, located on the left side of the

COLT MKIV SERIES '80 .380 GOVERNMENT MODEL

Manufacturer	Years Produced	Caliber/Capacity	Dimensions
Colt Industries Firearms Division Hartford, CT	1983 – Present	.380 ACP/7 rounds	Barrel Length: 3.25" O.A. Length: 6.0" Height: 4.2" Width: 1.0" Weight: 21.75 oz. (unloaded) 25.25 oz. (loaded)

frame, pushes up to "safe" and down to "fire." In its safe setting, the manual safety locks the sear lever, trigger, hammer and slide. When pushed down into its fire position, a red dot appears on the frame, warning that the weapon is not in its safe setting.

Another change in the .380 Colt design is the elimination of the M1911 grip safety. On a large gun like the M1911—one that will most likely be carried in a holster—a grip safety does not necessarily increase safe handling; in fact, it can actually prevent some shooters from firing the pistol when needed. For guns small enough to be carried in a pocket, though, a grip safety makes more sense. It's significant that John Browning designed all of his small pistols for FN and Colt to include a grip safety. Today's .380 Colt thumb safeties are much more positive in operation, and much less likely to be rubbed accidentally into firing position, than the tiny safeties on Browning's old pocket pistols. Therefore, eliminating the grip safety probably makes sense and certainly holds down the complexity and cost of the pistol. Particularly with a small automatic pistol, the number of moving parts should be kept to an absolute minimum so as to reduce the chances of something going wrong.

Despite its tiny size, the Colt Mustang Pocketlite fits nicely in the hand and is comfortable to hold and shoot. Other small guns, though, can be as uncomfortable to shoot as a large gun—a point that should not be lost on recoil-sensitive shooters. Even the Mustang Pocketlite, the smallest and lightest of the Colt .380 series, has good handling characteristics. The slightly larger and heavier .380-caliber Colts are even better. Their rear grip tangs, moreover, are large enough to prevent hammer bite, and the hammers themselves are rounded. Thanks to the locked-breech design, which makes rapid-fire follow-up shots possible, felt recoil is light. This capability—to "double tap" or "hammer"—is critical in a low-powered round like the .380 ACP, where one shot is effective in stopping an assailant only about half the time.

In order to reach their compact dimensions, many small, tightly fitted automatic pistols must sacrifice accuracy or reliability. But the Colt .380s, following the lead of the larger M1911A1 parent pistol, have retained both qualities. In testing a Mustang Pocketlite, a five-shot, 25-foot offhand group

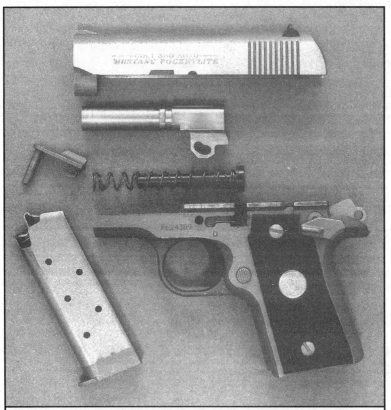

This disassembled Colt Mustang Pocketlite shows its locked breech construction, a direct descendant of the full-sized .45-caliber M1911.

The Colt .380 pistols, despite their small size and tiny sights, are capable of impressive accuracy; witness this 1-inch, 25-foot offhand group using Remington 88-grain jacketed hollowpoints.

measured a mere 1 inch, using Remington's excellent 88-grain jacketed hollowpoint. Other 25-foot offhand groups did not score as well, however. Cor-Bon's powerful 90-grain +P jacketed hollowpoint put five shots into a 2.6 inch group, while Samson's 95-grain FMJ round made a 2.9-inch five-shot group at the same distance. The best 50-foot five-shot group, using the Remington 88-grain JHP once again, measured 4.4 inches, an accuracy level that compares favorably with much larger service-type pistols. Automatic pistols generally tend to be fussy about the ammunition they use, so it's smart to experiment with several different brands before making a final selection.

The .380-caliber Colts are known, however, for their failure to feed on occasion. Once the pistol has been fired a few dozen times, though, the bearing surfaces begin to wear slightly against each other, thereby smoothing the action. This reinforces the point that any new handgun used for defensive purposes, especially an automatic pistol, should be taken to a shooting range and fired with several types of ammunition to determine: (1) which ammunition is the most reliable, and (2) which ammunition provides the best accuracy for that pistol. The most accurate round may not necessarily prove the most reliable in a given pistol. If you must choose, take a less-accurate round that is more reliable. An extremely accurate pistol that jams when you need it won't be much help, will it?

Overall, the Colt .380s, despite their small size, are excellent pistols that can be carried full-time with confidence. Their only weaknesses are the slightly undersized sights and an inherited single-action mechanism. With the latter, one cannot simply pull the trigger to fire the pistol; some action is required to carry the pistol in safety and then make it ready to fire. Otherwise, it's tough to find fault with the Colt .380s. Colt has done an excellent job in fitting a handy .380 pistol into the dimensions of a .25 ACP size.

COLT MKIV SERIES '80
MUSTANG, MUSTANG PLUS II, MUSTANG POCKETLITE

Manufacturer	Years Produced	Caliber/Capacity	Dimensions
Colt Industries Firearms Division Hartford, CT	1987-Present	.380 ACP/5 rounds .380 ACP/7 rounds (Plus II)	Barrel Length: 2.75" O.A. Length: 5.5" Height: 4.0" Width: 1.0" Weight (unloaded):18.5-20 oz.; 12.5 oz. (Pocketlite) (loaded): Add 2.5 oz. for 5 rounds, 3.5 oz. for 7 rounds

COLT WOODSMAN

In 1915, Colt introduced yet another John Browning design: the .22- caliber Woodsman pistol. Known primarily as a designer of military firearms, Browning also made many excellent sporting arms for Colt, Winchester and Fabrique Nationale. Among the best and most enduring of these was the Woodsman, long considered a favorite handgun for outdoorsmen/plinking/hunting. The First Issue Woodsman is shown at right. Although it saw some military service during World War II, the Woodsman was used largely as a training handgun.

The Woodsman was in production from 1916 until 1977, with only a short break during World War II (1943–1947), due to increasing government orders for other Colt arms, notably the M1911A1 pistol. Although it has been out of production for several years, copies of the Woodsman are still being made in Argentina and China, among other countries. In 1993, Interarms announced it would distribute a copy made by Norinco (China), and later that year Colt announced its plans to reintroduce the pistol.

Basically, the Woodsman is a single-action automatic pistol with an internal hammer concealed by the slide and an unlocked breech. Used primarily as a plinking or survival pistol, it is accurate and reliable enough to provide meat for the pot—and good service against human attackers in an emergency. Some variations of the Woodsman have attained the rarified atmosphere of "collectible" status and are generally reserved for hoarding and/or display rather than for practical purposes.

Several different versions of the Woodsman were made available, including the Target, Match Target, Sport, Challenger and Huntsman. Mechanically, these pistols were all about the same. Even the low-budget model, the Challenger—produced from 1950 to 1955 and replaced by the Huntsman—was well-made, reliable and accurate by modern standards. It cut costs by using cheaper plastic grips and simplified sights. Today, Woodsman pistols feature a single manual safety lever, located on the left side of the frame, which pushes up to safe and down to fire. On its safe setting, the manual safety locks the sear, hammer and slide.

The sights on all Woodsman pistols provide an excellent sight picture for easy and efficient aim-

In 1955, the Huntsman (above) replaced the Challenger (made 1950–1955) in the Colt Woodsman series.

ing. Their triggers are good, too, offering a crisp, light pull not found on most service pistols. These two factors, plus the almost total lack of recoil associated with the Woodsman's substantial weight and small .22 LR cartridge, all contribute to good accuracy. Using Challenger models, a five-shot, 25-yard (75-foot) offhand group measured 3.5 inches across.

The Woodsman pistols are also known for their reliability. Like their Ruger, High Standard and Buck Mark counterparts, they are big enough to avoid many of the feeding problems associated with rimfire cartridges in small pistols. As such, they offer good possibilities as a self-defense handgun. Although it's too big to conceal readily, the Woodsman definitely has the accuracy, reliability and ammunition capacity to help save your life should the need ever arise.

COLT WOODSMAN

Manufacturer	Years Produced	Caliber/Capacity	Dimensions
Colt Industries Firearms Division Hartford, CT	1916–1977; reintroduced 1993	.22 LR/10 rounds	Barrel Length: 6.5" O.A. Length: 12.4" Height: 5.5" Width: 1.0" Weight: 28 oz. (unloaded); 30 oz. (loaded)

CZ MODEL 83

When Ceska Zbrojovka (CZ) introduced its Model 83—also called vz.83 or CZ 83—in 1983, the world was a far different place than it is today. The original purpose of this pistol was to arm Czechoslovakia's police forces. Its predecessor, the vz.82, a 12-shot 9mm Makarov version of the same gun, was at the same time replacing the big vz.52 as Czechoslovakia's armed forces standard handgun.

The CZ 83 first appeared chambered in .32 ACP (7.65mm Browning) with a 15-shot magazine. Ceska Zbrojovka, sensing an export potential for this firearm, quickly added a .380-caliber version that held 13 shots. Today, the CZ 83 (now with 10-shot capacity) enjoys a growing popularity among law enforcement and military shooters in several countries.

Showing its Walther and Makarov influences, the CZ 83's disassembly is controlled by unlatching the front of the trigger guard from the frame, plus its double-action trigger mechanism. Among its numerous original touches, however, are a fully ambidextrous magazine release and safety, and an interlock between the magazine and the trigger guard (i.e., the magazine must be removed from the grip before the trigger guard can be lowered to begin disassembly). The CZ 83 is also more rugged than the Walther and, despite having twice as many parts, it even compares favorably with the Makarov in this regard.

Like most .32, .380 or 9mm Makarov pistols, the CZ 83 uses a blowback or unlocked-breech mechanism. Its all-steel construction and high-capacity magazine make it a large pistol for its caliber. The CZ 83s leave Czechoslovakia with a polished blued finish, although Magnum Research, the U.S. distributor, offers several special editions, including an all-chrome beauty. Fit and finish on the CZ 83 are excellent throughout.

The rear edge of the ramp front sight on the Model 83 is highlighted with a narrow white bar, while the rear sight has two white dots. The markings make the front sight more conspicuous than the rear sight, which is good. Unlike the CZ 75 (but like the later CZ 85), the top of the slide on the CZ 83 is serrated to break up glare.

The safety setup of the CZ 83 uses the same types of controls and safety mechanisms found on the later CZ 85 9mm pistol. When pushed up to its safe position, the manual safety lever on the CZ 83 locks the slide, hammer and sear, allowing cocked-and-locked carry. Like other CZ pistols, the manual safety on a CZ 83 can be applied only with the hammer cocked (applying the safety does not decock the hammer). Like the original CZ 75, it still has an inertial firing pin that requires considerable force before the firing pin can overcome spring pressure sufficiently to strike the hammer and fire the pistol. The CZ 83 also includes a firing-pin lock that releases only when the trigger has been pulled all the way back. The magazine/trigger guard interlock mentioned earlier is another safety feature; it helps ensure that the pistol is unloaded before the shooter begins to disassemble it. Many accidental shootings occur because the victim tried to disassemble a weapon without making sure it was unloaded.

The CZ 83 boasts a smooth trigger in both double-action and single-action modes. Being larger than the typical blowback pistol, it fits nicely in the hand and is comfortable to hold and shoot.

There's very little recoil, even with hot Cor-Bon +P ammunition. The CZ 83 is also quite accurate. One five-shot, 25-foot offhand group measured 1.3 inches using Cor-Bon's 90-grain +P jacketed hollowpoint ammunition. Another similar group, using Israeli-made Samson 85-grain FMJ ammunition, measured 1.5 inches. With Winchester's Silvertip 85-grain hollowpoint, two 25-foot offhand groups measured 1.8 and 1.9 inches across. Even the worst result, using CCI Blazer 88-grain jacketed hollowpoints, put five shots into a 2.4-inch group from 25 feet. This kind of consistency from one brand of ammunition to another is most impressive. At 50 feet, a five-shot group fired with Silvertip hollowpoint ammunition measured 2.9 inches across. Another five-shot group with Samson FMJ went into 3.5 inches; and still another five-shot group using Cor-Bon measured 4.6 inches. But when the double-action first shot was thrown out, the remaining four single-action shots went into a square measuring a mere 1.9 inches. That is truly sensational accuracy for most shooters, including those who test-fire larger pistols with a greater sight radius.

The CZ 83 is accurate and pleasant to shoot, as shown by this 1.3-inch, 25-foot offhand group fired with Cor-Bon +P hollowpoints.

In testing three different CZ 83 pistols over a period of not quite a year, the author experienced only one failure to feed. And that occurred with a hollowpoint bullet during the first firing of that particular pistol with a full magazine. In subsequent firings, using all other brands of FMJ and hollowpoint ammunition, that same pistol performed flawlessly.

If the CZ 83 has any shortcomings, it lies in the stiffness of its operating controls. The magazine, for one, is difficult to load to its full capacity. Nine or 10 rounds will go in without incident, though, and you can get in the full complement if you work at it. The magazine release is also quite stiff, but it will eject the magazine completely from the bottom of the grip (unlike CZ's larger 9mm pistols, the Models 75 and 85). There's some stiffness in the manual safety lever, too, but all of these controls do loosen up with extended use.

The only other objection to the CZ 83 is its size. Glock's Model 19 and a handful of other automatic pistols in 9mm and .40 S&W caliber are not much larger than the CZ 83. But if you are limited by official policy to .380 caliber, or if you prefer its milder recoil and less chance of overpenetration (compared to 9mm), then this is an excellent pistol.

CZ MODEL 83

Manufacturer	Years Produced	Caliber/Capacity	Dimensions
Ceska Zbrojovka Uhersky Brod, Czech Republic	1983–Present	.380 ACP/ 10–13 rounds	Barrel Length: 3.8" O.A. Length: 6.9" Height: 4.9" Width: 1.3" Weight: 26 oz. (unloaded); 32 oz. (loaded)

DAVIS D38 DERRINGER

Although Davis Industries makes its own P-32 and P-380 pistols, the company is better known as a maker of derringers. Most of these are small models chambered in .22 LR and .22 Magnum, but in 1993 the company introduced the slightly larger, more powerful Model D38, a two-shot .38 Special derringer.

The fit and finish of the Model D38 are excellent. Together with its attractive, bright-chrome finish and black composition grips, this model presents an imposing appearance well out of proportion to the gun's compact size and the limited ammunition capacity of a derringer.

Like most derringers, the D38 is a break-open type, with the barrel hinging controlled by a lever located behind the trigger on the right side of the frame. This opening latch locks in a detent (to hold the barrels closed) and swings forward to unlock and open the barrels for unloading or reloading. The empty cartridge is removed by a manually operated extractor on the right side between the two barrels. When this extractor is pushed rearward, it forces the two empty cartridges partway out of the breech end of the barrels. From this position they are then easily shaken or plucked loose so that two fresh cartridges can be inserted. When you have only two shots to work with before reloading, you need every advantage.

Firing is accomplished by a single-action mechanism. After loading, a spur hammer must be moved beyond the half-cock setting to its fully cocked position. The cross-bolt safety button is then pushed in from the left side of the frame toward the right side. This places the weapon on "safe," while pushing it from right to left arms the derringer. This safety arrangement, which allows cocked-and-locked carry, is better suited to left-handed shooters, who can easily push the safety to its "fire" setting with the shooting-hand thumb. A right-handed shooter, on the other hand, must push the safety to the fire position with the index finger.

Since derringers are strictly close-up weapons, the large sights on the Model D38 give a nice touch but are a wasted effort. In one test-firing, a two-shot, 10-foot offhand group measured 1.2 inch-

Despite its small size, single-action mechanism and tiny sights, the D38 can deliver two solid hits very fast at close range. This 1.2-inch offhand group, using two Federal Nyclad 125-grain +P rounds, was fired from a distance of 10 feet in about three seconds.

es, using Federal's Nyclad "Chiefs Special" 125-grain hollowpoint load for maximum expansion.

The D38's shortcomings are those found in most derringers: a limited capacity of only two rounds, a slow rate of fire (because the hammer needs to be recocked prior to each shot), and a severe recoil that seems inevitable whenever a manufacturer tries to obtain maximum power from a small package.

Although the Davis D38 is not a gun to be used for pleasure, it does offer two shots of a serious combat cartridge in a small but sturdy package. For those who prefer carrying a derringer, this is a good caliber to choose. You must, however, be prepared to accept the increased recoil over smaller, weaker rimfire models.

DAVIS D38 DERRINGER

Manufacturer	Years Produced	Caliber/Capacity	Dimensions
Davis Industries Chino, CA	1993–Present	.38 Special/2 shots	Barrel Length: 2.7" O.A. Length: 4.65" Height: 3.4" Width: 0.9" Weight: 11.5 oz. (unloaded); 14 oz. (loaded)

DAVIS P-380

Davis Industries introduced its Model P-380— a five-shot .380-caliber pistol—in 1991. Endowed with excellent accuracy and reliability, it was priced below $100 and continues to do very well. (A similar five-shot version in 32 ACP—the P-32—is also in production.) The Davis P-380 strongly resembles the smaller .25 ACP pistol made by Raven (*see* separate listing), chiefly in its method of disassembly and the use of a cocked-striker indicator (a pin that protrudes from the rear of the slide when the striker spring is compressed).

The Davis P-380 pistol disassembles in much the same way as Walther's Model 8: (top to bottom) slide, firing pin, removable recoil spring wrapped around one-piece barrel/frame and magazine. A number of other modern compact pistols, notably the Raven and the Jennings/Bryco pistols, are built similarly.

A tubby little gun, especially in width, the P-380 is available in either a bright chrome finish or in a black matte Teflon. The quality of workmanship, as with other Davis handguns, is excellent, especially considering the low price.

The P-380, with its blowback or unlocked-breech mechanism, is constructed mostly of investment-cast zinc alloys. This manufacturing technique greatly reduces costs compared to more traditional guns made of forged and milled steel.

Unfortunately, this method of manufacture also makes the P-380 a large and rather heavy pistol for its caliber, not to mention its limited five-round magazine capacity.

The P-380 has a manual safety lever located on the left side of the frame. When this lever is pushed up to its "safe" position, it locks both the slide and the sear to allow cocked-and-locked carry. Unfortunately, the safety lever is noticeably undersized and could prove disastrous for shooters as they try desperately to thumb it down to the fire setting.

Even with its undersized sights, the P-380 is a surprisingly good shooter. Moreover, its trigger pull is crisp and smooth, better than almost anything in its class. A five-shot, 25-foot offhand

The Davis P-380 is surprisingly accurate. This 25-foot offhand group measures 2.2 inches across.

group measured 2.2 inches using Israeli-made Samson 95-grain FMJ ammunition; and at 50 feet a similar group measured 5.2 inches across. Although the owner's manual advises against using hollow-point ammunition (because of possible feeding malfunctions), test-firing Winchester Silvertip 85-grain hollowpoint ammunition with the P-380 proved perfectly safe, reliable and accurate.

In addition to its undersized safety and sights, the P-380 has an irritating habit of ejecting the empty cartridge casings straight up and back at the shooter, much like Beretta's Model 1934. Also, its slide, in common with most small and inexpensive pistols, does not hold open on the last shot. And the magazine capacity—only five rounds—could be a real handicap in an extended firefight.

All in all, however, the Davis P-380 is an impressive pistol that can outshoot the Jennings/Bryco Model 38 *(see* separate listing) in its price range and even compete well with the Accu-Tek AT-380, which costs almost twice as much. For its price and caliber, this gun is a top buy.

DAVIS P-380

Manufacturer	Years Produced	Caliber/Capacity	Dimensions
Davis Industries Chino, CA	1991–Present	.380 ACP/5 rounds	Barrel Length: 2.8" O.A. Length: 5.4" Height: 4.0" Width: 1.25" Weight: 22 oz. (unloaded); 24.5 oz. (loaded)

E.A.A. .380 EUROPEAN

The "European" model pistol distributed in the
U.S. by European American Armory (E.A.A.
Corp. of Sharpes, FL), has been around for a long time. Made
by Tanfoglio in Italy, it was imported by FIE as the "Titan II" for
a number of years before that company went out of business. When
E.A.A. picked up a portion of FIE's import business, the company renamed the
Titan II the "European."

This medium-frame, single-action automatic pistol is marketed in the U.S.
mostly in .380 caliber, but Tanfoglio makes seven-shot .32 ACP and 10-shot .22 LR
versions as well. Blued and chrome finishes are available for the European model,
and its grips are smooth hardwood. Fit and finish are excellent. The gun is
smoothly contoured throughout, including its sights and wood stocks, both
desirable features for a concealed carry gun. The only prominent feature spoiling this sleek effect is the
European's Beretta-style hooked magazine extension, which adds nearly an inch to the height of the
pistol.

With its open-topped slide, the European reveals the strong influence of Beretta's two classic single-action pistol designs, the Models 1934 and 70. It is, like the Berettas, a sturdy and simple blowback pistol. Oddly, it has two manual safeties: a frame-mounted trigger-locking safety on the frame (as

*The .380-caliber E.A.A. European, a highly regarded Italian design, scored this five-shot offhand group from a
distance of 50 feet, measuring 3.1 inches.*

the Beretta 1934), and a slide-mounted safety that blocks the hammer. The frame-mounted safety, which is just above the trigger guard, is also involved in the takedown procedure. Actually, this overlapping of safety mechanisms is not a desirable feature; it adds unnecessary complications to the firing drill and could make it difficult to fire in a hurry.

For a pistol that has been in production for many years and has steadily evolved and improved, the European has become, not surprisingly, a solid and competent shooter. Its sights may be slightly undersized, but more important, its front sight shows up quite well. The trigger on this pistol is far smoother than that of Beretta's Model 1934 (although not quite as good as the Model 70 trigger). Comfortable to hold and shoot, with minimal recoil, the European is highly accurate. A five-shot, 25-foot offhand group measured 1.8 inches, while at 50 feet a five-shot offhand group measured 3.1 inches across. Samson 95-grain FMJ ammunition was used for both these groups, but the results were nearly as good with Winchester's Silvertip 85-grain hollowpoint. Reliability was flawless, with no failures to feed or fire even when using several types of hollowpoint ammunition.

Among the European's chief shortcomings are the stiffness of its operating controls. For example, the gun is difficult to load in a hurry; i.e., the magazine follower will hold the slide open on an empty gun only until the magazine is removed. Then the slide slams shut, demonstrating again the influence of Beretta's Model 1934. The magazine release, located on the heel of the frame, is quite stiff, too. The grips are attractive and comfortable to hold, but they work loose after extended shooting. The most serious problem, though, is the addition of a second safety catch. With two dissimilar styles of safety catch, a risky situation could arise in which one of the safeties is on when it should be off, and vice versa.

Despite these problematical operating controls, which can be overcome with practice, the European boasts a proven design. Accurate and reliable as well, it can outshoot many pistols costing far more.

E.A.A. .380 EUROPEAN

Manufacturer	Years Produced	Caliber/Capacity	Dimensions
Fratelli Tanfoglio Gardone, Val Trompia, Italy	About 1990 to date (Imported by E.A.A. Corp.)	.380 ACP/7 rounds	Barrel Length: 3.9" O.A. Length: 7.4" Height: 5.7" Width: 1.1" Weight: 26 oz. (unloaded); 29.5 oz. (loaded)

FÉG MODEL B9R

Century International Arms of St. Albans, VT, began importing this Hungarian-made pistol in 1993, but the .380-caliber gun actually went into production a year earlier. The most obvious feature of this high-capacity Model B9R manufactured by Fégyver es Gazkeszuelekgyara of Budapest is its large size. Those who wish to carry a handgun this big can easily carry any compact 9mm, .40 S&W, or even .45-caliber automatic pistol. Most pistols chambered in .380 caliber are much smaller than the B9R and more like Walther's famous PPK. As such, they are built to compete as personal defense guns with the smallest .38 Special revolvers.

Because of its bulk, the B9R fits into a strange niche, tactically speaking. That is, its primary appeal is limited to shooters for whom concealability is not a major concern, but for whom bullet overpenetration could cause problems. Obvious applications would include home and business defense, two legitimate and good reasons for owning such a gun.

Nearly identical in size and appearance to FÉG's 9mm compact steel-frame pistol (called the P9RK by Century International Arms), the B9R differs in its slightly shorter slide and barrel and its finely checkered slide top (to reduce glare across the sighting plane). The B9R also has an alloy frame, which makes it lighter in weight. Because the B9R uses a low-pressure round, it does not require a locking mechanism. Thus, the barrel is configured as a simple blowback, simplifying construction and lowering manufacturing costs.

The B9R handles well, with all controls easy to operate and logically arranged. For those accustomed to Colt and Browning pistols, the magazine release is located in the usual manner, while the manual safety with its Walther-style decocker works effectively. The disassembly procedure is identical to that of the P9RK pistol; but, with the B9R's recoil spring set to the lower power level of the .380 cartridge, less pres-

The B9R—FÉG's monster .380—is quite accurate and, because of its size, is pleasant to shoot. The author fired this 2.8-inch, five-shot offhand group from a distance of 50 feet.

sure is exerted against the shooter's hand.

The B9R's size also makes it comfortable to hold and shoot. The trigger pull is smooth and heavy in double action, while in single action, the trigger is light with plenty of slack. Still, the trigger is easy to learn and the gun can be made to shoot well.

As for its sights, the designers unfortunately failed to make the rear sight notch wide enough—a common failing among Hungarian-made handguns. With a slightly wider rear sight notch, this could be an excellent combat-style fixed sight system.

In test-firing the B9R, it did fine with an assortment of hollowpoint ammunition and there were no failures to feed or fire with any of the brands used (some brands, though, lacked enough recoil impulse to lock open the slide following the last shot in the magazine). The best groups were fired with Winchester's generic "USA" brand ammunition, which uses a 95-grain FMJ bullet. With this ammunition, a 25-foot offhand group placed five shots in a 1.7-inch pattern. And a 50-foot, five-shot measured only 2.8 inches across, more than acceptable accuracy for a combat pistol in .380 caliber.

While not quite as refined as the similar Model PT-58 made by Taurus (*see* separate listing), FÉG's B9R is highly competitive in this special niche of large, high-capacity, 9mm-sized, .380-caliber pistols. It's the best-shooting Hungarian-made .380 pistol available and costs only a few dollars more than any others of its kind. (Other Hungarian .380-caliber pistols, however, are designed for a greater level of concealment and are considerably smaller). For those who like the .380 caliber and are not terribly concerned about the size, this is a good gun to have on your side.

FÉG MODEL B9R

Manufacturer	Years Produced	Caliber/Capacity	Dimensions
FÉG, Budapest, Hungary	1992–Present	.380 ACP/15 rounds	Barrel Length: 4.0" O.A. Length: 7.0" Height: 5.3" Width: 1.35" Weight: 25 oz. (unloaded); 33 oz. (loaded)

FÉG PA-63 (AP9, PMK-380)

FÉG began making close copies of the Walther PP and PPK in the late 1940s. The first of these—the Model 48—was nearly identical to the PP, differing only in the location of its loaded chamber indicator pin, the shape of its manual safety lever, and the configuration of its magazine floorplate and grips. Chambered in .32 or .380 caliber, the Model 48 served Hungary's military and police forces, along with several foreign nations (notably Egypt), and sold well commercially throughout Western Europe as the "Attila."

In the late 1950s, FÉG grew adventurous and departed more boldly from the original Walther design. Its much-modified Model PA-63 in 9mm Makarov caliber became a standard Hungarian military and police sidearm. The PA-63 had a larger frame with a more curved backstrap for a better hold. It also dispensed with a loaded chamber signal pin altogether and replaced the steel frame with one made of lightweight aluminum alloy, reducing overall weight by several ounces.

Reducing weight to the absolute minimum made sense in a pistol meant to be concealed in one's pocket. Moreover, the reduced strength of the light alloy frame was not considered a problem in lower-powered calibers, as it can be in pistols chambered for 9mm Parabellum and other larger, high-pressure rounds. FÉG later made the PA-63 in a .32 ACP version for commercial sale and police use, and as .380 ACP versions: the Models AP9 and PMK-380.

In its 9mm Makarov military version, the PA-63 sports a brightly polished aluminum frame. Although the military does not ordinarily care for guns with such conspicuous

The FÉG PA-63 is reasonably accurate, although it suffers from the same heavy double-action trigger as other Hungarian-made Walther PP clones. This 2.0-inch, five-shot offhand group was fired from a distance of 25 feet using 9mm Makarov ammunition.

finishes, having the two-tone finish saved the time and expense of an extra process for these cost-conscious buyers.

Whereas the AP9 and PMK-380 are more reminiscent of the Walther PP, the PA-63 is more competitive with the Soviet-designed Makarov. With its more powerful cartridge, the PA-63 has more felt recoil than either of its .380-caliber variants. This, combined with its small sights and heavy trigger, hurts the gun's accuracy. A five-shot, 25-foot offhand group, using Norinco 94-grain FMJ, measured exactly 2 inches. And from a distance of 50 feet, it was very difficult to fire an acceptable group, the best try measuring 5.6 inches cross. There were, however, no failures in feeding, firing or ejecting three different brands of 9mm Makarov ammunition. The PA-63 was imported in large numbers by K.B.I., Inc., of Harrisburg, PA.

FÉG AP9. Imported by Century International Arms of St. Albans, VT, the AP9 is a commercial .380-ACP version of the PA-63 service pistol, with the same white alloy frame and two-tone appearance.

In general, the AP9 shares the same strengths and weaknesses of the Walther PP/PPK pistols. Its most obvious drawback is a very heavy double-action trigger pull. The magazine release is located just below the slide at the front of the left grip, rather than behind the trigger guard. As a result, the empty magazine protrudes 1/8 of an inch from the bottom of the grip instead of smoothly ejecting.

Despite a very difficult double-action first shot, the AP9 test-fired with surprising accuracy. One offhand group, using Federal 95-grain FMJ, placed five shots in a tiny 1.4-inch pattern; and a 50-foot group placed within an incredibly small 1.7-inch pattern. That was, however, after a first shot, fired double action, had landed some 2 1/2 inches away from the point of aim. The four remaining shots, all single action, were fired at the first bullet hole.

The AP9 is a good .380-caliber pistol that can be purchased for much less than any Walther on the market.

FÉG PMK-380. This .380-caliber commercial version, imported since 1992 by K.B.I., Inc., sports a black-anodized frame. Offering a much sleeker appearance than the other PA-63-type guns, the PMK-380 is nonetheless similar in construction and operation to the Walther PP. Due to a backstrap that curves out farther than the PP's, the Hungarian gun boasts a considerably larger grip that will fit, surprisingly, in most holsters made for the PP. Large-handed shooters will undoubtedly prefer the PMK-380's larger grip over the Walther's.

FÉG's PMK-380 is identical to the .380-caliber AP9, except its all-black alloy frame has been anodized to match the slide.

On the other hand, the PMK-380 is not nearly as refined or polished a gun as the Walther pistols. Its sights are undersized; it has a heavier trigger pull in both single and double action; the magazine release is much stiffer (causing the empty magazine to release only partially from the grip); and recoil is sharper because of its lightweight alloy frame.

The FÉG PMK-380 disassembles the same as a Walther PP or PPK. As a "poor man's Walther," the PMK-380 truly excels.

In test-firing, the PMK-380 produced a 2.9-inch pattern from a 25-foot offhand group, using Samson 95-grain FMJ. The double-action first shot landed more than two inches from the single-action follow-up shots, all of which went into a tight pattern less than 3/4 of an inch across. Other groups measured nearly 4 inches across, which is a poor showing at 25 feet, even when shooting offhand. In general, though, the PMK-380 is an acceptable handgun for those seeking a low-cost, double-action .380-caliber pistol.

FÉG PA-63

Manufacturer	Years Produced	Caliber/Capacity	Dimensions
FÉG, Budapest, Hungary	1950s–Present	9mm Makarov (9x18mm)/7 rounds .380 ACP/7 rounds	Barrel Length: 3.9" O.A. Length: 6.9" Height: 4.8" Width: 1.3" Weight: 21 oz. (unloaded); 26 oz. (loaded)

FÉG SMC-380/SMC-918

K.B.I., Inc., of Harrisburg, PA, began importing this small Hungarian-made pistol in mid-1993, but its history dates back to the late 1950s. At about the same time FÉG began making the Model PA-63 (*see* previous listing), it also developed a smaller PPK-sized 9mm Makarov caliber pistol, called the RK-59. An excellent little pistol, similar to Poland's Model vz.63, it is highly regarded in military circles, serving the Hungarian military and police forces.

In l991, Century imported about 3,000 RK-59s into the U.S. The small size of this gun makes it especially handy as a hideout gun, used mostly by high-ranking officers, pilots and various vehicle crews who occasionally need a pistol but are forced to work and fight in confined spaces. Handgun expert Leroy Thompson has argued that the RK-59 is perhaps the world's best military pistol, because it uses a fighting cartridge powerful enough to be taken seriously, yet is compact enough to carry comfortably on the person at all times.

A slightly improved version of the RK-59— the SMC-380—appeared in 1991. It's actually the same gun rechambered to the slightly less powerful, albeit better known, .380 ACP round. Its frame is still a lightweight alloy, but for commercial sales it is anodized black to match more closely the blued slide of the pistol. In its military version, the frame is left unfinished, as in the PA-63 described earlier.

The SMC-380 is of historical interest because it is the smallest gun ever imported legally into the United States since the passage of the Gun Control Act of 1968 (according to which a gun cannot be imported if it is less than 4.0 inches in height). The SMC-380, which is barely 4.1 inches high, had to have a target-type left grip installed to meet the government's stringent importation criteria. The left target-style grip widened the pistol from 1.1 inches to 1.3 inches, but that was a small price to pay. A thinner, flatter left grip panel is also available on request.

Like the PMK-380, the SMC-380 is available only in .380 ACP caliber.

When disassembled, the FÉG SMC-380 clearly shows its debt to the Walther PP. The left grip can be replaced by a thinner unit to eliminate the thumbrest.

Its alloy frame makes it smoother and two or three ounces lighter than the PPK. It also carries better in a pocket than the higher-priced German gun and fits the average hand better. Its sights, while tiny, are easy to line up quickly, thanks to the comfortable curve of the backstrap.

In testing an early SMC-380, the pistol proved quite accurate. One 25-foot offhand group placed five shots in a one-inch pattern, using the Remington 88-grain jacketed hollowpoint. The second-best group at the same distance measured 1.1 inches across, using Samson 95-grain FMJ. Unfortunately, the pistol used required an extended breaking-in period of several hundred rounds before it fed consistently and reliably. Later, though, a second SMC-380 tested much better, with only one breaking-in jam. It's always a good idea to run at least 200 rounds (four boxes) of any particular brand of ammunition through any gun, without a single malfunction, before relying on that gun/ammunition combination for personal protection.

In general, the FÉG SMC-380 offers a Walther PPK level of performance for much less cost than the German-designed gun.

FÉG SMC-918. When K.B.I. observed the popularity of the SMC-380 in the U.S., it decided to import the 9mm Makarov version, the SMC-918. The Hungarians had made this model (with slight modifications) since the late 1950s, with importation beginning in late 1994.

The debate continues whether the 9mm Makarov or the .380 ACP is a better defense cartridge. Neither is particularly powerful, though some of the loadings—particularly the faster hollowpoints and exotic rounds (such as MagSafe)—have caused incapacitating wounds when fired in self-defense.

The SMC-918 we tested handled well. With its clean lines and rounded corners, this pistol car-

FÉG's SMC-918 is capable of good accuracy at close ranges. This five-shot offhand group fired from a distance of 25 feet measures an acceptable 1¹/₂ inches across.

ries comfortably in one's pocket and is light and handy. It also boasts good instinctive pointing, with a trigger pull that is noticeably smoother and lighter than that found in the SMC-380s tested. Despite the improved trigger pull, however, the SMC-918 proved slightly less accurate than the SMC-380. Whether this is a quirk of the 9mm Makarov cartridge or an inherent situation is difficult to tell. Regardless, the test pistol had no trouble feeding any ammunition tested, including Hornady's XTP hollowpoint. Recoil with the SMC-918 was sharp, similar to firing a small .38-caliber revolver. The shape of its backstrap could be at fault. By rounding it off much more than that of the Walther PPK, for instance, the Hungarian designers have created a gun that is smoother in contour but a bit more difficult to fire. Compact guns are, after all, an exercise in compromise.

The SMC-918 offers the 9mm Makarov cartridge in a package that is appreciably smaller and lighter than the Soviet-designed Makarov pistol or its derivatives. The SMC-918 is, in fact, the smallest pistol currently in production for the Makarov round. The price to pay is a gun that is easier to carry and slightly more difficult to shoot. Given its mission of self-defense, though, that's a compromise many buyers will surely find acceptable.

FÉG SMC-380/SMC-918

Manufacturer	Years Produced	Caliber/Capacity	Dimensions
FÉG, Budapest, Hungary	1961–Present (380) 1950s–Present (918)	.380 ACP/6 rounds 9mm Makarov/ 6 rounds (918)	Barrel Length: 3.5" O.A. Length: 6.1" Height: 4.4" Width: 1.3" Weight: 18.5 oz. (unloaded); 21.5 oz. (loaded)

GRENDEL P-12

When it was introduced in 1986, The Grendel was considered a lot more radical than it would be today, what with its combination of features including a high-capacity .380-caliber magazine, its smooth shape (to prevent snagging), polymer frame for light weight and corrosion resistance, and double-action-only trigger mechanism. While the Grendel may not have been the first gun ever made with these features, it was probably the first to combine all of them in quite this way and still retail within a reasonable price range.

The original Grendel, called the P-10, had a fixed 10-round magazine and unloaded from the top of the open action, much like the old-fashioned Mauser C.96 "Broomhandle." The improved P-12, first released in 1992, features a detachable magazine that holds up to 11 rounds; it also has a lightened hammer to provide faster lock time and improve accuracy.

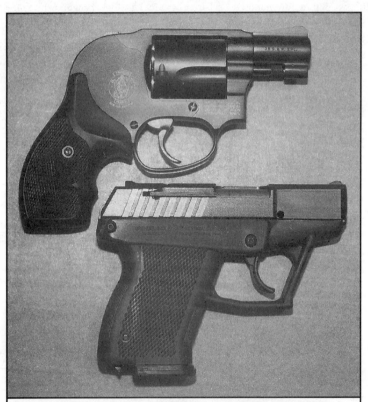

The Grendel P-12 (bottom), although hardly larger than Smith & Wesson's Model 38 Bodyguard (top), is only slightly heavier, yet it holds more than twice as many rounds.

But when test-fired at 25 feet, an early Grendel P-10 registered an unacceptable five-shot group of 4.5 inches. The trigger pull was too heavy and the gun proved generally unreliable, with repeated double feedings even with FMJ ammunition. The P-12, though, is much better, but still far from perfect. A five-shot 25-foot group measured 1.9 inches, while at 50 feet the grouping was 4.2 inches. The trigger pull was much smoother than the original P-10. With its heavy double-action trigger and firing-pin lock, this improved Grendel does not require a manual safety, thus ensuring a sleek contour with no levers or other protrusions. The sights are a nice size for a pistol meant for concealed carry, and the rear sight has a proper radius to avoid snagging.

Reliability is something else. The P-12 is much better than the P-10 in this regard, but it is

The clean lines and relatively light weight of Grendel's P-12 make it a strong candidate for a carry pistol. Its double-action-only trigger is manageable after some practice, as this 1.9-inch, 25-foot offhand group illustrates (point of aim was the bottom of the black portion of the target).

far from perfect, suffering from an occasional jam— usually because of its failure to feed with hollow-point ammunition. Since reliability is the primary requirement of a defensive pistol, it must shoot with maximum dependability, regardless of its other attributes. And while the test P-12 works better with FMJ bullets, the .380 really needs all the help it can get; i.e., an expanding hollowpoint bullet. The large magazine capacity may offset the use of ball ammunition somewhat, but fewer, more powerful shots are preferable (such as the .38 Special Smith & Wesson J-frame revolvers.

Since the P-12 is priced at a little under $200, buyers are probably well-advised to set aside enough funds for a gunsmith to polish the feed ramp and tune the gun. Having done that, this could be a good choice for those who desire a small but reasonably powerful automatic pistol with a large magazine capacity.

GRENDEL P-12

Manufacturer	Years Produced	Caliber/Capacity	Dimensions
Grendel, Inc. Rockledge, FL	1992 –1995	.380 ACP/11 rounds	Barrel Length: 3.0" O.A. Length: 5.3" Height: 4.5" Width: 1.3" Weight: 13 oz. (unloaded); 19 oz. (loaded)

HECKLER & KOCH P7K3

In the late 1970s, Heckler & Koch introduced its radical 9mm pistol— the Model PSP—as the first of what has become a highly successful line of similar handguns. These include the 13-shot 9mm Model P7M13, the 10-shot .40 S&W caliber Model P7M10, and the .380-caliber Model P7K3 (H&K also developed a .45-caliber variant that was abruptly cancelled). The Model P7K3 was first made available to civilians in the U.S. in 1988, although it had been developed several years before that.

In most P7-series pistols, the number that follows the "P7" designation refers to the magazine capacity, but in the case of the "K3" designation it stands for the three interchangeable calibers: .22 LR, .32 ACP (7.65mm Browning) and .380 ACP. To convert a P7K3 from .380 to .32 caliber, one simply exchanges the barrel. To convert from either centerfire caliber to .22 LR rimfire caliber, the barrel, slide and magazine must all be exchanged. The P7K3 is not the first Heckler & Koch pistol to offer this feature; in fact, the company's very first pistol, the HK 4, featured it.

Like other Heckler & Koch P7-series pistols, the P7K3 uses a cocking indicator at the rear of the slide. This indicates when the cocking lever (located at the front of the grip) is depressed far enough for the pistol to fire. Note also the two-dot markings on the rear sight, which combine with the single dot on the front sight.

While the P7K3 shares many of the same features as the larger P7-series pistols, it has dispensed with the latter's gas-retarded mechanism. Instead, the P7K3, because of the less powerful cartridges it uses, employs a simple blowback or unlocked breech mechanism, and its fit and finish are flawless.

Whereas the Models P7M8, P7M13, and P7M10 are all service handguns (*see Complete Guide to Service Handguns*), H&K clearly intended to market the P7K3 as a training pistol. It shoots superbly and has no equal, thanks to its extraordinarily smooth, crisp trigger, and its 3-dot sight systems. Its pebbled grips fit well in the hand and little recoil is felt while firing, no matter what brand of ammunition is used, including Cor-Bon's hot 90-grain +P jacketed hollowpoints. The P7K3 is a superb performer in rapid fire and is extremely accurate. Three five-shot, 25-foot offhand groups, using three different brands of ammunition, each measured 1.5 inches across. That says a lot for the gun's standard of workmanship, especially for an automatic pistol. Another five-shot offhand group fired at 50 feet measured only 3.2 inches across,

Within the Heckler & Koch P7 series is the 9mm P7M8, another compact, smooth-operating "best choice."

using Samson 95-grain FMJ ammunition.

The only real shortcoming of the Model P7K3 is its high price: more than $1,000 (1995). Even the .22 LR conversion kit costs as much or more than some complete handguns. Still, the P7 series remains the smoothest-operating set of guns available today. When seconds count and you must hit the target with every shot, these are the easiest and most reliable guns to have—assuming price is not a factor. In that regard, one of H&K's design and manufacturing imperatives is to create a new USP pistol designed to hold down costs.

If you can afford one, any of the P7 pistols will do the job as well as any pistol on the market—and far better than most. Within the P7 compact pistol family, the P7K3 or the 9mm P7M8 remain the best choice.

HECKLER & KOCH P7K3

Manufacturer	Years Produced	Caliber/Capacity	Dimensions
Heckler & Koch GmbH Oberndorf, Germany	1970s–1995	.380 ACP/8 rounds	Barrel Length: 3.8" O.A. Length: 6.3" Height: 4.9" Width: 1.14" Weight: 26.5 oz. (unloaded); 30.5 oz. (loaded)

HI-POINT MODEL CF

Introduced in 1994, the Hi-Point Model CF is a
.380-caliber version of the 9mm Model C pistol,
dating back to the Maverick or Stallard pistol first produced
in 1987. With their single-action triggers, single-row magazines
and manual safeties (on the left side only), all these pistols are
old-fashioned. In other respects, though, they are quite modern, using the
most cost-effective mass production methods and materials currently available
to the firearms industry. These include various kinds of plastics, investment cast
alloys, stamped steel, roll pins, and inexpensive but durable finishes.

Like most .380-caliber pistols, the Model CF employs an unlocked breech
and a polymer frame similar to the Glock and Sigma pistols. It's also flawlessly reliable with a variety
of ammunition, including hollowpoints, particularly after a breaking-in period. Owners of all automatic pistols, by the way, should fire several types of ammunition before determining which ammuni-

*A large gun by .380 standards, the Hi-Point CF produced this five-shot offhand group measuring 1 1/2 inches
across, fired from a distance of 25 feet.*

tion to use. Reliability and accuracy, in that order, should be the two main criteria affecting one's choice.

Accuracy with the Model CF, due in large part to its smooth single-action trigger release, is at least acceptable. In testing, the best five-shot offhand group fired at 25 feet measured 1.7 inches. The sights, which are fixed, use the popular three-dot highlights to aid in rapid aiming. To minimize snagging, they are located low to the slide, offering a good sight picture for better aim. The manual safety, although small, is well placed for right-handed shooters, who merely press down to fire and up to safe. Left-handers are stuck, though, with "Condition Three" carry.

The first thing a shooter notices about this gun is its massive slide, which weighs about 20 ounces, making the gun top-heavy while doing nothing to enhance its handling. In the interest of economy, makers of this pistol have eliminated some other refinements found in more expensive designs. For example, there's no hold-open device to lock back the slide after firing the last round. In addition, the slide serrations are too shallow for a good grip, making the slide surprisingly difficult to draw back in a hurry despite the gun's relatively weak recoil spring. The magazine release (located on the frame just behind the trigger guard) is hard for short-fingered persons to reach, and it doesn't always drop the empty magazine fully free of the grip. To disassemble this model, the slides can be separated from the frame only by forcing out a retaining pin with a punch. Unfortunately, a number of modern compact pistols share this negative characteristic.

To sum up, the Hi-Point Model CF is not recommended for the dedicated automatic pistol enthusiast, lacking as it does many of the refinements found on more traditional designs. It's not for weak-handed people, either, because its slide requires such a vigorous tug to the rear before the pistol can be loaded and cocked. Nevertheless, it offers protection to people on a budget.

HI-POINT MODEL CF

Manufacturer	Years Produced	Caliber/Capacity	Dimensions
Beemiller, Inc. Mansfield, OH	1994–Present	.380 ACP/8 rounds	Barrel Length: 3.5" O.A. Length: 6.7" Height: 4.9" Width: 1.3" Weight: 35 oz. (unloaded); 38 oz. (loaded)

INTRATEC PROTEC 25

When Intratec announced its Protec family of pistols in 1991, it was to consist of two calibers: .22 LR and .25 ACP, plus several different finish options. By 1992, the .25-caliber Protec was already in distribution, but the .22 LR version was either unavailable or at least not widely advertised.

The Protec is closely related to the highly regarded Czech CZ-45 pistol, a double-action-only pistol in .25 ACP and itself descended from an earlier CZ design made between 1936 and 1940. Its barrel was attached to the frame with lugs, similar to the Browning-designed FN Model 1906. The CZ-45's manageable trigger mechanism and extremely compact dimensions have attracted a loyal following, even in the U.S. Deteriorating relations with communist-dominated Czechoslovakia, followed by the Gun Control Act of 1968, conspired to halt importation of the CZ-45 altogether.

Interestingly, small automatic pistols in .25 caliber far outsell larger automatic pistols and revolvers. Even though the U.S. market is closed to foreign makers of these tiny pistols, there exist significant markets in Europe and other parts of the world for this type of low-powered but highly concealable pistol. As recently as 1992, the Czechs introduced yet another weapon of this type.

The Intratec Protec 25's disassembly procedure, based on early Browning practice, is a little more complicated than that of most pocket pistols.

Because a loophole in the Gun Control Act allows U.S. manufacturers to build pistols locally that are too small to be imported legally, Intratec decided to go ahead with a close copy of the CZ-45: the Protec 25. It was a good choice. The two pistols are so similar that most of their parts are interchangeable. The Protec 25 is better shaped, though, and it's made of more modern materials.

Like most small pistols, the Protec 25 uses a blowback or unlocked-breech mechanism. The overriding priority is to make a gun of this type as small as possible. A handgun that is too large for concealment or easy carrying will most likely be left behind by its owner. What Ceska Zbrojovka (CZ) tried to do so many years ago— and what Intratec has attempted to emulate— is build a gun small enough to be carried at all times, yet contain acceptable shooting characteristics.

As a result, the Protec 25 is extremely slim—less than an inch thick at its widest point. While many gun manufacturers have figured out how to make a handgun short in length and small in height, few have taken the extra step to make a gun thin enough to conceal well and carry comfortably. A person who carries a gun that's too thick will always be worrying about the pistol's concealability. Indeed, thickness is such a critical element in a gun's concealability that we have included the thickness (along with height) of each gun covered in this book.

The need to miniaturize is also apparent when one looks at the Protec's sights, which consist of a simple groove running down the top of the slide. This pistol is extremely well-shaped for concealed carry, too, with no protrusions to snag on clothing. There are no manual safety levers or other controls to mar the smooth profile either. As with a revolver, the hammer automatically decocks after each shot; all that's needed to fire the Protec 25 is a firm trigger stroke. Further, a magazine disconnect safety prevents the trigger from operating the hammer when the magazine is detached. That way, the gun cannot be fired unless the magazine is fully inserted.

Considering its diminutive size, the Protec 25 shoots reasonably well. In a test-firing at distances of 10 and 25 feet only, accuracy was acceptable. A nine-shot, 10-foot off-hand group measured 1.3 inches across, and another group at 25 feet came in at 3.5 inches. The primitive sighting groove was difficult to pick up against a dark target, and the rounds were starting to keyhole (tumble end over end) at 25 feet. The trigger is pretty stiff, making the gun a bit slower than other small .25 ACP pistols; but there were no feeding problems with FMJ or hollowpoint

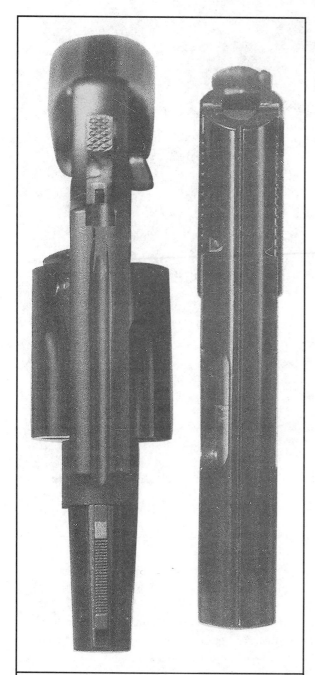

Intratec recognized that a gun's length and height are less important to concealment than its width. Comparing the Smith & Wesson Chiefs Special revolver (left) with the Protec 25 (right) shows how important it is to reduce a gun's width to ensure carrying comfort and easy concealment.

At close range, the Protec's .25 ACP cartridge is both accurate and deadly. This rapid-fire offhand group, shot from a distance of 10 feet and measuring 1.3 inches across, took slightly more than three seconds to empty the eight-shot magazine (plus one in the firing chamber).

ammunition, and very little recoil.

The Protec 25 is a reasonable choice for a minimum-sized hideout pistol, one that works best when carried in a holster (several manufacturers offer excellent pocket holsters for this type of gun). For those who prefer to carry this pistol in a pocket, make sure the pocket is sturdy enough to hold almost a pound of weight. Lint can also be a problem, for it can gum up the pistol's mechanism and cause it to fail at a moment of crisis.

INTRATEC PROTEC 25

Manufacturer	Years Produced	Caliber/Capacity	Dimensions
Intratec Miami, FL	1991–Present	.25 ACP/8 rounds	Barrel Length: 2.5" O.A. Length: 5.0" Height: 3.6" Width: 0.75" Weight: 14 oz. (unloaded); 16 oz. (loaded)

JENNINGS/BRYCO MODEL 38

The Bryco Model 38 was released by Jennings
Firearms in 1988 and quickly proved to be a pistol
with the firepower of a Walther PPK at about a quarter of the
cost. Borrowing features from the Browning "Baby" and
Walther Model 9 (*see* page 96), its updated design utilizes the
most modern manufacturing techniques to help hold down the cost.

Unfortunately, the reality does not live up to the promise. The Model 38
is, to its credit, compact, well-shaped to the hand and comfortable to carry. Its
light weight is made possible by an investment-cast light alloy frame, a manufacturing technique that also reduces costs. Finishes are available in blue, bright
chrome, satin nickel and black Teflon. The grips are ribbed black plastic, walnut or resin-impregnated
wood. In addition to the .380-caliber model discussed here, Jennings also makes .22 LR and .32 ACP
variations, as well as larger 9mm versions.

Like the early pocket pistols on which its design is based, the Model 38 has a single-action trigger. Its manual safety is mounted on the left side of the frame, which, in its up or safe setting locks the

*The Jennings/Bryco Model 38 boasts better sights than most pocket pistols. Low to the slide and unlikely to
snag, it offers a reasonably sized sight picture. The only weakness is its heavy trigger pull, which resulted in this
excessively large 5.2-inch, 25-foot offhand group.*

sear and slide (push down to fire). The safety lever is easy for right-handed shooters to operate but is virtually inaccessible to a left-hander.

In addition to a magazine disconnect safety, the Model 38 features a cocked-striker indicator—a small pin that protrudes from the rear of the slide whenever the striker spring releases the firing pin into the firing chamber. While not actually a loaded-chamber indicator, this pin does help indicate when the gun is ready to fire (though one should not rely wholly on it).

The Model 38 boasts better sights than most pocket pistols. Low to the slide and unlikely to snag, it nonetheless offers a reasonably sized sight picture. And yet, this is not a particularly good shooting pistol. Its trigger is much too heavy, making accuracy beyond point-blank range a matter of luck. The author's two best five-shot, 25-foot offhand groups measured 5.2 inches using Winchester Silvertip 85-grain hollowpoints, and 6.5 inches using Winchester's generic USA 95-grain FMJ.

Reliability was also a problem, with the gun jamming or misfiring five times in 50 rounds using the Winchester ammunition. Surprisingly, though, the pistol was totally reliable with the Silvertip. In all fairness to the gun and its manufacturer, the frequency of functional failures tapered off after about a box of ammunition had gone through the test gun, although it never became wholly reliable.

Despite some rough spots, the Jennings/Bryco Model 38 offers lots of potential. With a little work to improve the trigger, and with a brand of ammunition that it likes, this model could become a promising defensive handgun.

JENNINGS/BRYCO MODEL 38

Manufacturer	Years Produced	Caliber/Capacity	Dimensions
Jennings Firearms, Inc. Irvine, CA	1988–Present	.380 ACP/6 rounds	Barrel Length: 2.8" O.A. Length: 5.3" Height: 3.7" Width: 1.0" Weight: 16 oz. (unloaded); 19 oz. (loaded)

JENNINGS J-22

When Jennings Firearms introduced its models J-22 and J-25 in the early 1980s, the two pistols were identical, except the J-22 was chambered in .22 LR caliber and the J-25 in .25 ACP. Both guns featured six-shot magazines with releases located on the bottom rear, or heel, of the grip. Satin nickel, chrome and black Teflon finishes were available, and the grips were either black plastic, ivory or hardwood. The gun has evolved into an exceptionally sleek model with smooth lines that make it suitable for concealed carry, as does its light weight, due in part to an alloy frame.

Jennings pistol controls are typical of modern single-action pocket models; i.e., the safety, which is located on the left side of the frame, pushes up to safe and down to fire (on early J-22 and J-25 pistols a sliding safety catch was pushed back to safe and forward to fire).

Despite its modern appearance, the Jennings pistol is really no different in features and performance than the millions of single-action, striker-fired blowback pistols produced by literally hundreds of manufacturers during the past 100 years or so. In its construction and disassembly procedures, the Jennings pistol is quite similar to Walther's classic Model 9 made prior to World War II. That is not meant as a criticism of the Jennings, whose design has worked well over the years in its role as a limited defensive pocket pistol of minimal size and cost.

Although it is small—and consequently difficult to hold— the Jennings is a reasonably good shooter. Its sights are acceptable, but the trigger, like the Bryco Model 38 discussed earlier, is much heavier than it needs to be; in fact, the competing Raven (*see* page 172) has a much better trigger. Nevertheless, accuracy is good, considering the ranges one can expect from a pocket pistol. A six-shot offhand group fired from a distance of 10 feet measured only .9 inch; while at 25 feet, the six-shot magazine emptied into a group 2.5 inches across. Still another group fired at 50 feet measured an unacceptable 8.2 inches across (due almost entirely, however, to the author's inability to master this tiny gun's heavy trigger). Still, accuracy at 10- and 25-foot distances was very good. After a number of breaking-in jams during the first three loads, the Jennings pistol settled down nicely.

What every handgun owner should learn from this is the importance of buying a large quantity of ammunition— preferably several different brands—and test-firing the gun at a local shooting range. The goal is to gain experience in handling the gun, learning what it can do, and determining what ammunition works best in it. Many automatic pistols, including some of the finest and most expensive models, will occasionally jam or malfunction before they're broken in. It's far better to have those breaking-in jams occur on a firing range than during a burglary or break-in in the middle of the night. That's when a properly functioning handgun can literally make the difference between life and death.

Considering their low price (under $100), these Jennings J models are well-made and serviceable pocket pistols. If you can live with the small caliber, they can be perfectly acceptable and efficient.

JENNINGS J-22

Manufacturer	Years Produced	Caliber/Capacity	Dimensions
Jennings Firearms, Inc. Irvine, CA	1980s–Present	.22 LR/6 rounds	Barrel Length: 2.5" O.A. Length: 4.94" Height: 3.4" Width: 0.9" Weight: 13 oz. (unloaded); 14 oz. (loaded)

IVER JOHNSON (AMAC) PONY

The history of Iver Johnson's Pony .380-caliber pistol is at once confusing and convoluted. The Spanish company, Star, introduced the ancestor of this pistol, known as the Model DK or Starfire, in 1958. Its importation into the U.S. ended in 1968 when it fell afoul of the U.S. Gun Control Act.

In 1973, Colt commissioned the Garcia Corporation, then the importers of Star pistols from Spain, to produce a .380-caliber Starfire-type pistol, to be called the Colt Pony. Soon after Garcia's subsidiary, the Firearms International plant in Accokeek, MD, began producing the pistols, Colt quickly terminated the arrangement because it was dissatisfied with the quality of the guns. Colt then began to develop its own .380-caliber Government Model (*see* separate listing).

Garcia then made arrangements to have the parts imported from Spain and to assemble the pistols, advertised as "Model D," at the Firearms International plant. Later production took place completely in America between 1974 and 1977. The following year, Iver Johnson acquired Firearms International's tooling operation and reintroduced the little .380, calling it the "X-300 Pony." Intermediate in size between the Colt .380 Government Model and the smaller Mustang, the Iver Johnson Pony is mechanically about the same as a .380-caliber Colt—but with some subtle differences. The Iver Johnson Pony features a spur hammer (carried over from the earlier Spanish design) instead of the rounded one used by the .380 Colts, and it has a tiny adjustable rear sight instead of Colt's fixed sights.

The Pony's adjustable rear sight is so small that it's next to useless. Its grip tang is slightly longer than the .380 Colts, and it has a small projection on the lower edge of the front gripstrap for better third or fourth-finger support (the Colts, in contrast, have a straight front gripstrap). The Pony also has checkered wooden grip plates or stocks on its blued version (a nickel-plated Pony with black plastic grips has also been offered), whereas the Colt's grips are checkered plastic.

The author's impressions after examining one of these pistols some years ago was that it worked reasonably well, but was less smooth and refined than the .380 Colts. Accuracy was reasonably good—no worse than a Mustang—but the Pony did put its bullets several inches high at 25 feet. According to some critics, some Pony pistols have been poorly made, causing frequent jamming. So, before you consider buying one of these little pistols, test-firing may be a wise move.

As a used gun, the Pony does not hold its resale value as well as a Colt .380, but when loaded with good ammo, it offers a reasonable backup in an emergency situation.

IVER JOHNSON (AMAC) PONY

Manufacturer	Years Produced	Caliber/Capacity	Dimensions
Iver Johnson/AMAC Jacksonville, AR	1978 (c.)–1988	.380 ACP/6 rounds	Barrel Length: 3.2" O.A. Length: 6.0" Height: 4.35" Width: 1.1" Weight: 20 oz. (unloaded); 23 oz. (loaded)

MITCHELL ARMS

MITCHELL ARMS TROPHY II

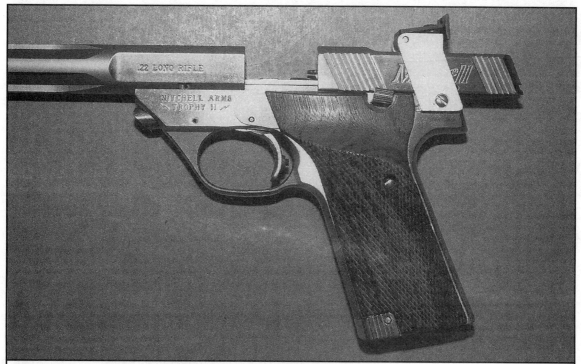

Those who are knowledgeable about .22-caliber
target pistols will immediately recognize the name "High Standard."
Between 1932 and 1984, this company produced some of the world's
finest .22-caliber pistols, many of which were used in everything from international shooting competition to wartime use during World War II, Vietnam and
beyond.

After High Standard closed its doors in 1985, Mitchell Arms revived several High
Standard models, including the Victor, Sharpshooter, Olympic I.S.U., Sport King,
Citation and Trophy. These new High Standard renditions were built at a factory in Fort Worth, TX,
and are now available in blued or stainless versions, with long fluted barrels or shorter bull barrels,
plus interchangeability of parts with the former High Standard guns. The Trophy, for example, dated
from 1959 with a military version following in the early 1960s. An M1911-type grip was added to
enhance the gun's value as a training pistol for military use. It remained in production until 1984;
then, after a short hiatus, Mitchell Arms revived the design and began shipping the Trophy II in 1993.

The Trophy II's grip, weight and operating controls are, with few exceptions, closely modeled on
those of the M1911 military-caliber pistol. The manual safety lever, which is located on the left side of

Note how the rear sight on the Trophy II is mounted on a bridge above the moving slide. Anchored firmly to the stationary receiver (rather than moving back and forth with the slide), this kind of rear sight is much less likely to shift its zero.

Mitchell Arms's reincarnation of the Trophy II, like its High Standard ancestor, is an excellent and accurate pistol. This five-shot, 25-foot offhand group measures a mere 2/3 inch across. At 50 feet, another five-shot off-hand group spanned just two inches. Many pistols can't shoot that well at half the distance.

the frame, pushes up to safe and down to fire. In the safe setting, the manual safety blocks the sear and hammer and disconnects the trigger linkage. But unlike the safety on the Colt M1911, the one on the Trophy II does not lock the slide, which means that loading and unloading operations can be carried out with the manual safety lever on safe. Despite this safeguard, shooters should always rely on sensible safety precautions rather than trusting wholly in a mechanical safety device to prevent accidental firings.

The magazine release on the Trophy II is located at the bottom of the grip frame; but it's at the front, or toe, of the grip rather than at the rear, or heel. The slide release, located on the right side of the frame, is also placed differently on the M1911-type pistol, where the release is on the left side. The front and rear backstraps are stippled, and the grips are made of high-quality checkered walnut for a secure hold. The left grip has a prominent thumbrest (left-handers, take note).

Not surprisingly for a target pistol, the Trophy II has a smooth, light trigger and excellent sights, which are quite unusual. The front sight is an undercut Patridge pattern not unlike that found on the Ruger Mark II; but the rear sight, which is mounted on a bridge over the slide, is connected to the frame, not the slide. Clearly, the reasoning behind this arrangement is to prevent the recoiling slide from disrupting the rear sight alignment. The rear sight can be adjusted for windage and elevation with a regular screwdriver (or even a dime), a nice touch compared to the tiny, jeweler-type tools required for sight adjustments on so many other pistols. The sight picture is large and very clear, too, with no dots on the sights. On the stainless Trophy II, the sights are dull black to avoid reflections.

The Trophy II is as comfortable to shoot as the competing Ruger Mark II and Browning Buck Mark pistols. Its trigger is extremely light and there is almost no recoil, thanks to the gun's weight and the low power of the .22 LR cartridge. The Trophy II excels both in precise aimed fire and in rapid-

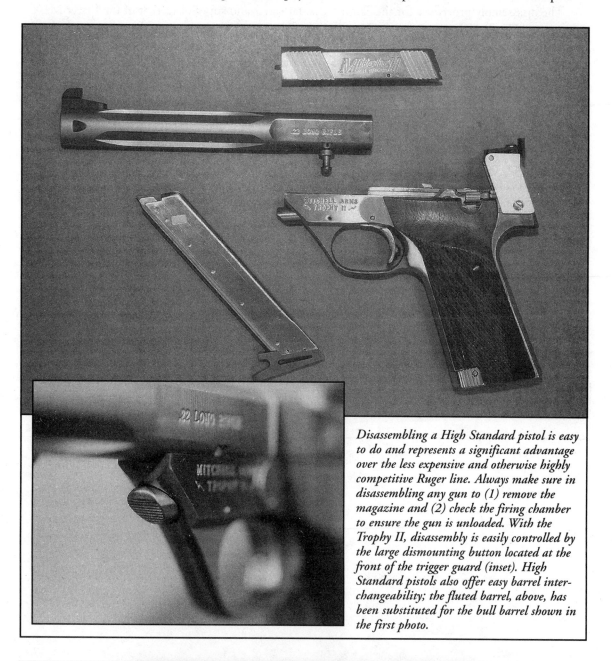

Disassembling a High Standard pistol is easy to do and represents a significant advantage over the less expensive and otherwise highly competitive Ruger line. Always make sure in disassembling any gun to (1) remove the magazine and (2) check the firing chamber to ensure the gun is unloaded. With the Trophy II, disassembly is easily controlled by the large dismounting button located at the front of the trigger guard (inset). High Standard pistols also offer easy barrel interchangeability; the fluted barrel, above, has been substituted for the bull barrel shown in the first photo.

fire follow-up shots. Not surprisingly, the test pistol proved highly accurate. One five-shot, 25-foot offhand group, using CCI Blazer 50-grain FMJ ammunition, measured only ²/₃ inch across. At 50 feet, using the same ammunition, the group measured 2.0 inches. Next, a five-shot, rapid-fire group, fired offhand at 25 feet, measured 3.2 inches across and was well centered, with two hits in the 10-ring and three in the 8-ring. After two failures to feed the top round from the magazine into the firing chamber, the Trophy II had no further failures to feed or fire with any of the half-dozen brands of ammunition tested.

The disassembly procedure for the Trophy II is far easier and superior to that of the Ruger Mark II (*see* page 177). To fieldstrip a Trophy II, you must first remove the magazine, then draw back the slide and pull it rearward to eject a round in the chamber (even if there's no round left in the chamber, it's always a good idea to do this as a way to develop safe habits). The slide is locked open by pushing the slide release lever up while the slide is back, then moving the safety lever up to its safe position. Next, while holding the pistol in your shooting hand, push the barrel-locking plunger (located at the front of the frame) with the thumb of the support hand, meanwhile pulling straight upward on the barrel (with the four fingers of the same hand). Once the barrel has been removed from the frame, pull the slide back slightly to unlock it, then ease it forward off the frame.

When drawing back the slide, be sure to release the trigger all the way after each shot to allow a follow-up shot. And be careful while drawing back the slide not to bruise your fingers on the rear sight bridge. And finally, whereas all modern semiautomatic pistols have a disconnecter linked to the trigger to prevent fully automatic fire, the Trophy II seems particularly sensitive to this. The shooter must, as a result, make a concious effort to release the trigger far enough to allow it to reset between shots.

The Trophy II costs quite a bit more than a Ruger Mark II or Buck Mark; but on the other hand, this pistol has a much classier design and is still far less expensive than a Smith & Wesson Model 41. In summation, the Trophy II is an excellent pistol for sporting, plinking, hunting and outdoor survival purposes; but it can, when necessary, serve the role of a good self-defense weapon.

MITCHELL ARMS TROPHY II

Manufacturer	Years Produced	Caliber/Capacity	Dimensions
Mitchell Arms Santa Ana, CA	1992–1995	.22 LR/10 rounds	Barrel Length: 7.25" (or 5.5") O.A. Length: 11.6" Height: 5.8" Width: 1.6" Weight: 40 oz. (unloaded); 42 oz. (loaded)

NAVY ARMS TT-OLYMPIA

Although Navy Arms announced its new TT-Olympia
pistol in 1992, the history of this superb pistol actually began more
than 60 years earlier, in 1926. That was the year Germany's world-
famous Carl Walther Waffenfabrik introduced the *Sport-Pistole*, a .22-caliber blowback pistol designed for plinking and target competition. A few years later, a
German marksman won a silver medal with one of these guns at the 1932 Los
Angeles Olympics. A. F. Stoeger shrewdly capitalized on the pistol's excellent showing
and renamed it the "Model 1932" (a name change that Walther did not recognize).
Suddenly the *Sport-Pistole* was a popular gun and Stoeger and Heyer (Nairobi, Kenya)
could not supply enough of them.

As good as the *Sport-Pistole* was, Walther, in its efforts to create the world's best .22-caliber competition pistol, saw room for improvement. In 1934, Fritz Walther, son of the late founder of the
company, redesigned the *Sport-Pistole,* chiefly by replacing the striker with an exposed round hammer
mechanism, similar to that of the Walther PP; but later models all used an improved internal hammer
with a much faster lock time. Walther later named the gun the *Olympia Pistole* in hopes it would bring
Olympic gold to Germany.

Eventually, Walther offered several versions of its *Olympia-Pistole*. The standard model fired the
.22 LR round, but variants intended for Olympic and other international competition used instead
the .22 Short cartridge with its lower recoil. Barrel lengths varied from 240mm (9.5 inches) in the
Funfkampfmodell to 100mm (3.9 inches) in the *Sportmodell*. Except for the *Funfkampfmodell*, which
held six rounds of .22 LR, the magazines of all other variants held 10 rounds. The .22 LR versions
were made of steel, while the .22 Short variants used a lightweight aluminum-alloy slide to ensure sufficient movement in chambering follow-up shots. Different barrel lengths, many variations in muzzle
weights and grip shape, all enabled skilled shooters to tailor their pistols to their own preferences.

In its final form, the *Olympia-Pistole* was a handsome, streamlined gun made of excellent materials. Based roughly on the earlier *Sport-Pistole,* plus the various influences of Walther's PP service pistol,
the *Olympia-Pistole* was admirably suited for competitive use in the late 1930s. In fact, during the
final prewar Olympic Games held in Berlin in 1936, German shooters using *Olympia-Pistolen* won
gold and silver medals in rapid-fire competition.

During the war, the *Olympia-Pistole* went out of production, but Germany's armed forces
increased demands for Walther's expertise concerning martial firearms. Shortly after the war, though,
the *Olympia-Pistole* got a new lease on life when Hämmerli AG of Switzerland licensed its version of
the pistol as the Model 200. (Walther was prohibited from manufacturing firearms for 10 years after
the war, as were other German arms makers). The Walther/Hämmerli deal was arranged in 1951, and
during the next 15 years variants of the Model 200 began to appear, including Models 201, 202, 203,
204 and 205. These guns differed only slightly from the prewar *Olympia-Pistole* and, like their
German predecessor, proved extremely successful in international shooting competition. Hämmerli's
updated Model 206, introduced in 1962, was internally almost identical to the *Olympia-Pistole*, but
without its graceful appearance. Hämmerli's later Model 230 series, made from 1970 to 1986, had
very little in common with its *Olympia-Pistole*, but the company still makes the Model 212, a slightly
modified Model 206. Thus do the *Olympia-Pistolen* remain alive and well in Switzerland, their second

home. Meanwhile, the Carl Walther Waffenfabrik, having painfully reconstituted itself following World War II, introduced several lines of target pistols—but it has never revived the *Olympia-Pistole*.

Interestingly, the Olympic winner also found another home in Communist China. Val Forgett, former president of Navy Arms Company, who has an almost uncanny knack for creating top-quality modern replicas of historic firearms, worked closely with China North Industries Corporation (Norinco) to develop the TT-Olympia, a faithful reproduction of the *Jagermodell* version of the *Olympia-Pistole*. The *Jagermodell* had been popular in prewar Germany both as a target pistol and a sportsman's outdoor pistol, much like the Colt Woodsman (*see* page 132). It was a versatile handgun, one that was not so awkwardly specialized (for Olympic competition) as to be useless for any other purpose.

The TT-Olympia is a single-action pistol with a crisp trigger. The rear sight, faithful to the prewar originals, is a simple pattern adjustable only for windage. The sight picture is quite good, and the pistol is a pleasure to shoot. The manual safety lever, located on the left side of the frame, pushes up to safe and down to fire. The magazine release, located just above the safety lever, is about the same size and shape as the safety, which could cause confusion. On the bottom of the 10-shot magazine is a wooden extension that fits flush with the bottom of the large checkered-walnut stock. The left grip, like many target pistols, has a prominent thumbrest suitable for right-handed shooters. Disassembly procedure for the TT-Olympia is the easiest of all target pistols tested for this book.

An elegant pistol that performs well, the TT-Olympia is Navy Arms's reproduction of the Olympia-Pistole *produced by Walther in the 1930s. Since the original took gold and silver medals for marksmanship in the 1936 Olympics, it should come as no surprise that the replica TT-Olympia is also quite accurate—as demonstrated by this 1.3-inch, five-shot offhand group shot from a distance of 25 feet.*

While its days as an Olympic target pistol are over, the TT-Olympia remains an outstanding shooter, with an excellent trigger and enough weight to dampen the recoil. It excels both in precision firing and in rapid-fire shooting, functioning best with standard-velocity ammunition. Low-powered RWS subsonic rounds do not cycle the slide vigorously enough to feed the next cartridge, while high-powered CCI Stinger ammunition generally produces groups an inch larger at 25 feet than do standard-velocity CCI Mini Mags. A five-shot, 25-foot offhand group using Mini Mags went into 1.2 inches, while a 50-foot offhand group, firing a full 10 rounds from the magazine, measured 2.8 inches. A five-shot, rapid-fire group fired offhand at 25 feet measured only 1.3 inches across, which indicates exceptional accuracy. No failures to feed were experienced with any of the standard- or high-velocity ammunition tested, although the low-powered RWS subsonic rounds caused the shooter to draw back the slide by hand after each shot.

The TT-Olympia remains a beautiful, sleek and graceful pistol, perhaps the most impressive target pistol of all those tested. Moreover, it's still by far the least expensive pistol in its class.

NAVY ARMS TT-OLYMPIA

Manufacturer	Years Produced	Caliber/Capacity	Dimensions
China No. Industries Corp.(Norinco), China	1992–Present by Navy Arms (importation banned since 1995)	.22 LR/10 rounds	Barrel Length: 4.7" O.A. Length: 7.9" Height: 4.9" Width: 1.45" Weight: 28 oz. (unloaded); 30 oz. (loaded)

PSP-25

People who are knowledgeable about the history of firearms design will immediately recognize the lines of the PSP-25 as being copied from FN's famous 1932-vintage "Baby" Browning. Actually, the origins of the PSP-25 date back much further— to Fabrique Nationale's Model 1906, which introduced the .25 ACP cartridge (called the 6.35mm Browning in Europe). This excellent little gun, which has been widely copied, is still used by thousands of people because it fits easily into a vest pocket or the palm of a shooter's hand.

After John M. Browning died in 1926, FN hired his star pupil, Dieudonne Joseph Saive, to rework several of Browning's designs, a collaboration that produced a large 9mm pistol— the immortal High Power. At the opposite end of the scale, Browning created the tiny Model 1906, which in 1932 Saive reworked into the even smaller "Baby" Browning. To do this, Saive simplified and improved the slide contours and omitted the Model 1906's grip safety. The Baby was an immediate success and, although production largely ceased during World War II, FN resumed production following the war. The U.S. was among FN's best customers for the Baby, selling it in this country with a prominent Browning marking on the grip.

Unfortunately, like so many small handguns, importation of the Baby into the U.S. was scuttled by the passage of the Gun Control Act (GCA) in 1968. Under its rules, no handgun less than four inches high could be imported into this country. In an attempt to make up for this loss of Belgian-made imported

Like many other small automatic pistols, the cocked-striker indicator on the PSP-25 is a pin that protrudes from the rear of the slide when the striker is cocked and ready to release once the trigger is pulled. When the striker is not cocked, the pin retracts into the slide.

Baby Brownings, Bauer Firearms Corporation (Fraser, MI) began in 1972 to make close copies. As mentioned earlier, a loophole in the Gun Control Act allowed the domestic manufacture of guns considered too small for legal importation by the GCA. It even allowed domestic arms makers to assemble these undersized guns from imported parts. Bauer marketed its Baby pistol until 1984, further contributing to the history of the PSP-25 by crafting the Baby design in stainless steel—a first.

Enter Precision Small Parts of Charlottesville, VA, which obtained a license from Fabrique Nationale Herstal in 1990 to build the Baby in the U.S. Since then the PSP-25, which is available in both a blued and a hard-chrome finish, has gained a modest following. Its main claim to fame is its small size, stemming from the Browning/Saive design for a blowback single-action .25 auto. It is

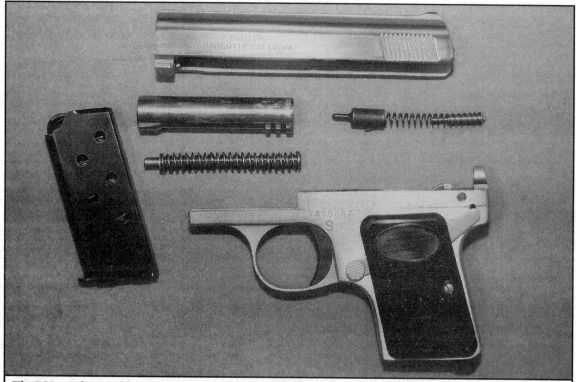

The PSP-25 disassembles easily and conveniently into six parts.

almost inconceivable that something so small (4 inches long and less than 3 inches high) could become a deadly firearm—and yet the PSP-25 is exactly that. While it is by no means the only pistol available in this tactical niche, the PSP-25 has an advantage stemming from its FN/Browning pedigree and the marketing savvy of K.B.I. Its quality is outstanding and completely up to FN's exacting standards. In fact, so good is this U.S.-made beauty that PSP actually exports some of its production to FN for resale to its European and worldwide markets as an FN pistol.

Among the PSP-25's safety devices is a cocked-striker indicator that protrudes slightly from the rear of the slide, much the same as Walther's loaded-chamber indicator. The striker is cocked by pulling back the slide and releasing it. This same action brings the topmost round from the loaded magazine into the firing chamber. When the shooter sees (or feels) the cocked-striker indicator protruding from the slide, he can assume the pistol is ready for shooting. A manual safety lever, located on the left side of the frame, just forward of the upper front portion of the left grip panel, pushes up to safe (marked "S") and down to fire. When in its safe setting, the manual safety locks the trigger and slide. The safety also helps lock the slide back when field-stripping the pistol for cleaning. In addition, the PSP-25 features a magazine disconnect safety, which prevents the pistol from firing when the magazine is removed from the gun. Located at the lower rear of the grip frame, or "heel" of the pistol, the magazine release lessens the chance of accidentally separating the magazine from the pistol while it's under concealment in the shooter's pocket.

Another nice feature is the gun's easy and convenient disassembly procedure. Simply remove the magazine and empty all ammunition from it. Then draw back the slide and pull it rearward to eject a round in the chamber (if there is one). Then, reinsert the unloaded magazine into the grip and move the safety lever down to fire. Next, dry-fire the pistol to uncock the striker, and remove the magazine once again. Pull the slide back slightly until the notch on top of the safety lever fits into the farthest of two notches found on the underside of the slide. This operation locks the slide open, exposing about 5/16 inch of the front end of the barrel. Now rotate the barrel about 90 degrees counterclockwise (as viewed from the front). This takes the lugs that are machined under the barrel out of alignment with matching grooves cut into the frame. You can now release the safety/disassembly lever and push the slide and barrel forward off the frame. With the slide removed, all working parts are available for cleaning and inspection.

The PSP-25 is a faithful copy of the FN "Baby" Browning, a smaller version of John Browning's FN Model 1906. The PSP-25 has virtually no recoil and is very accurate, as this 1.8-inch, five-shot 25-foot offhand group indicates.

Despite its tiny size, the PSP-25 is comfortable to shoot, with a short, light trigger stroke and minimal recoil because of the low pressures generated by the .25 ACP cartridge. Its sights, while low-profile in the extreme, work quite well too. This gun excels in rapid-fire follow-up shots; in fact, a skilled shooter can empty its magazine in two seconds or less, which is probably the best way to handle a single assailant.

In testing the PSP-25, we found a surprisingly high level of accuracy. The usual 50-foot course of fire was bypassed (because of the .25-caliber ammunition used) and instead we tried some rapid-fire shooting at a more likely distance of 10 feet for a gun of this type. Typical groups at this distance went into about two inches. A five-shot, 25-foot offhand group, using CCI Blazer 50-grain FMJ ammunition, measured 1.8 inches. Another group fired at 25 feet using CCI Blazer 45-grain jacketed hollowpoint produced five shots in a 2.4-inch group (four of the five landed in a tight 1.2-inch pattern). In addition, the PSP-25 produced no failures to feed or fire with several types of FMJ and hollowpoint ammunition tested.

As with most small pistols, however, the slide will not hold open with the last shot fired, which means the shooter must count rounds—an unlikely proposition, indeed, in the midst of a serious gunfight. The only other problem encountered with the test gun was the stiffness of its safety lever, especially when pushing it down into its firing position. Perhaps this is an intentional move on the manufacturer's part to lessen the chance of an accidental discharge or simply a quirk of this particular pistol. Previously tested Model 1906 and Baby Browning pistols did not exhibit such hard-to-operate safety levers. Many owners of the Baby Browning and pistols of similar design leave the safety on the fire setting and the firing chamber empty, then rack the slide immediately before shooting. That's the only way a left-hander can operate this gun, by the way, since the safety lever is on the pistol's left side only.

A true pocket pistol in size and weight, the Model PSP-25 will fit almost anyone's wallet or purse. For those who are unable, for whatever reason, to carry a larger pistol in a more powerful caliber, it's a good choice.

PSP-25

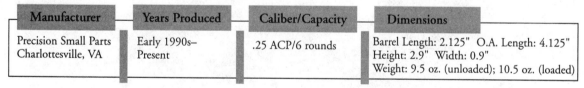

Manufacturer	Years Produced	Caliber/Capacity	Dimensions
Precision Small Parts Charlottesville, VA	Early 1990s–Present	.25 ACP/6 rounds	Barrel Length: 2.125" O.A. Length: 4.125" Height: 2.9" Width: 0.9" Weight: 9.5 oz. (unloaded); 10.5 oz. (loaded)

RAVEN

The Raven, which dates back to the early 1970s, has become one of the top-selling guns in the U.S., mostly because of its low cost, small size and reliable performance. Its finish—whether in blue, nickel, chrome or black Teflon—is quite good, as are its smooth hardwood grips.

Like the Davis P-380 (*see* page 137), the Raven features a simple zinc-cast frame that is inexpensively cast to allow the gun to sell for less than $100. Its design, while reminiscent of Walther's Model 9, is larger and less refined than that prewar classic; still, for a small pistol, the Raven boasts good sights, an above-average trigger, and shoots surprisingly well.

During test-firing, a five-shot, 10-foot offhand group went into 1.4 inches, followed by a five-shot, 25-foot target, fired offhand, that also measured 1.4 inches across. Even a 50-foot offhand group—something one would ordinarily not even attempt with a small .25-caliber pistol—went into

The underrated Raven is successful because it is inexpensive, reliable and, as the photo shows, quite accurate.

a mere 4.2 inches. This sort of performance would put many larger and far more expensive guns to shame.

For such an inexpensive gun, though, some weak spots are bound to appear. To begin, the manual safety is too small, and the magazine release is located at the bottom of the grip, which bothers most shooters (but actually makes sense on a pistol with a small grip). The Raven is also top-heavy, with a large, thick slide, and it's not much of a natural pointer, either. Then there's the extractor, which is located on top of the slide instead of on the right side, as is usual with most automatic pistols. As a result, the spent cartridge, which is usually very hot, flies straight up into the air for a few feet before raining down on the shooter's head.

The Raven, like any .25 ACP pistol, is sadly underpowered and unnecessarily large for such a small cartridge. Still, considering its low price, it offers excellent performance. For shooters who are on an extremely limited budget, this gun ranks high among the best choices.

RAVEN

Manufacturer	Years Produced	Caliber/Capacity	Dimensions
Raven Arms (Orig.) City of Industry, CA Phoenix Arms (Current) Ontario, CA	1972–Present	.25 ACP/6 rounds	Barrel Length: 2.4" O.A. Length: 4.75" Height: 3.4" Width: 0.9" Weight: 15 oz. (unloaded); 16 oz. (loaded)

REMINGTON MODEL 51

In 1919, Remington introduced its Model 51 in
.380 ACP caliber, and two years later it added a .32 ACP-caliber
model. Both calibers remained in production until 1927, reaching
a total production of some 54,000 .380s and 11,000 .32s. Actually,
Remington had developed the Model 51 from a larger .45 ACP-caliber pistol—
created by the noted firearms designer John Pedersen— to compete with Colt's
then popular M1911 pistol. The .45-caliber Pedersen pistol was, by all accounts, an
impressive performer that came close to gaining acceptance by the U.S. Navy over
the M1911. Unfortunately, World War I intervened and the U.S. armed forces,
forced to standardize and rationalize production as much as possible, ordered the Navy to take the
M1911 instead. Remington then shelved the Pedersen pistol for the time being and turned its pistol-
making efforts to producing M1911 pistols for the duration of the war.

 After the war, Remington revised the design into a much smaller pistol in .380 ACP caliber, with
a .32 ACP-caliber version following later on. Although the .380/.32 version retained the separate
breechblock of the .45 model, the spur hammer was discarded in favor of a concealed hammer
designed to smooth the contours of the pistol for pocket
carry. The shape of the grip was also the subject of much
research. In fact, the whole pistol became noticeably sleek
and comfortable to carry as well as to shoot. Its breech-locking mechanism dampened recoil to a considerable extent
compared to the straight blowback designs offered by Colt
and other competitors.

 The breech-locking mechanism of the Model 51, however, contributed to the pistol's two great weaknesses: it was
a difficult gun to fieldstrip for cleaning and maintenance,
and it was expensive to manufacture. As a result, despite its
excellent fit and finish and top-notch performance, the
Model 51 never seriously threatened the Colt Pocket Model
for market share. Still, it has served many police forces suc-
cessfully as an undercover gun, and it even gained fame
among military personnel, its most notable proponent being
General George S. Patton.

Remington's Model 51, manufactured between 1919 and 1927, and long considered one of the most elegant pocket pistols ever made, is now highly valued as a collector's item.

 Comfortable to carry and shoot, accurate almost to a fault, and reliable even with modern
ammunition, the Model 51 remains a popular gun for armed civilians. If one can find an example at a
good price, it's well worth considering as a defensive pistol.

REMINGTON MODEL 51

Manufacturer	Years Produced	Caliber/Capacity	Dimensions
Remington Arms Co. Ilion, NY	1919–1927	.380 ACP/7 rounds .32 ACP/8 rounds	Barrel Length: 3.5" O.A. Length: 6.6" Height: 4.5" Width: 1.0" Weight: 21 oz. (unloaded); 24.5 oz. (loaded)

RUGER MARK II GOVERNMENT TARGET MODEL

Ruger began updating its original Standard pistol in 1982. What emerged—
the Mark II—was a significant improvement over the classic Ruger Standard,
the gun that started Ruger's fabulously successful gunmaking career in 1949. Among
other improvements, the Mark II features a bolt hold-open capability once the last shot in
the magazine has been fired; a manual safety that can be left in its on-safe position when
working the slide; and an improved magazine and trigger arrangement. In short, it remains
Ruger's classic target pistol, with its sleek lines, comfortable handling and rapid, accurate 10-shot firepower. The regular Mark II Target Model has a lighter barrel that gently tapers to the muzzle, while
the barrel on the Government Target is a heavier bull-barrel type with no taper.

The "Government" label, by the way, is no mere marketing gimmick. The U.S. armed forces

The Ruger Mark II Government Target Model is capable of sensational accuracy, as this .8 inch, five-shot 25-foot offhand group clearly indicates.

Except for its magazine release, which is mounted at the bottom rear "heel" of the frame, the Ruger Mark II's controls mimic those of the M1911A1. Top photo shows the newer stainless steel Standard Model; a new 22/45 version with injection-molded Zytel frame (bottom photo) is even more like the classic .45 ACP M1911A1 service pistol; note the difference in the grip angle.

have used Ruger pistols for many years, both as suppressed survival/assassination arms and as training/competition pistols, all with excellent results. Moreover, its long barrel is ideally suited for use with an integral suppressor (an efficient silencer that surrounds the barrel). A Ruger rimfire pistol with an integral suppressor is extraordinarily quiet.

The Mark II is, like other Ruger firearms, so well designed for efficient and economical mass production that it costs only about half of what other government-issue rimfire pistols cost—including the Colt, High Standard and Smith & Wesson Model 41. The Mark II may not be quite as refined as a top-of-the-line High Standard or S&W Model 41, but it comes close in performance—and the price is right. Moreover, because Ruger designed the Mark II from the outset for economy of manufacture, with no compromise in quality, it will undoubtedly remain competitive in price.

Not surprisingly, the Mark II Government Target pistol, despite being somewhat muzzle-heavy because of its long barrel, is extremely accurate. Its Luger-like grip angle makes it awkward for some shooters to hold, but it's easy to shoot with precision and accuracy. One 25-foot offhand group loaded with CCI Mini Mag ammunition placed five shots in a pattern only .8 inch across, with four of the shots in the 10-ring and the fifth in the 9-ring almost touching the 10-ring.

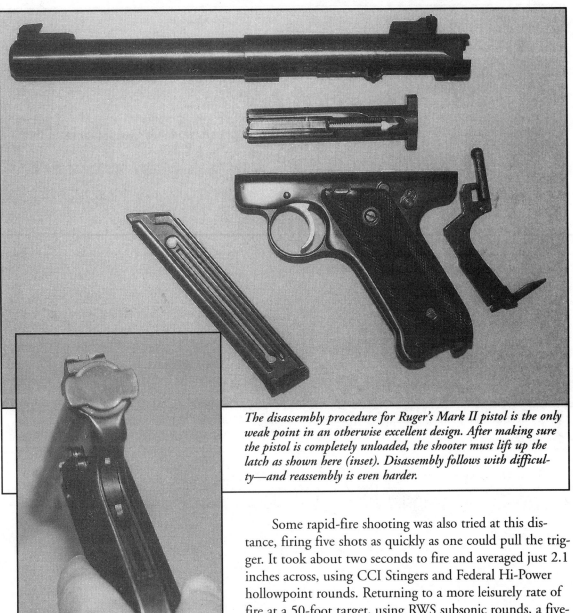

The disassembly procedure for Ruger's Mark II pistol is the only weak point in an otherwise excellent design. After making sure the pistol is completely unloaded, the shooter must lift up the latch as shown here (inset). Disassembly follows with difficulty—and reassembly is even harder.

Some rapid-fire shooting was also tried at this distance, firing five shots as quickly as one could pull the trigger. It took about two seconds to fire and averaged just 2.1 inches across, using CCI Stingers and Federal Hi-Power hollowpoint rounds. Returning to a more leisurely rate of fire at a 50-foot target, using RWS subsonic rounds, a five-shot offhand group measured only 1.9 inches across.

If the Mark II has any shortcomings, they are in the pistol's disassembly/reassembly procedures, which are something of an ordeal. In that regard, Smith & Wesson's Model 41, the Navy Arms TT-Olympia and the Mitchell High Standard pistols (*see* separate listings), among other competitors, enjoy a huge advantage over the Ruger. Otherwise, the Mark II is an excellent pistol that offers performance and features closely competitive with pistols that cost considerably more.

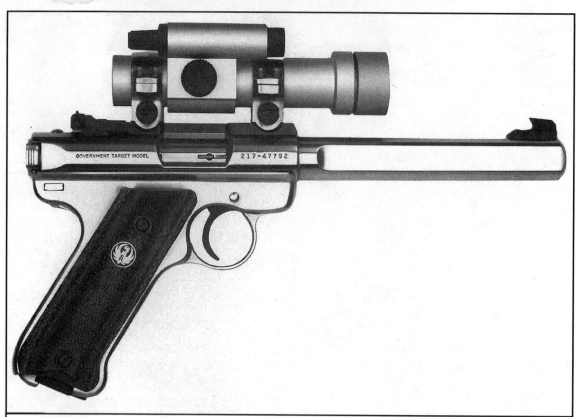

For competition purposes, the stainless steel Government Target Model has been designed to mount an optical sight.

RUGER MARK II GOVERNMENT TARGET MODEL

Manufacturer	Years Produced	Caliber/Capacity	Dimensions
Sturm, Ruger & Co. Southport, CT	1986 – Present	.22 LR/10 rounds	Barrel Length: 6.9" O.A. Length: 11.12" Height: 5.5" Width: 1.2" Weight: 46 oz. (unloaded); 48 oz. (loaded)

RUSSIAN PSM

The extraordinarily compact PSM, which appeared late in the Soviet regime, first became known to Western intelligence sources in 1983, when samples captured in Afghanistan made their way back to the West. Since then, the PSM has also appeared in the Middle East, Western Europe and Cuba, although never in large numbers. This pistol appears to have replaced the similar but older and larger Makarov Model PM *(see* page 79). It was used previously by the Soviets as a service pistol, but only to a very limited degree and in highly specialized applications. The Makarov remains by far the more common of the two pistols.

The gun's official designation—PSM—is a Russian acronym for *Pistolet Samozariyadniy Malokaliberniy*, which translates to "Pistol, Self-loading, Small Caliber." The caliber—a 5.45x18mm round unique to this gun—follows the traditional Russian practice of making a pistol in the same caliber as the service rifle (in this case, the 5.45x39mm AK-74). In doing so, one must accept a loss in pistol bullet efficiency in order that the barrels on both weapons may be rifled using the same machinery. The bullet itself weighs 40 grains and has a muzzle velocity of slightly over 1,000 feet per second. Although barely taller than a .25 ACP round, the 5.45x18mm round is far more powerful and has gained fame for its ability to pierce helmets and other body armor at close ranges.

Similar in construction to the Makarov PM, the PSM utilizes a double-action trigger mechanism, with its magazine release located in the heel of the frame. Slightly longer and taller than a Walther PPK, it is also extraordinarily slim, making concealment easy. And its weight, just over a pound, is made possible by an aluminum-alloy frame. The Russians have demonstrated with the PSM that they

Despite its double-action capability, the Russian PSM is designed to be cocked on the draw. The same thumb motion that cocks the hammer also serves to deactivate the nearby manual safety. Here the trigger is shown cocked and the safety down in its fire position.

The magazine release on the PSM is mounted in the bottom rear, or heel, of the frame. Note the pebbled plastic grips on this commercial model. The original military-style grips are made of metal with vertical serrations. The hole just above and behind the magazine release is for attaching a lanyard.

The PSM is so thin that its drawbar has to be located outside the frame. The Russians have extended the leading edges of the grips forward to cover and protect this vulnerable part (as Colt did with its Double Eagle).

The commercial PSM rig shown includes a military-style leather holster, spare magazine and a cleaning rod.

are far ahead of U.S. and Western European gun designers in resolving the problems that relate to the most critical factors in handgun concealment: thickness and weight. Despite its double-action capability, the PSM is designed to be cocked on the draw; the same thumb motion that cocks the hammer also deactivates the manual safety (for right-handed shooters). Otherwise, its handling properties are identical to those of the more common Makarov pistol, which was itself a very scarce pistol in the U.S. prior to the 1990s.

For all of its advanced features, the PSM is not an easy pistol to shoot. Its odd shape and short grip make it awkward to hold, and its thin frame is no help in getting a solid grip on the weapon. The double-action trigger pull is also heavy, especially considering the weapon's small size. Nevertheless, its easy concealment, together with an ability to fire a cartridge disproportionate to its modest size, make the PSM far superior to comparable .22- and .25-caliber pocket pistols commonly available in the U.S. and Europe.

With the breakup of the Soviet Union, the PSM has become commercially available in Western Europe, at least for the time being. Frankonia Jagd, a well-known German sporting goods dealer, offers PSMs for sale in Germany, albeit at a stiff price. For that reason, a small number of these interesting handguns is trickling back into the U.S.(mostly via Germany-stationed GIs, who buy them there and later sell them in this country). In any event, the PSM will certainly never become easily available here unless some enterprising American manufacturer arranges to build it under license or copies it outright.

RUSSIAN PSM

Manufacturer	Years Produced	Caliber/Capacity	Dimensions
Izhevsk Ordnance Factory Izhevsk, Russia	1980-Present	5.4x18mm/8 rounds	Barrel Length: 3.4" O.A. Length: 6.3" Height: 4.1" Width: 0.7" Weight: 16 oz. (unloaded); 17 oz. (loaded)

SEECAMP LWS-32

This tiny Seecamp pistol, which replaced the earlier .25-caliber version, is one of the most radical, sought-after pistols in the world. Because of its desirable compactness, it's also one of the most difficult to obtain, having been extremely popular since its inception among police officers, federal agents and others who require a small but powerful backup pistol.

Mechanically, the Seecamp pistol is closely based on previous Czech pistol designs, including CZ's excellent .25-caliber pocket pistols. Intratec's Protec pistol (*see* page 154) is another example of a U.S.-made pistol whose design was closely influenced by Czech gunmakers.

Everything about the Seecamp is optimized to make it smooth in contour, light, compact and easy to carry. Its all-double-action mechanism does away with the need for a manual safety lever, which would only add bulk to the pistol. It has no sights, relying instead on a shallow groove that runs down the top of the slide. While some may object that this lack of sights makes the gun unsuitable for use much beyond contact distance, that is exactly the point; i.e., this gun is intended specifically for emergency shooting at point-blank range.

Because of Seecamp's desire to achieve the greatest degree of miniaturization, its pistol calls for a series of compromises. For example, its Model LWS-32 was designed to work only with the fairly expensive Winchester Silvertip cartridge, because of that round's short overall length. Fortunately, the Silvertips's little 60-grain hollowpoint bullet has proven more effective than the average .32 ACP as an anti-personnel round. On the other hand, the Seecamp is not always 100% reliable and requires an extensive break-in period. It also has a sharp, stinging recoil, a long reach to the trigger, and a stiff trigger pull. And yet, unpleasant as it

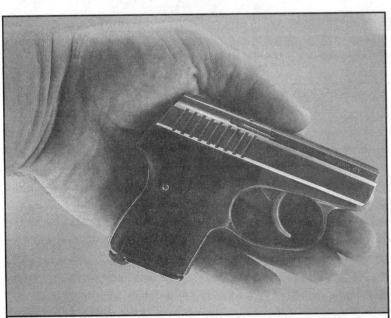

The diminutive size of the Seecamp LWS-32 has made it extremely popular among police, federal agents and others who require a small but powerful backup pistol.

This fairly recent example of the Seecamp LWS-32 bears serial number 13219, indicating that production has been slow over the past decade or so. High demand for the arm has driven the price up as well as forced buyers to look elsewhere to fulfill their needs.

may be to shoot, this little pistol could prove a real lifesaver under the most dire circumstances.

The worst feature of the Seecamp, however, is its exorbitant price. The Seecamp factory is a relatively small operation as gun manufacturers go, and production is therefore limited. This combination of short supply and tall demand results in "street" prices of up to $1,000 or more for one of these little guns. Those who buy direct from the factory pay a more reasonable price, true, but they must lay down a substantial deposit and then wait for as long as several years for delivery.

Because the Seecamp is so difficult to buy, many shooters are willing to settle for something more accessible, such as the Colt Mustang Pocketlite, North American Arms' Mini-Revolver, or Smith & Wesson's Sigma .380.

SEECAMP LWS-32

Manufacturer	Years Produced	Caliber/Capacity	Dimensions
L.W. Seecamp Co., Inc. New Haven, CT	1985–Present	.32 ACP*/6 rounds *(Winchester Silvertip only)	Barrel Length: 2" O.A. Length: 4.1" Height: 3.1" Width: 0.8" Weight: 10.5 oz. (unloaded); 12 oz. (loaded)

SEMMERLING LM-4

Semmerling's LM-4, certainly one of the more unusual handguns available, came about from a desire (shared by other pistol-makers covered in this book) to pack a defensive handgun cartridge into the most efficient space. Although its designers succeeded in making the LM-4 small, so many compromises were involved in its creation that its appeal and utility were severely limited. The pistol appeared sometime in 1975 and was made for almost ten years before the Semmerling Corporation closed its doors, whereupon American Derringer of Waco, TX, took over production.

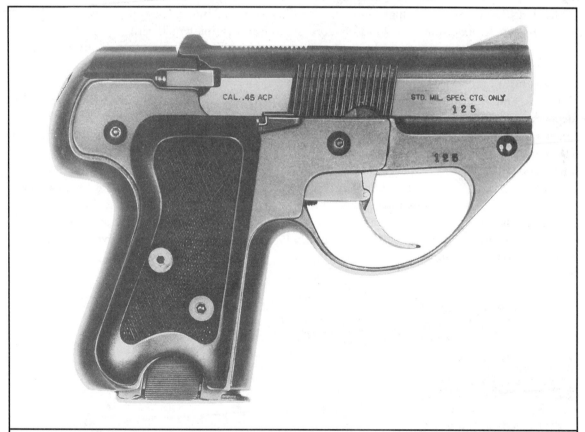

The original Semmerling LM-4 designers had in mind miniaturizing the gun as much as possible without sacrificing its ability to use a powerful handgun cartridge. What evolved was an automatic pistol look-alike slightly more than 5 inches long, under 4 inches high, and a mere 1 inch wide. A true work of art, the LM-4 is in fact a manually operated, four-shot repeater in .45 ACP—with the price tag to match.

The LM-4 is available in either a blued finish with checkered plastic stocks, or a stainless finish with smooth wooden stocks. Although it looks like an automatic pistol, the LM-4 is in fact a manually operated, 4-shot repeater in .45 ACP, the dominant caliber for which this gun is made. After the magazine is loaded and inserted into the grip, the shooter places the thumb of his support hand on the loading grooves along the side of the slide, pushes the slide forward, then pulls it back into place. This action—pushing the slide to the front—ejects an empty round and, by pulling the slide back to its rest position, chambers a new round. The LM-4 is fired with a double-action-only trigger. Rearward slide movement in an automatic pistol is caused by recoil forces; the slide's subsequent movement forward is provided by a powerful return spring. But, in the LM-4, the slide travels only about 1^1/$_2$ inches. There are no springs to resist its motion. Thus, with practice, a reload takes only a second or so. The worst feature of this process is that two hands are required to reload the gun. And, since the LM-4 requires such close tolerances, it is extremely expensive to make. In addition, according to the manual, the LM-4 is reliable only when used with milspec FMJ ("ball") ammunition.

The designers of this pistol had in mind miniaturizing the gun as much as possible without sacrificing its ability to use a powerful handgun cartridge. What evolved was a gun slightly more than 5 inches long, less than 4 inches high, and a mere 1 inch wide. For another perspective, consider that the LM-4 weighs about the same 24–25 ounces as a Makarov pistol, which, although small, measures an inch longer and taller than the LM-4. Moreover, 9mm Makarov ammunition is a long way from the powerful 230-grain .45 ACP ammunition used in the LM-4.

Because of the LM-4's double-action-only trigger, no manual safety mechanism is provided. The gun cocks and fires with one long pull on the trigger. Recoil is best described as impressive or severe, depending upon the shooter's physical endurance and threshold of pain. Because of this recoil, the heavy trigger pull and the small sights, accuracy is compromised. However, considering that the LM-4 is designed for "contact" range, or slightly beyond, the sights (ramp front and rear notch) are actually pretty good.

Despite the LM-4 designers' gallant attempts to combine such compact dimensions with a powerful caliber, its uncommon two-handed method of operation makes it impractical as a defensive handgun, where one needs that support hand to fend off an opponent rather than operate the pistol. The LM-4 is a work of art, true, but it's also priced like one—so shooters are well advised to leave this little jewel to the collectors.

SEMMERLING LM-4

Manufacturer	Years Produced	Caliber/Capacity	Dimensions
Semmerling Corp. (Orig.) American Derringer (Now) Waco, TX	1975– Present	.45 ACP/5 rounds 9mm/7 rounds	Barrel Length: 3.625" O.A. Length: 5.2" Height: 3.7" Width: 1.0" Weight: 24 oz. (unloaded); 29 oz. (loaded)

SIG-SAUER P230

When Walther in 1973 introduced its Model PP Super— an improved and slightly enlarged Model PP chambered in 9x18mm Police (Ultra) caliber—the Swiss police looked at it with interest. Like the then West Germans, they wanted something that was slightly more powerful than the PP and PPK models, but without much added bulk. As so many countries rich in natural pride and blessed with a strong industrial base, the self-reliant Swiss balked at the idea of buying foreign guns. Consequently, in 1976 they developed their own 9x18mm police pistol— the Model P230 — manufactured by SIG (Schweizerische Industrie-Gesellschaft) of Neuhausen am Rheinfall in their native Switzerland. Since that beginning, the P230 has been chambered in three additional calibers—.22 LR, .32 ACP and .380 ACP—and ranks among the world's finest pistols in its size range.

This right side view of the SIG-Sauer P230 is reminiscent of Walther's PPK in appearance. The P230, shown blued, has a lightweight alloy frame; a heavier all-stainless version is also available.

Mechanically, the P230 is quite similar to the Walther PP or one of its many clones. It features a blowback mechanism with the barrel pinned to the frame and the recoil spring wrapped around the barrel. The P230's one unique touch is a decocking lever mounted on the left side of the frame, a design contributed by the J.P. Sauer & Sohn Company of Eckenförde, Germany, now a SIG subsidiary that manufacturers the gun. Sauer had used a similar device on its Model 38H pistol of World War II fame. By lowering this lever, one safely decocks the hammer onto a loaded chamber. The pistol is then ready to fire simply by pulling through on the trigger. Even though the decocking lever springs up into its firing position once the shooter has released his hold, the chances of an accidental firing are remote. That's because the firing pin stays locked until the trigger has been pulled back all the way. When all parts are in good working order, even dropping the weapon should not cause it to fire.

In addition to the decocking lever, the P230 differs from the Walther PP in its disassembly. For instance, it is not controlled by a hinged trigger guard; instead, there's a separate disassembly lever on the left forward portion of the frame which the shooter pushes down and forward (but only after removing the magazine and drawing back the slide to make sure the firing chamber is unloaded). The slide is then pulled to the rear and lifted off the frame in PP/PPK style. The P230 also has a loaded-chamber indicator; but, unlike the Walther pistols, this is a Beretta-style marked extractor that protrudes slightly to expose a red dot when the firing chamber is loaded.

Because it was designed as a service pistol in the slightly larger 9x18 caliber, the P230 is larger than the Walther PPK and some of the other .380-caliber pistols developed from .32-caliber ancestors. The P230 is, in fact, almost exactly the same size as the Makarov pistol, which also started out in a 9x18 caliber. Interestingly, the Makarov, which uses a bullet 9.2mm, or .362 inch, in diameter, can also handle the Western 9x18mm Police round, while the Soviet-designed 9x18 Makarov round is slightly too wide to fit the PP Super and P230 models, whose barrels are designed for a .355-inch bullet.

Its superior trigger, large comfortable grip and excellent sights all contribute to making the P230 an easy and pleasant gun to shoot. Using a stainless Model P230SL, the author fired (as fast as he could pull the trigger) an eight-shot, 25-foot offhand group measuring 3.8 inches across. It took only two or three seconds to fire eight rounds, causing the range owner to yell out, "One shot per second maximum!" Four of the shots landed in the central X-ring of the target and the remaining four landed just outside it.

Overall, the P230 is an impressive shooting piece, but its occasional reliability problems cause one to doubt the gun's ability to come through in a life-and-death situation. Also, with Makarov pistols now widely available, shooters have a better option. The Makarov is more ruggedly built, fires a more powerful cartridge, and is a lot less expensive. The Czech CZ 83 also is no larger, but it holds nearly twice as many rounds and costs considerably less. In short, there are plenty of .380-caliber pistols available that are smaller, thinner and less expensive than the SIG-Sauer P230.

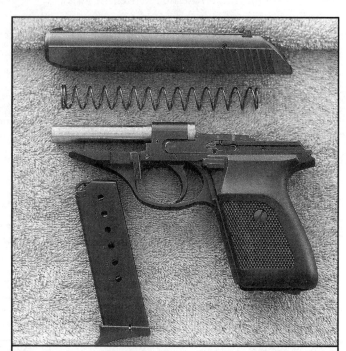

The SIG-Sauer P230 is similar to the Walther PPK in general construction, although it uses a decocking lever on the frame to lower the hammer; it also features a disassembly latch (rather than a hinged trigger guard) to disassemble the pistol for cleaning. When the P230 is disassembled, however, the similarity between the two pistols is evident.

SIG-SAUER P230

Manufacturer	Years Produced	Caliber/Capacity	Dimensions
SIG—Neuhausen am Rheinfall, Switzerland J.P. Sauer & Sohn, GmbH Eckernförde, Germany	1976 –Present	.380 ACP/7 rounds	Barrel Length: 3.6" O.A. Length: 6.7" Height: 4.8" Width: 1.2" Weight (alloy frame): 16.25 oz.–18.5 oz. (stainless): 23 oz.–25.25 oz.

SMITH & WESSON MODEL 41

In 1957, after a grueling phase of development
that lasted a full decade, Smith & Wesson finally introduced its .22
LR Model 41. In its original version it had a 7³/8-inch barrel with integral muzzle brake; but two years later S&W introduced a new Model 41
with a 5-inch barrel designed for field use. Its easy interchangeability of barrels gave
shooters two guns for the price of one. That same year, the Model 46 went into production, intended primarily for use by the U.S. Air Force for competitive shooting.
This inexpensive model with its 7-inch barrel lacked the fancy frills of the Model 41.
Later, Smith & Wesson introduced variants with barrel lengths of 5¹/2 inches and 5 inches.

In an effort to capture civilian interest in the gun, the company introduced a Model 41-1 in
1960 chambered for the .22 Short cartridge, but this model proved unsuccessful and few were pro-

Those who prefer a Smith & Wesson automatic pistol to a revolver can choose the superbly accurate Model 41 in .22 Long Rifle caliber

Except for the classic checkered grips, the restyled Model 41, introduced in 1995, takes on a new high-tech look.

duced. A few years later, a heavy-barrel version with a 5¹/₂-inch barrel was brought out, followed by a similar pistol featuring an extendable front sight for a longer sight radius.

As an extremely accurate and refined target pistol, the Model 41 has consistently ranked among the top sellers in the Smith & Wesson line. Its sleek, graceful design demonstrates the considerable influence of Walther's *Olympia-Pistole*, a prewar design of exceptional grace and beauty. The Model 41's disassembly procedure, similar to Walther's *Olympia* and PP/PPK Series, is controlled by a trigger guard hinged at the front.

Despite its high cost compared to guns like the High Standard Trophy II and Ruger Mark II, the Model 41 is an excellent and versatile gun. Its great accuracy gives it a viable self-defense capability against human attackers despite the low power of the .22 LR round. Unfortunately, it's also an expensive pistol, so shooters who seek Smith & Wesson quality in a less expensive rimfire design might be better served with the Model 422/622 series, or the Model 2214— the next S&W gun discussed.

SMITH & WESSON MODEL 41

Manufacturer	Years Produced	Caliber/Capacity	Dimensions
Smith & Wesson Springfield, MA	1957–Present	.22 LR/10 rounds	Barrel Length: 5.5" O.A. Length: 9.0" Height: 5.3" Width: 1.4" Weight: 44 oz. (unloaded); 46 oz. (loaded)

SMITH & WESSON MODEL 2213/2214

In 1990, Smith & Wesson introduced the Model 2214, a smaller version of the company's popular Model 422 designed especially for fishermen or hunters who wanted alternatives to the more traditional .22 LR "kit gun" revolvers. The Model 2214 "Sportsman" is light, compact and extremely accurate—characteristics that are ideal for home-defense purposes as well as outdoor use.

Like most of Smith & Wesson's other .22 LR pistols (except for the deluxe Model 41), the Model 2214 is fashioned from the pistol designed by John Browning at the dawn of automatic pistol design, FN's Model 1900 (*see* page 75). Like that venerable workhorse, the Smith & Wesson Models 422, 2204, 2206 and 2214 all have their barrels positioned underneath the recoil spring, unlike most other automatic pistols. The effect places the barrel close to the hand, which, combined with the weak impulse of the .22 LR cartridge, reduces recoil almost to nothing.

In keeping with its plinking or target functions, the Model 2214 trigger is grooved, and its fixed sights are marked prominently with three large white dots, making it look like a combat gun. In terms of handling and shooting, it offers mixed results. The good news is that the Model 2214 is accurate, even in rapid fire, and it has very little recoil. While many shooters dislike marked sights, preferring a wide, square notch rear sight and a black front post sight, the 3-dot system on this gun is really quite good. One five-shot, 25-foot offhand group measured 1.0 inch across, while a five-shot, 50-foot offhand target came in at 3.5 inches. In terms of accuracy, CCI Blazer worked best in this gun, but other brands did fine.

Right from the box, the gun's reliability was flawless—even with the wide variety of ammunition tested. This kind of reliability is unusual in an autoloading pistol, many of which experience at least a few "breaking-in" jams early on. For a .22 LR pistol, especially one this small, and with its cantankerous rim-fire cartridge, this author applauds Smith & Wesson's design and workmanship in that the gun feeds reliably right from the start.

In addition, the smooth contours and lightweight alloy frame of Models 2213/2214 allow for easy carry in one's pocket. Incidentally, the only difference between the two models is the composition of the slide: Model

In the manner of the FN Browning Model 1900, the Model 2214's barrel lies beneath the recoil spring. This unusual relationship of barrel to spring sets the barrel low, near the hand, which diminishes recoil and allows for easier shooting.

Smith & Wesson's Model 2214 "Sportsman" is a smaller version of the company's popular Model 422, shown above in its 4¹/2-inch barrel Field version. The 2214 was designed especially for fishermen or hunters who wanted alternatives to the more traditional .22 LR revolvers.

The author's best five-shot offhand group with the Model 2214 fired from a distance of 50 feet measured 3.5 inches across. Right from the box, the gun's reliability was flawless — even with the wide variety of ammunition tested.

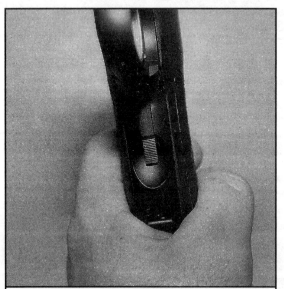

The magazine release on the Model 2214 is located on the front gripstrap, an odd location but one that makes the pistol ambidextrous and unlikely to release by mistake.

The Model 2214's awkward safety lever is shown pivoted down and back to its fire position, exposing a red dot on the frame.

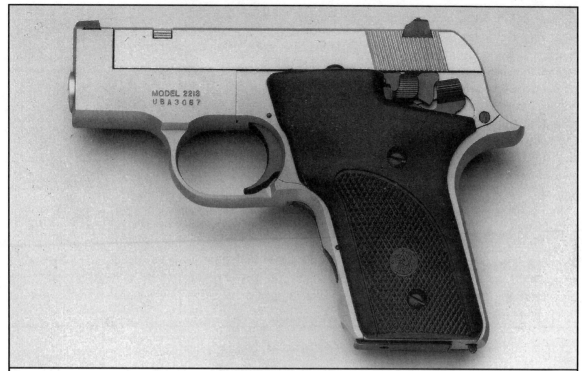

The Model 2213 with stainless steel slide is light, compact and extremely accurate—characteristics that are ideal for home-defense purposes or outdoor use. With its small size, smooth contours and light weight, it is a convenient pistol to carry in a pocket, backpack or tackle box.

2213's is of stainless steel, the 2214's is of blued carbon steel.

Less welcome features of the Model 2214 include an almost vertical grip that fails to point instinctively as most modern pistols do. Perhaps the reversed relationship of barrel to breechblock (to reduce recoil) is partially responsible for this. The manual safety catch pushes rather awkwardly down and back to its fire setting, a motion akin to cocking a hammer. In the safety's favor, it can be left on while operating the slide, something not possible with the Colt M1911, the Browning High Power and many other pistols. A final weak point with the Model 2214 is its magazine release. Located in the front of the grip, it is awkward to release and requires a firm push with the middle or ring finger. This requires the shooter to relax his grip on the pistol and perhaps cause him to drop the magazine.

Despite these minor faults, the Model 2214 is a good pistol for easy, convenient carry and is useful for accurate rapid fire. The low recoil and good sights make it quite versatile as an outdoor gun that can double for emergency self-defense purposes.

SMITH & WESSON MODELS 2213/2214

Manufacturer	Years Produced	Caliber/Capacity	Dimensions
Smith & Wesson Springfield, MA	1990–Present	.22 LR/8 rounds	Barrel Length: 3.0" O.A. Length: 6.1" Height: 4.4" Width: 1.1" Weight: 18 oz. (unloaded); 19.5 oz. (loaded)

SMITH & WESSON SIGMA .380

Smith & Wesson introduced its Sigma pistol in .40 S&W caliber in 1994, then quickly added a compact version plus full-sized and compact 9mm models. An even handier .380 version, greatly reduced in size, was introduced in mid-1995. It's much smaller than its 9mm and .40 caliber brethren, but the family resemblance is obvious. Like the larger members of the Sigma line, the .380 version is equipped with a steel slide and polymer frame. It also features Sigma's original patented two-piece trigger, whereby the firing pin does not become engaged until the shooter has correctly pulled the trigger through a complete arc.

Despite its rather blocky slide, the .380-caliber Sigma is well shaped for carry in a pocket or an ankle holster, with no protrusions of any kind. The sight is simply a groove recessed into the slide top, and there's no manual safety. The trigger is double-action for each shot (requiring an 8- to 10-pound trigger pull) and the magazine release is recessed into the side of the grip. Even more important, Sigma's weight is less than one pound. Keeping the weight down is absolutely crucial to pocket pistol

Smith & Wesson's Sigma in .380 caliber boasts an innovative and well-conceived design. It features a patented two-piece trigger, whereby the firing pin does not become engaged until the shooter has correctly pulled the trigger through a complete arc.

design. Many handguns advertised as "pocket pistols" are in reality too heavy to be carried in one's pocket, even though they may otherwise fit in terms of length, height and width. Keeping the weight within limits seems to be a particular problem with automatic pistols more so than revolvers.

Before the introduction of the .380-caliber Sigma, the only handguns suitable for pocket carry all had serious shortcomings. Even the smallest revolvers have that telltale bulge where their cylinders are located, thus compromising concealment. Derringers are usually limited to two shots, and they never have more than four. Classic pocket automatic pistols, such as the Baby Browning and Walther TPH, are underpowered .22- or .25-caliber models. And the .32-ACP Seecamp (*see* separate listing) may be more powerful, but it is ultra-rare. The Colt Mustang Pocketlite and AMT Backup .380 are suitably small, but they're not always reliable and are limited by a single-action trigger, which is an impediment in a pocket pistol intended for close-range defensive use.

The polymer technology needed to keep down the weight of an automatic pistol has been available since Glock brought out its first pistol in the early 1980s. Now Smith & Wesson, to its credit, has become the first company to take advantage of polymer technology by creating a true pocket automatic with acceptable caliber and magazine capacity.

SMITH & WESSON SIGMA .380 COMPACT

Manufacturer	Years Produced	Caliber/Capacity	Dimensions
Smith & Wesson Springfield, MA	1995–Present	.380 ACP/6 rounds	Barrel Length: 3" O.A. Length: 5.9" Height: 4" Width: 0.8" Weight: 14 oz. (unloaded); 16 oz. (loaded)

TAURUS MODEL PT-22/PT-25

When Taurus introduced its PT-22/PT-25 series in 1991, it marked the end of a protracted period of development spanning a decade or more for the Brazilian-based company. The obvious ancestry of the PT-22 goes back to the prototype Beretta Model 21, with its tip-up barrel system and slightly longer barrel. Like the Beretta pistol, the Taurus tip-up-barrel pistol is offered in two different versions: a .22 LR caliber with nine-shot magazine (Model PT-22) and a .25 ACP caliber with eight-shot magazine (Model PT-25). The PT-22/PT-25, made in the U.S. by Taurus International of Miami, is available in blued or nickel finish, originally with smooth Brazilian hardwood stocks, but now with checkered wood stocks.

The features, controls and handling characteristics of the PT-22 are virtually identical to the Beretta Model 21 (*see* page113), except the PT-22 is slightly larger. It also differs from the Beretta by having a magazine release button mounted on the left rear of the trigger guard (the pre-

The Taurus Model PT-22 shows considerable Beretta influence, particularly its open-topped slide and tip-up barrel. The right-side view (inset) displays the partially exposed drawbar located just above the trigger on the frame.

The PT-22 proved gratifyingly accurate, as this five-shot 25-foot offhand group measuring 1.9 inches clearly demonstrates.

In this photo of a disassembled PT-22, note the open-topped slide and the large extension added to the magazine bottom, making the gun easier to hold.

ferred position for most American shooters); and the trigger mechanism is double action for each shot rather than the first shot only. One advantage enjoyed by the PT-22 over Beretta's Model 21 is that its sights are larger and thus more functional.

The Taurus PT-22 is the result of fine workmanship, is large enough to hold comfortably (yet remains easily concealed), and is highly accurate. Its trigger pull is light and easy, and the sights are excellent for a pistol of this size. In test-firing the Taurus pistol, a five-shot, 25-foot offhand group, using CCI Stinger hyper-velocity hollowpoints, measured only 1.9 inches. The Stinger is an excellent round to use in .22 LR pistols that are strong enough to take it, offering performance comparable to a

The Taurus .25 ACP PT-25, shown above in nickel finish, is probably a better bet than the PT-22 in terms of ammo-feeding reliability.

.22 Magnum in a .22 LR loading (many manufacturers of .22 LR pistols, however, warn against using "high velocity" or "hyper velocity" ammunition in their pistols).

While testing an early PT-22, several jams occurred, serving as a rather forceful reminder that using a .22 LR pistol for self-defense may be hazardous. One jam was caused by a failure to feed the second-to-last cartridge in the magazine. When the cartridge did not feed, the bullet nose went straight up, while the cartridge rim remained caught in the magazine lips. All attempts to unstick the cartridge, or even to remove the magazine, failed until one of the wooden stocks was removed. We then pressed down on the magazine follower with a screwdriver to ease the tension on the two cartridges that were left. Obviously, a problem like this arising in the middle of a defensive situation could be disastrous. This jamming experience is not meant as a condemnation of the PT-22, which has many good points, but rather a warning against using the .22 LR cartridge in small automatic pistols when one's life is on the line. Should one of these guns jam with a rimfire cartridge, it can be a real bear to fix—and when you're shooting to save your life, there may not be time to clear the jam.

If you prefer a .22 LR for self-defense and are willing to accept the compromises in power and reliability inherent in the cartridge, then the Taurus PT-22 is a reasonable choice. As for feeding reliability, the PT-25 is probably a better bet than the PT-22.

TAURUS MODEL PT-22

Manufacturer	Years Produced	Caliber/Capacity	Dimensions
Taurus International Mfg. Inc. Miami, FL	1991–Present	.22 LR/9 rounds (PT-22) .25 ACP/8 rounds (PT-25)	Barrel Length: 2.75" O.A. Length: 5.25" Height: 4.1" Width: 1.0" Weight: 12 oz. (unloaded); 13 oz. (loaded)

TAURUS MODEL PT-58

When Forjas Taurus of Brazil began making its own version of the 9mm Beretta Model 92 in the early 1980s—a private commercial venture called the PT-92— the company introduced a much-modified version for civilian use in Brazil. Called the Model PT-57, it used the .32 ACP cartridge instead of the more powerful 9mm Parabellum round. The reason for this was that Brazilian firearms laws forbade the use of military-caliber firearms by Brazilian civilian shooters. The much smaller, lower-powered .32 ACP cartridge in the PT-57 made possible the elimination of the 9mm PT-92's locked breech. However, to keep retooling costs down, Taurus did not reduce the frame size of this pistol. Thus, the PT-57 is essentially the same size as the PT-92, along with its double-column, high-capacity magzine.

When the PT-57 proved successful, Taurus decided to build a 12-shot (now 10-shot) .380-caliber version—called the PT-58— for export to the U.S. market. Production began in 1988, with importation by Taurus International of Miami. This gun reveals traces of its Beretta ancestry, chiefly in its open-topped slide, its disassembly procedure, and its double-action trigger mechanism. Like the Beretta Model 92 and Taurus's own P-92, the PT-58 has a steel barrel and slide, both assembled on an aluminum-alloy frame. The chief difference between it and the parent PT-92 is that, because of the reduced caliber, the PT-58 does not require a locked breech.

The PT-58 is considerably thicker—especially in the slide and grip area—than the competing Beretta Model 84, the Browning BDA, or the CZ 83. The only large, high-capacity .380-caliber pistol that approaches it in size is FÉG's Model B9R (*see* separate listing). It's also an especially large pistol for its caliber, with a platform that's large even by high-capacity 9mm standards.

The Taurus PT-58 is available in blued or stainless steel finish (it was originally produced also in satin nickel, which has been discontinued). Fit and finish are excellent, especially on the satin nickel version, quite good on the blued model, and not quite so good in stainless steel. Its front sight, which in typical Beretta fashion is integral with the slide, is highlighted with a white dot; the rear sight, featuring two orange or white dots, is dovetailed into the slide and is drift-adjustable for windage. The rear sight is rather narrow for rapid acquisition in a combat situation, but the more important front sight shows up extremely well.

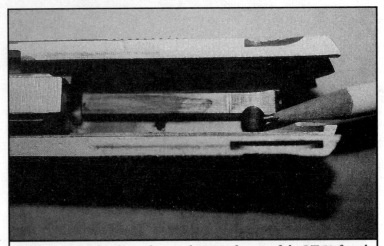

The pointer in the photo above indicates a feature of the PT-58 found in many automatic pistols: a spring-loaded plunger that automatically locks the firing pin in place until the trigger reaches the rearmost point of its travel just before firing.

Like other Taurus pistols made since the early 1980s, the PT-58 has a recurved trigger guard with deep serrations on its leading edge. The front and rear gripstraps, originally made of smooth Brazilian hardwood (now checkered wood) are also deeply serrated. Among its many safety features are an inertial firing pin, a firing-pin lock that is released only when the trigger is pulled all the way back, an ambidextrous manual safety that can be applied with the hammer either cocked or uncocked, a loaded-chamber indicator on the extractor, and a half-cock notch on the hammer.

The PT-58 shoots well, despite being rather oversized. The safety levers move easily on and off, and in what most serious shooters consider to be the right direction: down to fire and up to safe. The trigger on the PT-58 is quite heavy in both double- and single-action modes, with the latter indicating some creep prior to its release. The pistol's large size makes it a bit awkward to hold, but by the same token it's comfortable to shoot and recoil is reduced to a minimum. Typical of Beretta-designed clones, the PT-58 is flawlessly reliable and most forgiving of ammunition shape and bullet configuration.

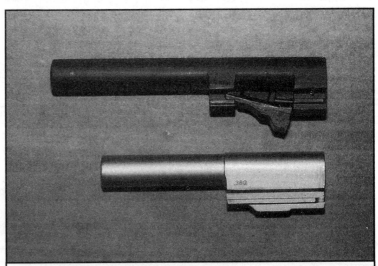

This comparison of barrels— the Taurus PT-99 (top) and PT-58 (bottom)—shows the former's locked breech, whereas the unlocked barrel of the PT-58 operates by straight blowback.

TAURUS

Despite its rather unresponsive trigger, the PT-58 is quite accurate. One five-shot, 25-foot offhand group measured exactly 2 inches across, using Samson 95-grain FMJ ammunition. Another five-shot, 25-foot offhand group, using Winchester Silvertip 85-grain hollowpoints, measured 2.2 inches. From 50 feet, a five-shot group with Silvertips made a pattern 3.9 inches across, while a 50-foot, five-shot group with Samson FMJ went into 4.2 inches. Discounting the double-action first shot, the remaining four shots of that last group all fired single-action into a pattern only 1.3 inches across.

The large size of the PT-58, shown here with its updated checkered grips, makes it a bit awkward to hold, but by the same token it's comfortable to shoot and recoil is reduced to a minimum. Typical of Beretta-designed clones, the PT-58 is flawlessly reliable and most forgiving of ammunition shape and bullet configuration.

The chief shortcoming of the PT-58 remains its size. If one is willing to carry a gun this large and heavy, then any compact 9mm or .40 S&W caliber automatic pistol, or even a powerful revolver, would be preferable. On the other hand, if one is limited to .380 caliber, or simply prefers it to the larger calibers, then the PT-58 is a good gun to have. Like all Taurus handguns, it's well made, reasonably priced and capable of good service.

TAURUS MODEL PT-58

Manufacturer	Years Produced	Caliber/Capacity	Dimensions
Forjas Taurus S.A. Sao Paulo, Brazil	1988–Present	.380 ACP/10 rounds	Barrel Length: 4" O.A. Length: 7.2" Height: 5.3" Width: 1.45" Weight: 30 oz. (unloaded); 36 oz. (loaded)

WALTHER MODEL TPH

For many years, tiny vest-pocket pistols formed the bulk of Walther's pistol business. So it should come as no surprise that one of the company's best offerings is a tiny pistol— the TPH—which stands for *Taschen Pistole* [mit] *Hahn* (meaning "Pocket Pistol [with] Hammer"). At first, Walther placed the double-action TPH in production in 1968 alongside the earlier single-action Model TP (introduced in 1961). Basically, the Model TP was a well-made but pedestrian rehash of Walther's prewar Model 9. By 1971, the TPH had totally supplanted the TP, which Walther eventually stopped making.

Mechanically, the TPH is a Model PP greatly reduced in size. It has the PP's double-action trigger mechanism and the same basic shape. In size, though, the TPH is more like a downsized PPK. In its frame construction, the TPH more closely resembles that of the larger PP. The metal frame of the TPH is exposed at the rear, whereas the PPK frame is covered by a wraparound grip design. Like the PP and PPK, the TPH features a manual safety on the left side of the slide which, when depressed to its safe position, automatically decocks the hammer. In those guns produced in Germany, the TPH is chambered either for .25 ACP or .22 LR calibers, with a lightweight aluminum alloy frame and a weight of only 11.5 ounces (unloaded).

For many years the TPH, due to its small size (3.7 inches high), could not be exported to the U.S., so it was a great rarity in this country, although widely distributed elsewhere. Finally, in 1986, Walther licensed Interarms to make the TPH, along with the PPK and PPK/S, at Ranger Manufacturing in Gadsden, Alabama. Initial production of the TPH in the U.S. was confined to a stainless steel version in .22 LR. Then in 1992, Interarms added a .25 ACP-caliber version, introducing that same year a blued finish. Today, the U.S.-made TPH is available with steel frame only, adding 2.5

The Walther TPH, a small-sized descendant of the PP series, was so small that few German-made versions ever made it into the U.S. Interarms began making a U.S. version, pictured above, in its Alabama plant in 1986. This gun has been used by the U.S. government, including Navy SEAL teams.

The accuracy of the TPH in .22 caliber is excellent. The author fired this five-shot, 25 foot offhand group measuring 1.4 inches.

ounces to its weight compared to the German version. Having tested the U.S.-made TPH in .22 and .25 caliber, the author can testify from firsthand experience that the U.S.-built version is every bit as good as the German gun—and a lot less expensive.

The TPH magazine, which holds six rounds (the same as the earlier TP), is easy to load to maximum capacity. Unlike the Models PP and PPK, when the last round is gone, the slide on the TPH does not stay back—a common omission in small automatic pistols. But despite its small size, the sights on the TPH are excellent, with the rear sight being especially good. It's shaped to provide a large square notch that remains in deep shadow under most lighting conditions. This feature automatically draws the eye to the sight and makes the front sight easy to see. Sight markings on the blued version are white, while the stainless version's are orange. The rear sight marking is a vertical bar and the front sight marking is a dot, which makes the proper sight picture like dotting an "i". Many full-sized service pistols would do well to have sights as good as those found on this Walther pistol.

Partly because of its sights, but also due to its smooth trigger and excellent shape, the TPH is a sensational shooter, especially when one considers its diminutive size. One 25-foot, five-shot effort with the .22 version measured 1.4 inches using CCI Stinger ammunition; the .25 ACP version measured 3.4 inches. At 50 feet, a five-shot group measured 5.2 inches (.22 version); the .25 version came in at 7.4 inches. Both versions exhibited flawless reliability.

Significantly, the TPH has become a highly favored small pistol for use by spies and special forces. So useful is the TPH in this application that several companies now make suppressors (silencers) specifically for this type of pistol. For those who want a small, flat, lightweight gun and one that's easy to carry under light clothing, the TPH is a top choice. ALthough low in power—neither the .22 LR nor the .25 ACP is an especially good round on which to stake one's life—it beats using your fists in a deadly attack. The TPH isn't cheap, of course, but quality always costs extra—and in this instance top quality is what you are definitely getting.

WALTHER MODEL TPH

Manufacturer	Years Produced	Caliber/Capacity	Dimensions
Carl Walther Waffenfabrik Ulm/Donau, Germany Interarms	1968–Present (in the U.S. since 1986)	.22 LR or .25 ACP/ 6 rounds	(U.S. version) Barrel Length: 2.8" O.A. Length: 5.3" Height: 3.7" Width: 0.9" Weight: 14 oz. (unloaded); 15 oz. (loaded)

5.9MM, .40 AND .45 CALIBER BACKUPS

CONTENTS

AMT Backup 204
Astra Model A-70 205
  Model A-75 "Firefox" 208
Beretta Model 92FC 210
  Model 92 Type M 210
Colt "Enhanced" Officer's ACP 213
  Double Eagle Officer's ACP 215
  Double Eagle Lightweight Officer's 217
  M1991A1 Commander 218
  M1991A1 Compact 220
CZ 75 Compact 221
Detonics CombatMaster MC-1 224
  Pocket 9 Pistol 226
European American Armory
  Witness Subcompact 228
  FAB-92 Compact 229
FÉG GKK-92C/P9RK 230
Glock Model 19 Compact 232
  Model 23 235
  Models 26 and 27 237

Hi-Point Model C 240
Intratec CAT-9 242
Llama Minimax 244
Para-Ordnance P12•45 246
SIG Models P225/P239 248
  Model P229 249
Smith & Wesson
  Model 3900 Series 252
  Model 4013 258
  Model 6906 259
  Sigma Compact 261
Springfield 1911A1 Compact 262
Star Models
  BM/BKM 264
  Firestar 265
  Firestar Plus 271
  Model PD 272
  Ultrastar 274
Walther Model P5C Compact 275
  Model P88 Compact 278

A fairly recent development in compact pistols has been the appearance of larger caliber compact models in 9mm Parabellum, .40 S&W and .45 calibers. The reason is obvious: compared to small-caliber pistols in .25, .32 and .380 calibers, the larger cartridges represent a major leap forward in power.

Such large-caliber compacts have been made available for many years by enterprising gunsmiths, who greatly modified existing service-pistol designs. These custom guns, however, have been too scarce and expensive for the average gun owner. In recent years, though, Star's Firestar, Glock's Models 26/27, the AMT Backup and others have become available from the factory in compact configurations. While these guns have not yet shrunk to true pocket-pistol size, they represent a significant step in that direction.

AMT BACKUP

Although available in .38 Super, .40 S&W, .357 SIG and .380 ACP, Arcadia Machine & Tool (AMT) has, with its .45-caliber Backup pistol, produced a major technical accomplishment. AMT took the powerful .45 ACP cartridge and fit it into a gun that is barely larger than many .380-caliber pistols, including its own .380 Backup. Amazingly, this gun includes a locked breech and, thanks to modern methods of investment casting, it is reasonably priced. Its trigger is double-action for each shot, similar to those of the double-action .380 Backup (not to be confused with the company's single-action Backup, an older and altogether different design) and the Seecamp LWS-32 (*see* page 181). The hammer of the .45-ACP backup pistol is visible from the rear but cannot be cocked—either manually or by the slide—for single-action shooting. Firing a compact gun in the double-action mode only virtually eliminates the need for a manual safety.

As with other so-called "pocket rockets"—i.e., guns that are shrunk to the smallest possible dimensions to accommodate the cartridge in question—the .45-caliber AMT Backup is a study in compromises, enough to make it a less effective weapon than a full-sized handgun in the same caliber. First, AMT's pistol has only a rudimentary sighting system that features a narrow groove running down the top of the slide, as in the .32-caliber Seecamp and 9mm CAT-9. In disassembling this pistol, a punch is required to remove the retaining pin that holds the barrel and slide together. More serious is the horrendous trigger pull, which in testing required about 20 pounds of pressure to fire the pistol. At a distance of 25 feet, the bullets went all over the target paper. Granted, AMT's little pistol is intended primarily for close-range shooting; but don't assume any accuracy to occur beyond that point. Otherwise, there's little not to like about the .45-caliber AMT Backup. Its recoil, while far from pleasant, is manageable. For a gun that has to be carried around often and fired once in a while for practice (or under life- threatening conditions) the AMT Backup is an excellent choice—especially for shooters who like the .45 ACP cartridge and don't trust anything smaller.

AMT BACKUP

Manufacturer	Years Produced	Caliber/Capacity	Dimensions
Arcadia Machine and Tool (AMT) Irwindale, CA	1992–Present	.40 S&W, .45 ACP/ 5 rounds .38 Super, .357 SIG, .380 ACP/6 rounds	Barrel length: 3" O.A. Length: 5.9" Height: 4.4" Width: 1.2" Weight: 24.5 oz.(unloaded); 30 oz. (loaded)

ASTRA A-70

Astra, which has been making firearms since
1908, got its first big break during World War I
when France and Italy ordered hundreds of thousands of the
Spanish company's Victoria and Ruby pistols. Between the World
Wars, Astra created the Models 300 and 400 pistols for military use
and sold its Model 900 machine pistol—a small submachine gun inspired by
the Mauser C96—in great numbers. Following Spain's Civil War, Astra was one
of the few arms factories allowed by the country's pro-German Nationalist government to continue making pistols. During World War II, Astra made the Model
600 for the Germans; and later, in 1969, it introduced the highly successful
Constable line, followed in 1982 by the A-80 line, which, in turn, spawned the Model A-70.

From the beginning, one of Astra's chief talents has been copying and improving on already
accepted foreign designs. The Ruby was based largely on the classic FN Model 1903, while the
Models 300, 400 and 600 were fashioned after FN's Model 1910. In addition, the Constable is a

The clean, sleek lines of Astra's Model A-70 make it ideal for concealed carry under clothing. The absence of an ambidextrous manual safety further reduces the width of this compact pistol.

Without tools, the A-70 disassembles easily into the following parts (top to bottom): slide, barrel, slide stop (behind barrel), magazine (behind slide stop), recoil spring/guide rod, and receiver.

clone of Walther's Model PPK, while other recent Astra Pistols, including the A-70, have borrowed heavily from the SIG line of pistols.

The A-70 first emerged in 1992. Like the competing Star Firestar M-43, this single-action automatic pistol is made entirely of steel, thus adding weight that limits carrying options. On the other hand, the all-steel construction does make the pistol much stronger than an alloy framed model and gives it good shooting qualities by reducing recoil.

The breech-locking mechanism on the A-70 features the Petter/SIG short recoil system, which substitutes a squared-off portion at the rear of the barrel for the precisely machined barrel/ slide interface of, say, the Browning High Power. This system was used as early as the French Model 1935T pistol of World War II and was later popularized by SIG's P220.

The feed lips on the A-70's magazine, which holds up to eight rounds in the 9mm and seven in the .40 S&W version, are well-rounded and the gun is easy to load. The magazine release forcefully ejects the magazine from the pistol; and there is no magazine safety, so the gun can still be fired as a single-shot should the magazine not be available. The well-rounded sights on the A-70, which use the popular 3-dot system, are acceptably large for accurate shooting, but the rear sight needs to be widened slightly for a better sight picture.

The safety mechanisms on Astra's pistol include an automatic firing pin safety, which is released only when the trigger has been pulled all the way to the rear upon firing. There's also a half-cock notch on the hammer and a manual safety that can be locked on with the hammer cocked. The safety lever goes up to safe and down to fire, as the M1911A1 pistol.

Despite its small size, the A-70 fits comfortably in the hand. Recoil is no problem in the 9mm version, which weighs nearly 30 ounces, and it excels in rapid double-taps (a popular combat technique in which two rounds are fired in succession as fast as possible). As for accuracy, the A-70 is more than acceptable for a combat pistol. Two five-shot offhand groups measured only 1.7 inches at 25 feet and 2.7 inches at 50 feet—good shooting indeed even for a big handgun. Typical for an out-of-the-box, single-action pistol, the trigger pull on the A-70 is rather rough and heavier than it needs

This Astra A-70 target illustrates a rapid double-tap, in which two bullet holes appear only .9 inch apart. While this is difficult to accomplish with a double-action pistol, a single-action pistol with a good trigger can do it with ease. In test-firing from a distance of 25 feet, the Astra A-70 placed five shots in a 1.6-inch pattern, with four shots going into one inch.

to be. Before taking it to a gunsmith, however, it would be wise to fire the gun unaltered for several weeks or even months. It's possible for a gun—and a shooter, for that matter—to get broken in after a while. If the trigger pull is still too stiff, make sure you go to a reputable gunsmith to have the work done.

The A-70 tested for this book had only one breaking-in jam in the first magazine; after that, it performed flawlessly using all brands of ammunition, including Winchester 115-grain Silvertip hollowpoint, Winchester 115-grain "USA" generic FMJ, Norinco 124-grain FMJ, and Hansen Combat 115-grain jacketed hollowpoint. Overall, the pistol shoots as well as a much larger pistol. Some shooters may, however, prefer a double-action pistol with a mechanical decocking feature; and left-handed shooters won't like the A-70's one-sided safety lever. Aside from that, the A-70 is an excellent pistol. It's highly competitive with Star's Firestar M- 43 (*see* separate listing) and in many ways surpasses it in handling and shooting.

ASTRA A-70

Manufacturer	Years Produced	Caliber/Capacity	Dimensions
Astra Unceta y Cia. Guernica, Spain Imported by European American Armory, FL	1992–Present	9mm/8 rounds .40 S&W/7 rounds	Barrel Length: 3.5" O.A. Length: 6.5" Height: 4.75" Width: 1.2" Weight: 29.3 oz. (unloaded); 33 oz. (loaded)

ASTRA A-75 "FIREFOX"

The Model A-75 is part of Astra's A-80 series, which in turn is based on SIG's excellent P220 line. The A-75, which came out in 1993, is mainly a double-action version of the single-action A-70, discussed in the previous listing. Although thicker than the Walther PPK, the A-75 boasts a much higher power level and holds up to two extra rounds in its magazine.

Slightly larger than Astra's single-action A-70, the A-75 resembles SIG's P225 in size, magazine capacity and double-action trigger system. Unlike the SIG's lightweight alloy frame, though, the A-75 is made of steel, which adds five ounces to its weight while improving its durability. The pistol tested for this book sported a matte blued finish, but nickel and stainless-steel finishes are also available. The breech-locking mechanism uses the Petter/SIG modified Browning short recoil system.

The magazine feed lips on the A-75 are well-rounded and the gun, which holds up to eight rounds in the 9mm caliber, is easy to load. The magazine body is supplied with seven witness holes, making it easy to determine how many rounds are left. The magazine release is reversible to suit both right-handed and left-handed shooters; when depressed, it pops the magazine free of the pistol (a function demanded by most American shooters).

The sights on the A-75, featuring the popular 3-dot configuration, are well-rounded to avoid snagging, an important consideration in concealed carry. As with the single-action A-70, the A-75's rear sight needs to be made slightly wider for an improved sight picture, but it is certainly adequate. The heart of this gun's safety is its automatic firing-pin safety, which is released only when the trigger is pulled all the way to the rear at the moment of firing. A half-

Compared to Smith & Wesson's Model 3913 LadySmith (top), the Astra A-75 offers competitive performance and similar features at a lower price.

cock notch on the hammer helps lower the risk of accidental firing, and a decocking lever (located on the left rear portion of the frame) drops the hammer when pushed down. Once the pistol is spring-loaded, the decocking lever automatically returns to its firing position upon release.

Despite its short grip, the A-75 fits comfortably in the hand. Its grip panels or stocks are made of roughened black plastic that feels like medium-grit sandpaper, and the front and rear grip-straps are heavily checkered, making the gun comfortable

This target, fired offhand with Astra's Model A-75 (not an A-70, as erroneously marked), placed five shots into a 1.5-inch pattern.

and secure to hold. It's also heavy enough (35–36 ounces) so as not to produce excessive recoil.

As for accuracy, test results with the A-75 were not as good as obtained with the Model A-70. Two five-shot offhand groups measured 2¹/4 inches at 25 feet and 3.9 inches at 50 feet. The trigger pull, even in its double-action mode, was smooth but heavy. At 50 feet, the double-action first shot fell consistently about two inches wide of the single-action follow-up shots. There was also a breaking-in jam on the A-75's first magazine, though that was followed by flawless reliability throughout the remainder of the testing using both hollowpoints and full-metal-jacketed ammunition.

Overall, the comparably sized Smith & Wesson Model 3900 pistols (*see* page 252), which seem a little sleeker and handier, are superior to the A-75. Still, the Astra pistol is a well-made and serviceable gun that will hold up better in the long run than an alloy-framed Smith & Wesson or SIG—and it's a lot less expensive.

Astra also makes a .40 S&W caliber version of the A-70, which is identical in size but loses one round of magazine capacity. In 1994, European American Armory, the U.S. importer, unveiled two exciting new versions of this gun. One is the A-75 Featherweight with a lightweight duralumin-frame (weighing 23.5 oz. in 9mm only) and the other is a .45 ACP model. These and other features ensure a bright future for this pistol.

ASTRA A-75 "FIREFOX"

Manufacturer	Years Produced	Caliber/Capacity	Dimensions
Astra Unceta y Cia. Guernica, Spain Imported by European American Armory, FL	1993–Present	9mm/8 rounds .40 S&W, .45 ACP/ 7 rounds	Barrel Length: 3.5" (3.7" in .45 ACP) O.A. Length: 6.5" (6.75" in .45 ACP) Height: 4.75" Width: 1.25" Weight: 31 oz. (unloaded); 35 oz. (loaded)

BERETTA MODEL 92FC

When Beretta introduced its Model 92SB in 1981, the company also unveiled its first cut-down compact version of the Model 92, the Model 92SBC. It became an immediate success. A more recent compact introduced by the company is the 92FC, which is essentially a Model 92FS with a shortened frame, barrel and slide. It includes the same Bruniton finish, chromed bore, squared trigger guard, slide retention device and safety features found on the Model 92FS. The most current compact version is the Centurion, introduced in 1993 in both 9mm and .40 calibers, which combines the best features of the compact and full-sized Model 92s. It features a compact barrel/slide unit mounted on a full-size frame (pictured above).

In testing the Model 92FC, it handled well and proved only slightly less accurate than the full-sized Model 92. One five-shot offhand group from 25 feet measured 1.8 inches, using Cor-Bon's +P load with a 115-grain jacketed hollowpoint bullet. Another five-shot group at 25 feet, using Winchester Silvertip with a 115-grain hollowpoint bullet, measured 2.2 inches across. The best five-shot 50-foot group, which spanned 3.2 inches, also used the Silvertips.

Like the full-sized Model 92S, the Model 92FC is completely reliable. Its open slide and alloy frame are, in fact, its only real shortcomings. Actually, the Beretta Compact is a good-sized pistol in its own right and should probably be regarded as a full-sized service pistol for use as a primary weapon rather than an undercover gun.

BERETTA MODEL 92FC

Manufacturer	Years Produced	Caliber/Capacity	Dimensions
Pietro Beretta SpA Gardone, Italy Imported by Beretta U.S.A. Accokeek, MD	1986 –Present	9mm/10 rounds	Barrel Length: 4.25" O.A. Length: 7.8" Height: 5.3" Width: 1.45" Weight: 31.5 oz. (unloaded); 37.5 oz. (loaded)

BERETTA MODEL 92 "TYPE M"

Soon after Beretta introduced the Model 92SB Compact, the need for an even more compact version became evident, causing Beretta to develop a single-column version—called "Type M"—in late 1982. Despite its attractive appearance and outstanding handling, this pistol did not reach the U.S. in large quantities until 1989.

The Type M features a Compact barrel and slide joined to a brand-new frame carrying a slim eight-round magazine. The frame is significantly thinner and narrower (1.1 inches) than those of the 10-shot standard Model 92 or Compact, which are 1.4 inches wide for the full-sized Compact Model frames. This reduction of .3 inch may not sound like much, but it makes a world of difference in handling. The high-capacity Berettas are so chunky that their grips often feel like you're holding a 2x4 or a baseball bat by the wrong end. The Type M, on the other hand, has an excellent feel to it. Because of its reduced grip, though, it must be fitted with a nonreversible magazine release (the magazine release on Beretta's larger pistols is reversible). The ambidextrous safety levers of the larger standard and Compact models are also fitted; in fact, the slide width on these pistols is the same as on the full-sized Model 92FS.

Beretta's Type M pistol is capable of absolutely sensational accuracy. This five-shot offhand group, made with the older SBCM from a distance of 25 feet, measured .8 inch. Another five-shot offhand group from 50 feet measured only 1.9 inches across.

The Type M comes in two configurations. The discontinued Model 92SBCM (a reduced Model 92SB) had the highly polished blued finish and rounded trigger guard of that earlier pistol. And the current Model 92FM is made to Model 92FS standards, with matte Bruniton finish, squared trigger guard, chrome-lined bore, and a slide retention device (shown on page 210).

In testing a Model 92SBCM made in 1989 together with a Model 92FM made in 1992, both guns proved sensationally accurate, even better than the full-sized models—and much better than the Compact, which was also tested for this book. A five-shot offhand effort measured .8 inch at 25 feet with the SBCM and .9 inch at 25 feet with the FM. At 50 feet, a five-shot group measured 1.9 inches with the SBCM and 3.1 inches with the FM. Top results were attained with Winchester 115-grain Silvertip hollowpoints and 124-grain Federal Hydra-Shok hollowpoints. But the Type M proved equally accurate and reliable with all other hollowpoints and FMJ ammunition tested.

Although it is an attractive and reliable pistol, the Type M's bulky underbarrel locking block makes it what is generally considered a "compact" gun. Its slide is noticeably wider than one finds on a Smith & Wesson Model 3900-series pistol, too, and it's slightly longer than necessary. Some also object to the Type M's limited eight-shot magazine capacity, but that is a small price to pay for improved handling. For those who shoot well and use a good modern hollowpoint round, eight rounds of 9mm ammunition is a formidable load of ordnance, especially when carrying a spare magazine or two.

Overall, the Type M is a superb handgun. It retains the accuracy of the larger Beretta pistols, along with their reliability; and, for those with small hands, it is by far the best military-caliber Beretta pistol available.

BERETTA MODEL 92 "TYPE M"

Manufacturer	Years Produced	Caliber/Capacity	Dimensions
Pietro Beretta SpA Gardone, Italy Imported by Beretta U.S.A. Accokeek, MD	1982–Present (92FM) (SBCM Discontinued)	9mm/8 rounds	Barrel Length: 4.3" O.A. Length: 7.8" Height: 5.3" Width: 1.5" Weight: 32 oz. (unloaded); 36 oz. (loaded)

COLT "ENHANCED" OFFICER'S ACP

Colt first introduced the Officer's ACP, or Officer's Model, in 1983. Although gunsmiths had been cutting down M1911-type pistols for many years prior to this, the probable source of Colt's inspiration for this pistol was one it didn't build—the M15 General Officer's Handgun of 1971. Originally, this was a government project undertaken at Rock Island Arsenal, where Colt pistols were cut down for use by high-ranking officers. Colt undoubtedly figured that such a reduced-size version of its trusty old M1911A1 might sell well.

The Officer's ACP—1¼ inches shorter than the full-sized Government Model and ½ inch shorter than the Commander—has a shortened frame containing a reduced-size magazine that holds only six rounds (the full-sized magazine in a Government Model or Commander will fit the Officer's ACP, but it will protrude slightly from the bottom of the grip). Early Officer's Models came in blued, nickel and stainless steel finishes and sported black checkered walnut stocks. Colt now makes the Officer's ACP in matte stainless, bright stainless and blued finishes. Colt also offers the pistol in a lightweight, aluminum-alloy frame version (the Officer's LW) that reduces its weight a full 10 ounces

In this view of an Officer's ACP barrel bushing and recoil spring plug, the small lug on the upper left has a tendency to shear off, jamming the gun.

The disassembled Enhanced Officer's ACP reveals both a flared barrel muzzle and separate barrel bushing.

This 1.8-inch group was fired offhand with Colt's Enhanced Officer's ACP from a distance of 25 feet.

(to 24 oz.) while increasing recoil. The Officer's ACP now also comes with pebbled neoprene grips instead of the more desirable checkered wooden grips found on older Officer's ACP pistols.

Because of how late Colt introduced it, the Officer's ACP has always used the MK IV Series '80 firing-pin safety lock. This undoubtedly reduces the chances of a discharge should the gun be dropped accidentally. On the other hand, there's no doubt that the firing-pin lock introduces extra mechanical linkages that can only complicate the trigger pull and possibly cause other things to go wrong. But given the litigious society in which we live today, firing-pin locks are here to stay, and anyone who deactivates such a device, or any other safety feature, is looking for trouble in court should he or she ever be involved in a shooting. In any case, a good gunsmith can work with the firing-pin lock and still provide a match-grade trigger pull if it's needed.

Because of its smaller grip, the Enhanced Officer's ACP is a little more difficult to hold than the Government Model, but the gun we tested seemed comfortable enough to shoot. Our best five-shot offhand effort at 25 feet measured 1.8 inches, while at 50 feet an offhand group measured only 2.4 inches.

The Enhanced Officer's Model costs more than its close cousin, the M1991A1 Compact Model (*see* page 220), and it has a smoother trigger pull, but it really doesn't seem to shoot any better. It all boils down to personal preference, of course, for in the long run the Officer's Model— and all M1911-type guns for that matter— are outstanding firearms.

COLT "ENHANCED" OFFICER'S ACP

Manufacturer	Years Produced	Caliber/Capacity	Dimensions
Colt Industries Firearms Division Hartford, CT	1983–Present	.45 ACP/6 rounds	Barrel Length: 3.5" O.A. Length: 7.2" Height: 5.1" Width: 1.25" Weight: (unloaded) 38 oz.; 44 oz. (loaded)

COLT DOUBLE EAGLE
OFFICER'S ACP

In 1991, following the example of the full-sized single-action Government Model and its numerous offspring, Colt introduced its first major variation on the Double Eagle— the Double Eagle Officer's ACP. Compared to the full-sized Double Eagle (*see Complete Guide to Service Handguns*), the barrel and slide on this new version were 1.5 inches shorter in length.

Like the Colt Officer's ACP single-action pistol, the barrel on the Double Eagle Officer's Model has been widened at the muzzle into a bell shape. In some pistol designs, notably those created by Detonics and Star, this type of barrel does away with the removable M1911-style muzzle bushing, a device that complicates the designs of many .45-caliber pistols. Unfortunately, the Double Eagle Officer's Model has retained this bushing. It also features a double recoil spring to handle the recoil of the .45 ACP cartridge more effectively. Unlike the single-action Officer's ACP, which has a reduced grip frame (hence a smaller magazine than the full-sized Government Model), the Double Eagle Officer's Model uses the same size frame as the big Double Eagle.

Disassembly of a Colt Double Eagle Officer's Model reveals its flared barrel and barrel bushing assembly, identical to that of the single-action Officer's ACP.

One advantage of a pistol with a shorter barrel is that an assailant who tries to disarm his victim has less to grab onto. If a longer barrel is not needed for accuracy or muzzle velocity, why carry around the extra weight and bulk? Despite its shorter barrel, the Double Eagle Officer's Model actually shot better during our tests than did the full-sized Double Eagle. Our best five-shot offhand effort at 25 feet measured 1.8 inches, while at 50 feet the pattern came in at 3.9 inches. As with the Double Eagle, the D.E. Officer's ACP has large fixed sights marked with the 3-dot system. Its trigger pull is slightly heavier as well. Its reliability was flawless using a wide variety of ammunition.

As in the single-action Officer's ACP, the disassembly process for this model is more complicated, mostly because of the two-spring recoil system it employs. A screwdriver is required to depress the recoil spring plug (located underneath the barrel) before the muzzle bushing can be rotated and removed. Next, the recoil spring plug must be given half a turn in either direction to unlock it. From there, the disassembly procedure generally follows along the same lines as an M1911.

Other than an overly aggressive magazine release spring, the design flaws in this pistol are relatively few. Its hooked, recurved trigger guard, with its deeply checkered front surface, is not called for in a handgun designed primarily for concealed carry. In addition, disassembly is more complicated than, say, the standard Double Eagle or M1911, which are already harder to take apart than most newer pistol models. Still, these minor objections do not alter the fact that the Double Eagle Officer's Model is a top compact pistol. It handles hollowpoints and even +P ammunition capably, and with its excellent handling and shooting qualities it is suitable for military and police use as well as for concealed carry by civilians.

This eight-shot 25-foot offhand group measuring 2.1 inches was fired with Colt's stainless steel Double Eagle Officer's Model. At 50 feet the same pistol produced a group measuring 2.9 inches.

COLT DOUBLE EAGLE OFFICER'S ACP MKII SERIES '90

Manufacturer	Years Produced	Caliber/Capacity	Dimensions
Colt Industries Firearms Division Hartford, CT	1991–Present	.45 ACP/8 rounds	Barrel Length: 3.5" O.A. Length: 7.25" Height: 5.5" Width: 1.3" Weight: 34 oz. (unloaded); 42 oz. (loaded)

COLT

COLT DOUBLE EAGLE LIGHTWEIGHT OFFICER'S MODEL

Colt introduced its Double Eagle Lightweight Officer's Model in 1992. Unfortunately, the gun has since been discontinued, but it was an excellent pistol and deserves a close look by those who are partial to the .45-caliber cartridge in a double-action Colt pistol, but who dislike the added length and weight of the full-sized or Commander-length Double Eagles.

Although this Lightweight Officer's Model was developed from the standard stainless steel Double Eagle Officer's Model, Colt lightened it by 10 ounces, using a lightweight aluminum-alloy frame instead of stainless steel. In keeping with Colt's high standards of fit and finish, the Lightweight Officer's Model is extremely well-made. With the same frame size as the Double Eagle and Double Eagle Officer's Models, it holds the full-sized eight-shot magazine now standard with all contemporary single-action Government Models and Double Eagles chambered for the .45 ACP caliber. The Double Eagle Lightweight Officer's Model is indeed a handsome weapon, with its slide flats finished in highly-polished blue and its frame and most of the slide in matte blue. The grip panels and the mainspring housing are made of checkered Xenoy plastic.

As all Double Eagle pistols, the Double Eagle Lightweight Officer's Model is highly accurate and fun to shoot. Its smooth trigger and excellent sights are much like the full-sized Double Eagle's. And, despite its lightweight alloy frame, recoil is light, thanks to the double recoil spring carried over from the original design of the single-action Officer's ACP. Another agreeable feature of this alloy-framed pistol is its excellent balance. Whereas the standard Double Eagle is slightly muzzle-heavy, the weight of this Lightweight Officer's Model is concentrated directly over the grip and the shooter's hand.

These positive qualities all contribute to good performance and shootability. A full magazine plus one round in the chamber (nine rounds) at 15 feet, fired in rapid succession, measured 3.5 inches across, with 2.0 inches taken up by one flyer, leaving eight rounds in just 1.5 inches. Our best five-shot, 25-foot offhand group measured 2.5 inches across, while at 50 feet the best five-shot offhand group measured 2.9 inches. Overall, the model tested performed flawlessly with all brands of ammunition, including hollowpoints.

For those who desire a light, compact double-action pistol, yet insist on a gun that uses the powerful .45 ACP cartridge, Colt's Double Eagle Lightweight Officer's Model makes an excellent choice.

COLT DOUBLE EAGLE LIGHTWEIGHT OFFICER'S MODEL

Manufacturer	Years Produced	Caliber/Capacity	Dimensions
Colt Industries Firearms Division Hartford, CT	1992–Discont.	.45 ACP/8 rounds	Barrel Length: 3.5" O.A. Length: 7.25" Height: 5.5" Width: 1.3" Weight: 25 oz. (unloaded); 32 oz. (loaded)

COLT M1991A1 COMMANDER

The Commander variation of the Colt
Government Model pistol has been around since
1950. Shortly after World War II ended, the U.S. Army expressed
an interest in replacing its M1911/1911A1 pistols with something
lighter and handier. The Commander, which resulted, differs from the
standard M1911A1 or Government Model pistol with its shorter barrel and slide
(.75") and a frame made of lightweight aluminum alloy instead of steel.
Interestingly, Colt retained the full-sized frame in its Commander with a seven-shot
(now eight-shot) magazine, perhaps feeling that shortening the barrel and slide and
choosing aluminum for the frame were enough to make an acceptable compact pistol.
Many shooters feel that the Commander (or the heavier steel-framed Combat Commander added to
the line in the early 1970s) is the most well-balanced pistol in the entire M1911 series. Another popular feature on the Commander was its rounded hammer, which people have for years placed on full-
sized Government Model pistols, making them more comfortable to carry as concealed weapons
against the body.

Although the U.S. military contract for which Colt developed the Commander never material-
ized, civilian demand for this shorter and lighter version of the Government Model has remained
strong, with more than 100,000 pistols sold over the past 40 years or so.

Colt's M1991A1 line requires some explanation. In 1992, Colt decided that it would be wise to
appeal to those gun owners who retained a strong nostalgic attachment to the M1911 and M1911A1
pistols of World Wars I and II. The M1991A1 pistols, which are essentially reissues of the former mili-
tary pistols, lack most of the features added to the Enhanced series; they do, however, keep the Series '80 firing-pin block and also have larger, more useful sights than the government-issue pistols of the past. The M1991A1 pistols are available in a matte parkerized finish with the traditional straight mainspring housing and long trigger of the original M1911. The grips or stocks are checkered black plastic, similar to those found on many of the issue M1911A1 pistols, but with the famous Colt emblem on the stock (absent on all GI pistol stocks).

Colt makes the popular M1991A1 in three sizes: a full-sized version, the intermediate-size Commander (above), and the Officer's ACP-sized Compact Model.

The M1991A1 Commander is easy to shoot. This five-shot group, fired offhand from a distance of 25 feet, measures 2.4 inches across. At 50 feet, this Colt pistol fired a five-shot offhand group measuring 3.9 inches.

The M1991A1 is available in three sizes: the full-sized Government Model with 5-inch barrel, the Commander Model (covered here), and the Officer's ACP-sized Compact Model (*see* next listing). There never was, of course, a Commander-sized .45-caliber Colt automatic pistol in general U.S. military issue, so adding the Commander Model to the M1991A1 line is not, strictly speaking, historically valid. All the same, it's a fine pistol. Its workmanship is excellent, too, and it shoots superbly, retaining all of the Commander's traditional excellent balance. Despite its light frame, recoil seems light, due no doubt to the gun's superb shape and fine handling characteristics.

In test-firing, a five-shot offhand effort at 25 feet measured 2.4 inches across, with three of the five shots going into a pattern only .75 inch across. The Commander also produced a five-shot group from 50 feet away measuring 3.9 inches.

In summation, the M1991A1 Commander is an excellent compact pistol. It's easier to carry around than a full-sized Government Model and it's fast handling, all the while retaining the full-capacity magazine of the standard Government Model.

COLT M1991A1 COMMANDER

Manufacturer	Years Produced	Caliber/Capacity	Dimensions
Colt Industries Firearms Division Hartford, CT	1992–Present	.45 ACP/8 rounds	Barrel Length: 4.25" O.A. Length: 7.75" Height: 5.4" Width: 1.3" Weight: 27.5 oz. (unloaded) 35.5 oz. (loaded)

COLT M1991A1 COMPACT

After Colt introduced its M1991A1, the company modified its plain-Jane, military-style pistol to include the Commander variant (*see* previous listing), followed by the Officer's ACP-sized M1991A1 Compact. This Compact variant is essentially an Officer's ACP with a parkerized finish and the Series '80 firing-pin block. Introduced in 1993, it was intended to give shooters who wanted a traditional M1991A1-type pistol one that was easier to carry.

Not surprisingly, the M1991A1 Compact shoots much the same as the Officer's ACP. Our best five-shot off-hand effort at 25 feet went into 2.4 inches, while at 50 feet the best pattern measured 2.7 inches. One noticeable feature of this Compact version is its heavy (but bearable) trigger, which feels more like a military pistol's. The sights are a big improvement over those found on the GI-issue Government Model. Although unmarked, they're larger than the original sights and feature a conspicuous square notch in the rear. Overall, the M1991A1 Compact earns high marks and offers a lower-cost alternative to the fancier Officer's Model ACP.

The M1991A1 Compact produced this 2.4-inch, five-shot offhand group at 25 feet.

COLT M1991A1 COMPACT

Manufacturer	Years Produced	Caliber/Capacity	Dimensions
Colt Industries Firearms Division Hartford, CT	1993–Present	.45 ACP/6 rounds	Barrel Length: 3.5" O.A. Length: 7.25" Height: 5.1" Width: 1.3" Weight: 34 oz. (unloaded); 40 oz. (loaded)

CZ 75 COMPACT

In November 1992, after a wait of several years, Action Arms introduced to the U.S. market a chopped version of the world-renowned CZ Model 75. Mechanically, this new gun, called the CZ 75 Compact, is almost identical to the regular CZ 75. It's smaller in length and height, though, and it has a rounded hammer, wooden grips and a removable front sight (to simplify the installation of optional tritium night sights).

The pistol tested and photographed for this book was finished in matte black lacquer. Magnum Research, the new U.S. distributor, also imports the CZ 75 Compact in matte and high-polish blued finishes. Like the original CZ 75, the Compact model features a sheet metal magazine brake in the grip. When the shooter presses the magazine release button, this brake prevents the magazine from falling clear. The Compact's shortened magazine has a capacity of two rounds less than the standard magazine of a full-sized CZ 75.

The safety features on the CZ 75 Compact are identical to those found on the parent CZ 75 except for a firing-pin lock that's been added to some versions of the CZ 85. (The CZ 85 is the same gun as the CZ 75, except for its ambidextrous slide release and safety.)

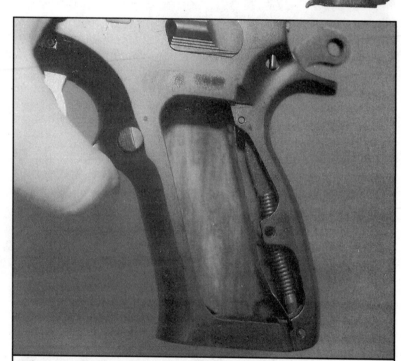

Like most other Czech CZ 75 variants, the CZ 75 Compact employs a sheet steel magazine brake, mounted (as shown) just ahead of the coil mainspring, with the left stock removed to prevent the magazine from falling completely out of the pistol.

Another feature inspired by the CZ 85 is the Compact's squared trigger guard, which unfortunately adds a sharp angle to the pistol's otherwise smooth lines. As we've pointed out often in this book, the smoother a gun's contours, the less likely it is to snag or catch during a draw. Another undesirable feature on the CZ 75 Compact is its magazine floorplate. It has a slight extension at the front that's intended to provide extra fourth-finger support on the Compact's shortened grip. This extension is sharply angled, however, and could easily snag. It also looks unsavory, as though someone took a pair

This photo of a disassembled CZ 75 Compact includes (top to bottom): slide, barrel, recoil spring guide rod, recoil spring, slide stop (in front of recoil spring), receiver (frame) and magazine.

of pliers and bent it down on purpose.

As for accuracy, the CZ 75 Compact proves acceptable, although not as good as the full-sized version. A five-shot group at 25 feet, using Samson 115-grain FMJ (an excellent Israeli brand) measured 2.3 inches. Another five-shot offhand group at 50 feet measured 3.9 inches with Winchester Silvertip hollow-points in the supersonic 115-grain bullet weight. What hurts this gun's accuracy is a double-action trigger pull that, while smooth, is excessively long. In testing, the double-action first shot opened up most five-shot groups by at least an inch, and sometimes by two or more inches. In single-action only, however, the accuracy levels of the Compact are competitive with those of the full-sized CZ 75 and 85. Fortunately, the Compact loses none of the reliability so typical of the CZ 75 series. In test

The CZ 75 Compact (bottom) is a worthy adjunct to the classic standard CZ 75 shown above it. Note the differences in slide length, height, stocks, cocking serrations on the slide and trigger-guard shape.

This five-shot 25-foot offhand group using the CZ 75 Compact measured 2.3 inches. Magnum Research now imports the Czech pistols.

firing, absolutely no jams occurred with this model using a variety of hollowpoint and FMJ ammunition.

In common with all Czech-made variations of the CZ 75, this Compact model is an excellent defensive pistol whose slightly smaller dimensions are preferred by shooters for concealment purpose. This pistol could use some refinements in its magazine and trigger pull, but those are minor objections to what is overall a fine handgun. In fact, the excellent design of the CZ 75 has inspired such copies and clones as the Italian-made EAA Witness Compact and Spain's Star Firestar.

CZ 75 COMPACT

Manufacturer	Years Produced	Caliber/Capacity	Dimensions
Ceska Zbrojovka Uhersky Brod, Czechoslovakia Imported by Magnum Research Minneapolis, MN	1992–Present	9mm/10 rounds	Barrel Length: 3.9" O.A. Length: 7.3" Height: 4.9" Width: 1.35" Weight: 32 oz. (unloaded); 39 oz. (loaded)

DETONICS COMBATMASTER/MC-1

Detonics' unique and innovative line of single-action .45 automatic pistols first went into production about 1975. Since then, a number of models have been offered, but the smallest and most interesting was the CombatMaster, or MC-1.

Based on the Colt M1911 Government series, the CombatMaster is not much longer or higher than a Walther PPK, albeit considerably thicker in order to contain the .45 ACP cartridge. It also incorporates a number of refinements ordinarily found only on expensive customized pistols, such as a barrel (without bushing) whose muzzle end flares slightly before returning into proper battery after each shot. Other refinements include a beveled magazine well to facilitate rapid reloading, an enlarged ejection port, and a double-coil recoil spring system. The latter has since been copied by, among others, the Colt Officer's ACP, which owes quite a lot to Detonics' gun. The CombatMaster also sports hand-polished internal parts, particularly in the trigger/sear linkage and the feed ramp, making operation easy, smooth and reliable.

Many of these improvements have since been copied by other manufacturers and put into their own factory pistols, but at the time the CombatMaster was unique. Not only did it offer these useful

Note the flared, enlarged ejection port in this right-side view of an early Detonics MC-1 CombatMaster.

features straight out of the box, it did so at a price that, while high, was still far lower than the alternative; i.e., buying a factory-standard Colt automatic pistol and paying a gunsmith to customize it.

Aside from the CombatMaster's small size, two recognizable features are its grip safety, which is permanently pinned and always flush with the rear of the slide, and the slide itself, whose upper rear surface is cut away to provide shooters better access to the hammer. Apparently, Detonics wanted the CombatMaster to appeal to those who carried single-action pistols with the hammer lowered (uncocked) and a round in the firing chamber, thereby forcing the shooter to cock the hammer before firing. The problem is, the pistol can still fire accidentally when dropped with enough force, or even when lowering the hammer onto the loaded firing chamber. On the other hand, a single-action pistol in this same mode is more difficult to fire than a pistol that's cocked and locked or with a loaded magazine in an empty firing chamber. This last example usually takes two hands to arm the pistol; but it's much easier for someone in a life-threatening situation to move the large slide than it is to find a tiny hammer and cock it. Moreover, it's difficult to cock most automatic pistols with one hand anyway, particularly with a hand that's dripping with sweat. Another problem with relieving the rear of the slide is that the front sight must be moved forward about an inch. The smaller the sight radius, the more difficult it becomes to line up the sights for consistent accuracy. That's one reason why most rifles are more accurate than most pistols. With their longer barrels, rifles usually provide a longer sight radius than do pistols, with their shorter barrels. The gun is so well made, however, that accuracy is still very good despite the reduced sight radius.

In the early 1980s, after solving the problem of galling (a destructive fretting caused by two metal surfaces rubbing against one another), Detonics perfected a stainless steel version of the CombatMaster. This represented one of the first successful solutions to the problem of making a stainless steel automatic pistol that did not rely upon such annoying requirements as special greases to prevent galling. The only reason for making a gun wholly or partly out of stainless steel is, after all, to reduce the need for continual maintenance. The CombatMaster made by New Detonics (which succeeded the original Detonics) featured extra gripping serrations at the front of its blued slide (in the photo on the preceding page, the slide is blackened stainless steel), along with a rounded hammer and a lightweight trigger with an overtravel stop. However, this modified version of the CombatMaster was featured in only a few firearms magazines before it was dropped, presumably because production was too low.

Despite its small size, the CombatMaster handles and shoots well. As one would expect in a small gun that fires a powerful cartridge, recoil is heavy but not at all excessive. Another interesting feature is that Colt's standard magazine will work in this pistol, although its greater cartridge capacity will cause the magazine to protrude from the bottom of the New Detonics gun. Unfortunately, the CombatMaster, despite its unique and innovative design, did not catch on, which means those who want one will have to haunt the gun shows and gun shops—and still need a large measure of good luck to find one.

DETONICS COMBATMASTER/MC-1

Manufacturer	Years Produced	Caliber/Capacity	Dimensions
Detonics Mfg. Corp. Seattle, WA and New Detonics Corp. Phoenix, AZ	mid-1970s–1992	.45 ACP/6 rounds	Barrel: 3.5" O.A. Length: 6.75" Height: 4.4" Width: 1.3" Weight: 29 oz. (unloaded); 35 oz. (loaded)

DETONICS POCKET 9

When Detonics went into business in 1975, one of its chief goals was to make smaller renditions of pistols using full-powered cartridges than what the competition offered. The result was an innovative line of smaller, full-caliber pistols, including the Pocket 9. Actually, Detonics' first compact 9mm pistol was the Model MC-1 rechambered from .45 ACP to 9mm. Only a few of these pistols were made, however, because Detonics quickly realized that further reductions in size were possible.

In the early 1980s, therefore, the company began experimenting with a new design—the Pocket 9—which went into production in 1985. It was taken off the market the following year, mostly because of its poor shooting characteristics and intense competition from Smith & Wesson and other makers of 9mm pistols.

For a double-action automatic pistol like the Pocket 9, recoil control with the high-pressure 9mm cartridge became a concern early on. Initially, the Pocket 9 employed a system of annular grooves machined into the walls of the firing chamber. Upon firing, the brass cartridge case swelled up into these grooves, delaying the opening of the slide long enough for chamber pressures to drop to a safe level. The slide then recoiled and, in standard automatic pistol fashion, ejected the spent cartridge case, cocked the hammer and compressed the recoil spring. On its trip forward, the slide stripped the next cartridge from the chamber and returned to battery, ready to fire the next shot in single-action mode.

The Pocket 9 sported ambidextrous safety levers, which rotated the firing pin out of reach of the hammer, which was then safely lowered by pressing the trigger. The firing pin utilized the inertia system typical of classic single-action pistols like the Beretta Model 34, Browning High Power, and Colt M1911 series. An inertia firing pin—which is too short to reach the primer of a chambered cartridge to begin with—is prevented from striking the primer by spring pressure until the pin has been smacked solidly from the rear by the hammer. Unfortunately, inertia firing pins may occasionally set off a chambered round in unintended ways—as when the gun is dropped. That's why many modern manufacturers have supplemented inertia firing pins with firing-pin locks. These devices can be deactivated only when the trigger has been pulled all the way to the rear.

The Pocket 9 featured a front post and a rear notch, which was recessed into a long groove that ran the length of the slide to prevent snagging. In fact, the design of this pistol throughout was streamlined to minimize snag, the one exception being its recurved front trigger guard. Whatever its size (especially one that's concealed under clothes), a pistol should be free of such protrusions.

An attractive and well-made pistol, the Pocket 9 was made of stainless steel, usually matte-finished (a high polish was also available), and came in a Long Slide (LS) model with 4-inch barrel and a .380-caliber version as well. It sported black Lexan grips with near-vertical grooving (to minimize slippage) and was similar in length and height to a Walther PPK. As for its role as a concealed-carry pistol, it gave up some of the shooting qualities of a larger gun in favor of minimum size. In attempting to achieve this goal, Detonics had mixed results, due in large part to its width, which exceeded that of the PPK. Another problem with the Pocket 9 was its weight, which eliminated it from contention as a true pocket pistol.

DETONICS

The Pocket 9 also failed to impress as a shooter. Cursed with a much too heavy double-action trigger pull, it was not especially accurate. In addition, despite the considerable weight, Pocket 9 shooters paid dearly for every shot with the gun's sharp recoil. Early on in the production run, Detonics discontinued the chamber grooving, which was supposed to delay the slide opening, and made the Pocket 9 a straight blowback pistol. Finally, the Pocket 9 was hard to take apart for cleaning, an important consideration in a weapon that was often carried under clothing or against the body.

With all its shortcomings, though, the Pocket 9 was an historic pistol, one that will probably become a collector's item someday. On the other hand, because of the concealment/backup role it fills, the Pocket 9 is probably marginally acceptable and useful.

An attractive and well-made pistol, the Detonics Pocket 9 (top, shown with a Walther PPK) was a short-lived attempt to create a 9mm Parabellum pistol that fit into one's pocket.

DETONICS POCKET 9

Manufacturer	Years Produced	Caliber/Capacity	Dimensions
Detonics Firearms Industries Bellevue, WA	1985–1986	9mm/6 rounds	Barrel Length: 3.0" O.A. Length: 5.75" Height: 4.1" Width: 1.3" Weight: 28 oz. (unloaded); 31 oz. (loaded)

EAA WITNESS SUBCOMPACT

European American Armory (EAA) was one of two companies—Quality Firearms, or QFI, being the other—formed when FIE went out of business in 1990. Upon its introduction in 1991, EAA's Witness line was little more than the latest version of Tanfoglio's near-copy of the CZ 75, and an equivalent to FIE's TZ-90, Excam's TA-90, or Springfield Armory's P9. Available in a number of configurations, the Witness line includes everything from competition guns to service pistols, with caliber choices in 9mm, .38 Super, .40 S&W, .41 Action Express and .45 ACP. The Witness Subcompact and FAB-92 Compact represent two of the smallest members of the family and are meant for concealed carry as defensive armament.

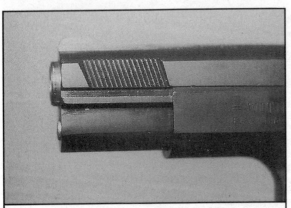

Current EAA Witness pistols feature cocking grooves machined into the front of the slide as well as the rear. Note also the slide rail that runs the full length of the slide, offering support all the way through the recoil stroke.

Like the CZ 75 Compact (*see* page 221), the Witness Subcompact is a double-action automatic pistol whose original 9mm 13-shot magazine (10 shots since January 1995) features a sloped finger extension on the bottom plant to provide additional fourth-finger support on the grip for large-handed shooters. (The gun is also available in .40 S&W with nine-round magazine or .45 ACP with eight-round magazine.) Mechanically, the Witness Subcompact is slightly smaller but otherwise almost identical to the reliable and durable CZ 75, including the single manual safety lever mounted on the left side of the frame. It also has, like many Tanfoglio-made CZ 75 copies, a rounded hammer for improved concealed carry, as opposed to the spur hammer found on the original CZ 75. Interestingly, the Czechs themselves have now moved to rounded hammers.

The slide on the Witness Subcompact, unlike the original CZ 75, features cocking serrations at the front as well as the rear. Its frame also has guide rails that run to the front of the frame, beyond the slide. A number of CZ clones have these full-length guide rails, which may make them easier to produce but could also allow dirt or sand to enter the gun's internal workings.

The Witness Subcompact comes in either a blued finish or a hard matte chromed finish, or a combination of the two. Overall, the Witness Compact handles much like a CZ 75, and in the course of testing it offered no problems in feeding with either FMJ or jacketed hollowpoint ammunition. The trigger pull, however, is considerably longer and harder than one finds on an original CZ 75. Still, the Witness Subcompact shot quite well during our tests. At 25 feet a five-shot offhand group went into 2.5 inches using Winchester 115-grain Silvertip hollowpoints; and another five-shot 25-foot group using Cor-Bon's +P 115-grain jacketed hollowpoints measured 2.8 inches. Our best 50-foot five-shot offhand group measured 4.8 inches across, using Silvertips (the double-action first shot adding almost an inch to the group size).

In summation, the Witness Compact, aside from its heavy trigger pull, is a functional and attractive pistol that competes in its capability with the CZ 75 Compact.

EAA WITNESS SUBCOMPACT

Manufacturer	Years Produced	Caliber/Capacity	Dimensions
Fabbrica d'Armi Fratelli Tanfoglio SpA, Gardone, Italy Imported by European American Armory (EAA), Hialeah, FL	1991–Present	9mm/10 rounds .40 S&W/10 rounds .45 ACP/8 rounds	Barrel Length: 3.66" O.A. Length: 7.24" Height: 4.9" Width: 1.35" Weight: 30 oz. (unloaded); 36 oz. (loaded)

EAA FAB-92 COMPACT

In 1992, European American Armory introduced a series of pistols called the FAB-92 (FAB stands for "Foreign American Brands"). It's a CZ-type pistol with ambidextrous slide-mounted safety levers which, when pushed down to the safe setting, also decock the hammer. By contrast, the CZ-type manual safety found on the Witness pistols blocks the sear but does not decock the hammer. Otherwise, the FAB-92 is identical to the Witness, including its blued, chrome or Duo-tone finishes and its handling capability.

The FAB-92 has the same stiff trigger of the Witness pistol, especially in double action, and a rear sight that lacks sufficient width for an optimum sight picture. But the gun handled a selection of FMJ and hollowpoint ammunition with perfect reliability. A five-shot offhand group fired from 25 feet with Winchester 115-grain Silvertip hollowpoints went into a 2.1-inch pattern, while a 50-foot group measured 5.8 inches across. Again, the double-action first shot widened that pattern by nearly 2.5 inches.

The FAB-92 Compact is unquestionably a viable defensive pistol. Whether a shooter prefers this gun over a CZ 75 Compact or a Witness Compact depends on whether you prefer a single-action or double-action first shot. If the former, then the FAB-92 should be chosen; alternatively, if a double-action first shot is preferred, then either the CZ 75 Compact or the Witness Compact deserves the nod.

EAA FAB-92 COMPACT

Manufacturer	Years Produced	Caliber/Capacity	Dimensions
Fabbrica d'Armi Fratelli Tanfoglio SpA, Gardone, Italy Imported by European American Armory (EAA), Hialeah, FL	1992–Present	9mm, .40 S&W/ 10 rounds	Barrel Length: 3.66" O.A. Length: 7.25" Height: 4.9" Width: 1.35" Weight: 30 oz. (unloaded); 36 oz. (loaded)

FÉG GKK-92C/P9RK

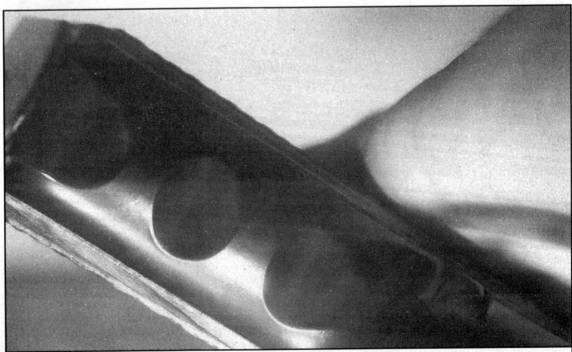

Introduced in 1992, the GKK-92C/P9RK is simply a FÉG-made P9R with a slightly shortened barrel, squared trigger guard and finger-grooved front gripstrap. The grip size—and consequently the magazine—remain the same as for the full-sized P9R. Slightly more expensive than the P9R, it's still highly competitive with other high-capacity 9mm pistols. Initial importation was handled by K.B.I. (as the Model GKK-92C), then, in 1993, by Century International (as the Model P9RK).

The GKK-92C/P9RK is a sensational shooter, superior even to the full-sized P9R (actually, it's not unusual for the compact version of a gun to outshoot the service model). In testing, the reliability of the GKK-92C proved flawless with a wide selection of loads. The GKK-92C also proved more consistently accurate from shot to shot than most automatic pistols, which indicates excellent quality control at the FÉG factory. To prove this point, four offhand groups five shots fired from 25 feet measured, in order, 1.7 inches with Winchester Silvertip 115-grain hollowpoints, 1.9 inches using Federal Hydra-Shok 124-grain hollowpoints, 2.4 inches with Cor-Bon +P 115-grain hollowpoints, and 2.9 inches with IMI Samson 115-grain FMJ. Ironically, the Samson round, which produced one of the least impressive groups at 25 feet, also boasted the tightest 50-foot group (3.5 inches), while Winchester Silvertips provided a group measuring 4.2 inches at 50 feet. The

A distinctive feature of the P9RK/GKK-92C is this pattern of finger grooves machined into its front gripstrap.

This five-shot, 25-foot offhand group from a P9RK/GKK-92C, fired with the powerful Cor-Bon +P round, measures 2.4 inches.

trigger pull, even in double-action mode, was smoother and lighter than the P9R could produce.

The GKK-92C/P9RK, despite being saddled with undersized sights, is an excellent pistol. In common with single-action PJK-9HPs, the GKK-92C sports a matte chrome finish through special arrangement with its importer K.B.I. (*see* I.D. photo on page 230). It is significantly less expensive than most American and West European high-capacity 9mm automatic pistols and is a very good buy.

FÉG GKK-92C/P9RK

Manufacturer	Years Produced	Caliber/Capacity	Dimensions
FÉG Budapest, Hungary Imported by KBI Harrisburg, PA and Century Int'l Arms St. Albans, VT	1992–Present	9mm/10 rounds	Barrel Length: 4.0" O.A. Length: 7.33" Height: 5.4" Width: 1.4" Weight: 32 oz. (unloaded); 37 oz. (loaded)

GLOCK MODEL 19 COMPACT

In 1983, Glock GmbH made its first pistol sale ever, selling 25,000 of its new P-80 pistols to Austria's armed forces. This gun, called the Glock 17 (for its magazine capacity), later equipped Norway's armed forces, followed by numerous police forces throughout the world. A furor arose over the construction of this pistol, which featured a strong polymer receiver. A rumor was spread irresponsibly by the press that the Glock 17 was supposedly an all-plastic pistol and therefore undetectable by X-ray machines, making it easy to smuggle in and out of countries by terrorists.

Once the rumor was quelled, Glock introduced a slightly smaller version—the Model 19—in 1988. Mechanically identical to the Glock 17, it is .4 inch shorter and weighs an ounce less. It also has the distinction of being the first variation on the Glock 17 ever produced, marking the advent of a comprehensive automatic pistol line that now includes both full-sized and compact guns in calibers 9mm Parabellum, 10mm, .40 S&W and .45 ACP. As the most compact and concealable pistol in its series, Glock's Model 19 is popular among civilians and police forces worldwide. It has also seen limited—but growing—use among the military units of several nations. For example, during the Gulf War of 1991, the naval aircrewmen of an entire U.S. squadron thought so highly of the pistol that they bought Glock 19s with their own funds and carried them on combat missions over Kuwait and Iraq.

The Glock 19 may not be much to look at, but it's well-rounded to avoid snagging—an important consideration in concealed carry—and its workmanship is excellent. All Glock pistols come in a durable, matte black finish, called Tenifer. Other user-friendly features of the Model 19 include the magazine, which has rounded feed lips and is a pleasure to load (no cuts or mashed thumbs to worry about). Also, because the magazine is liberally endowed with witness holes on its rear surface, it's easy to count rounds. For a secure, no-slip hold, even with sweaty hands, the Glock's polymer frame has excellent checkering on the front and

A disassembled Glock Model 19 reveals a combination of traditional and innovative features. The steel slide and barrel (top) use the Petter adaptation of Browning's short-recoil system, while the lightweight polymer frame and magazine (bottom) are as strong as steel, with much less weight or bulk.

rear gripstraps. This treatment is so good that Glock's Model 17, which once featured smooth gripstraps, has adopted the same style. The grip is so cleverly made, moreover, that it seems extremely small for such a large magazine capacity. It's comfortably curved as well.

Given its light weight, the Glock 19 shoots better than one might predict. The polymer frame seems to absorb some of the recoil; and because the pistol sits low in the hand, muzzle flip is reduced. The pistol also fits the hand comfortably, despite the short grip. While it may not be the most comfortable 9mm pistol to fire, that's a small price to pay for one of the lightest 9mm pistols extant. Neither is it the most accurate 9mm handgun—but it's certainly good enough. Our best accuracy results during testing occurred with Winchester Silvertips, although two other Model 19s tested were

Like other pistols using Browning's short-recoil system, the barrel on the Glock pistol tips down at the rear upon recoil, as shown. While theoretically less accurate than a fixed barrel, or one that recoils in a straight line, this short-recoil system remains simple and effective.

able to handle all ammunition types with perfect reliability. For example, one five-shot offhand group measured 2.0 inches at 25 feet and 5.3 inches at 50 feet.

Despite their good points, all Glock pistols take some getting used to. For one who's accustomed to more conventional handguns, the trigger on a Model 19 has an unusual feel to it. The safety, which is located in the trigger face, feels strange; and the pull, however light, has a pronounced two-stage effect, similar to that found on many military rifles. But it's consistent from pull to pull, and for that reason many shooters desire it. The standard trigger pull is five pounds, but for those who prefer a heavier trigger pull for safety reasons, Glock can supply trigger pulls of eight or 12 pounds instead.

Although the Glock 19 is short and light, its width (1.2") makes concealment by no means foolproof. Smith & Wesson's Model 3900 series pistols (*see* page 252) are thinner and therefore easier to hide. Because of this width problem, Glock has for several years been developing a smaller, more con-

This 2.0-inch offhand group was fired from a Glock 19 pistol at 25 feet.

cealable pistol with a single-column magazine in either 9mm or possibly .380 ACP. This new pistol is said to be about the same size as a Walther PP, although a prototype was unavailable for testing and comparison purposes at the time of this writing. Another objection to the Glock series is that its striker and trigger can be reset only when the slide is moved to the rear, making a misfired round very serious indeed. For further discussion of a dud or misfired round, see the chapter on Smith & Wesson's Model 3953 (page 255).

Despite their excellent performance and widespread, commendable service record, the Glock pistols remain controversial. Certainly they are in wide use, ensuring the availability of a host of accessories and aftermarket services and parts.

GLOCK MODEL 19 COMPACT

Manufacturer	Years Produced	Caliber/Capacity	Dimensions
Glock GmbH Deutsch-Wagram, Austria Imported by Glock, Inc. Smyrna, GA	1988–Present	9mm/10 rounds (13 for law-enforcement only)	Barrel Length: 4.0" O.A. Length: 6.9" Height: 4.9" Width: 1.2" Weight: 23 oz. (unloaded) 30 oz. (loaded)

GLOCK MODEL 23

In 1990, Glock's Model 23 became one of a select group of firearms to be adopted "sight unseen" by a major official body—in this case, the South Carolina State Police. Once Glock executives had seen Winchester's .40 S&W cartridge that year and recognized its potential, they put the Model 21 on the back burner and rushed development of the .40 S&W caliber Model 22 (full size) and Model 23 (compact) pistols. Both were in production by the end of 1990 and took off immediately in the U.S. police market.

Glock noticed right away that the .40 S&W cartridge offered a big-bore performance in a 9mm-sized platform. This appealed to those who claimed the 9mm was a "wimpy" cartridge as well as those who liked the easy carrying of medium-sized 9mm pistols. In fact, the Glock 23 is no larger than the Glock 19; and, practically speaking, it is well suited to uniformed carry and off-duty wear by police officers as well as concealed carry by private citizens. Glock claims its pistols have "33 parts, two pins and no screws," or about half the number of parts found in most 9mm pistols. Fewer parts should translate into fewer things going wrong. In fact, the Glock pistols are not perfect, but they have amassed an impressive record of reliable function since their inception.

The sights on a Glock 23 feature a white-outline rear and a prominent white-dot front. Despite its light weight, recoil is more pronounced than that of the Glock 19, which is similar

The Glock Model 23 (bottom) is slightly smaller and, because of its polymer frame, is appreciably lighter than the Astra A-100 shown at top.

in size. In addition to the standard five-pound trigger, Glock offers an optional trigger with about twice the pull weight, called the "New York Trigger." Its grooved face and secondary trigger make this an uncomfortable option for most shooters, however. Moreover, the magazine release on our test gun did not fully eject the magazine.

As for accuracy, our smallest five-shot offhand group fired from a distance of 25 feet measured only 1.9 inches across, using Winchester "Deep Penetrator" 180-grain jacketed hollowpoints. A follow-up five-shot offhand group from 25 feet measured 2.1 inches across, using Federal Hi-Shok 180-grain jacketed hollowpoints. At 50 feet, the best group measured 3.1 inches, using the Federal round. No malfunctions were experienced throughout the testing procedure.

Glock offers several interesting and useful accessories for which the company is justly famous. First, the storage case is designed so that one cannot leave a pistol in it until the trigger has been returned to its fired position. Glock also offers an ambidextrous sport/combat holster made of black plastic that fits any

The Glock Model 23 displays its great accuracy in this five-shot 25-foot offhand group measuring 2.1 inches. It also performs well at longer ranges; a five-shot offhand group fired from 50 feet measured 3.1 inches.

of its 9mm or .40 caliber pistols, accommodates all belt sizes, and uses a clever retention device that works off the pistol's trigger guard. A spare magazine holder similar in concept and design is also available.

The Glock 23 remains the company's most powerful small model and yet is one of the lightest pistols for its power level available. Once past its idiosyncrasies, shooters can rely on the Model 23 as an excellent personal defense firearm.

GLOCK MODEL 23

Manufacturer	Years Produced	Caliber/Capacity	Dimensions
Glock GmbH Deutsch-Wagram, Austria Imported by Glock, Inc. Smyrna, GA	1990–Present	.40 S&W/10 rounds (15 for law-enforcement only)	Barrel Length: 4.6" O.A. Length: 6.9" Height: 4.9" Width: 1.18" Weight: 22.4 oz. (unloaded) 30 oz. (loaded)

GLOCK MODELS 26 AND 27

In mid-1995 in response to passage of the U.S. "Crime Bill," the Glock mini-models 26 and 27 made their appearance. The most important provision of the Crime Bill, from a handgunning standpoint, is its prohibition against magazines holding more than 10 rounds (the large-capacity magazines are still legal for law enforcement; moreover, magazines completed before the bill took effect can still be owned and sold legally). As a result of this provision against high-capacity magazines, guns like the Beretta Model 92 and the larger SIGs and Glocks, for example, are not as practical for civilian shooters as they once were.

Because 10 rounds is now the legal maximum, a number of pistol manufacturers are taking an obvious step: creating small, truly portable pistols in serious calibers. Among the first to develop such

Although it is small, the Glock Model 26 is not awkward to hold and fire. Note how the shooter's pinky finger is wrapped comfortably around the magazine bottom.

pistols was Glock, who in June 1995 introduced the Model 26 (10-shot 9mm Parabellum caliber) and the Model 27 (9-shot .40 S&W caliber). Actually, several other truly compact 9mm pistols—notably the Kahr K9 (1994) and the Kel Tec P-11 (1995)—had already appeared. Since then, others have come on the scene, but the Glock handguns are arguably the best-designed among them. The Kel Tec has a polymer frame like the Glocks, and it is even lighter and considerably less expensive, but it has a plastic guide rod for the recoil spring, a feature that makes it questionable for long-term durability. It is also more difficult to disassemble than the Glocks. A cartridge is needed to withdraw a pin in the frame of the Kel Tec, whereas the Glocks can be disassembled without tools. The Kahr pistol, while it unequivocably boasts a slim, efficient design, is made completely from steel, rendering it much heavier than the compact Glocks. Admittedly, Kahr has an alloy-framed lightweight pistol under development, but alloy frames tend to be less durable than the advanced polymer perfected by Glock for its own pistol frames. Interestingly, the Glock Models 26 and 27, along with the larger Glocks and the competing Kahr, Kel Tec and SIG pistols, all use a variation of the short-recoil system and tipping barrel invented by John Browning in the early 1900s.

Identical in size and appearance, the Models 26 and 27 are the latest in a long series of pistols based on the famous Glock 17. Unlike the larger Glocks, of course, they have shorter slides, barrels and grips; internally, they also have a shorter and much more modified recoil-spring arrangement. And while there is considerable parts interchangeability with the larger Models 19 and 23, the compact pistols' major parts — their slides, frames and recoil spring — do not interchange. The Glock mini-pistols, however, will accept the high-capacity, longer magazines from the company's earlier and larger 9mm and .40-caliber pistols, although the magazine protrudes from the grips of the smaller models. Likewise, all controls on the Models 26 and 27 are located in the same places and work in exactly the same way as those on the other Glock pistols. This universality of operation helps sell many of the tiny Glocks, if only because the larger ones are among the most common handguns in official service worldwide.

Tests performed with the Model 26 showed excellent accuracy for a defensive pistol at 25 feet. One group of a full 10 rounds placed into a mere 1.5 inches. At 50 feet, groups were considerably wider, due most likely to operator inexperience (the guns have small handles that take some getting used to). A typical five-shot group fired at 50 feet spanned 3.4 inches. Not surprisingly, the Model 26 displayed perfect feeding reliability throughout extensive testing with a variety of different ammo brands and types.

Efforts to make the tiny Glock pistols easier to hold are already in evidence. The shortness of the grip on the Model 26/27 can be resolved with either a model 19 or 23 magazine. A steel magazine has been developed for the 9mm Glock 26, along with a .40-caliber Model 27 magazine. The 9mm mag-

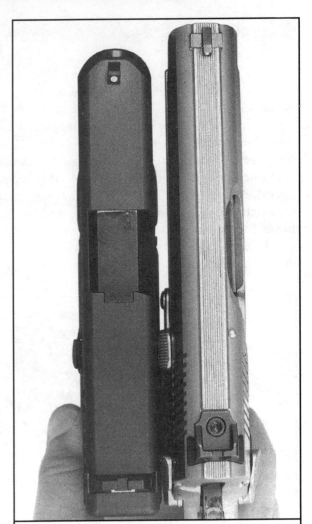

The width of the Model 26's slide (left) is compared with that of a chromed .45-caliber Star Firestar (right), indicating that Glock should perhaps consider re-engineering its slide to slim it down for better concealment.

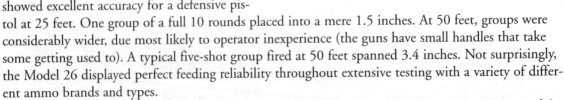

The mini-Model 26 is capable of good accuracy. Witness this 10-shot off-hand group fired from 25 feet, which measures a scant 1.5 inches across.

azine has a slight extension on the floorplate to give shooters more to hold onto, and a flared plastic magazine extension is also available, offering still more fourth-finger support while adding little to the pistol's bulk. But even with the standard Glock magazine, the short grip is nothing to worry about. Compactness is, after all, a desirable feature.

Recoil with the 9mm model is not at all objectionable. That's because the polymer frame does such an excellent job of flexing—enough to attenuate the gun's rearward impulse upon firing. The .40-caliber exhibits greater recoil, but also remains manageable.

The most impressive of the new breed of compact, full-caliber pistols is the Glock Model 26. Its small size, short grip and light weight make it perfect for concealed carry in a modern inside-the-waistband holster, shoulder, ankle or even a pocket holster. Its only design flaw—a wide slide—could easily be corrected by reverting to the same machined barrel top and intergral raised ribs found on traditional Browning-system guns like the Colt M1911—as opposed to the slightly wider, SIG-inspired locking system Glock now uses. Aside from that, the Glock Models 26 and 27 are at the top of the list. Despite competition from other compact models, the mini-Glocks' combination of small size, light weight and innovative design—along with their reliability and durability proven over years of arduous testing and service, place the Models 26 and 27 head and shoulders above the pack.

GLOCK MODELS 26 AND 27

Manufacturer	Years Produced	Caliber/Capacity	Dimensions
Glock GmbH Deutsch-Wagram, Austria Imported by Glock, Inc. Smyrna, GA	1995–Present	9mm/10 rounds (M26) .40 S&W/9 rounds (M27)	Barrel Length: 3.5" O.A. Length: 6.5" Height: 4.2" Width: 1.25" Weight: 22 oz. (unloaded); 27 oz. (loaded)

HI-POINT MODEL C

In 1987 an inventor named Ed Stallard introduced the Maverick, an unusual, inexpensive
handgun used primarily for personal defense. To hold
down costs, a simple blowback mechanism was employed rather
than a locked breech. It also had a single-action trigger mechanism, but it did not use ambidextrous controls, nor did it have a high-capacity
magazine. Instead, it came with a standard-capacity eight-round magazine. To
reduce costs even more, the Stallard-designed pistol used the most cost-effective
mass production methods available, including the extensive use of plastics, investment cast alloys, stamped steel, roll pins and inexpensive finishes. These methods
allowed Stallard to offer the Maverick at what was then the lowest price for a new
9mm pistol.

Traditionally, an unlocked-breech 9mm pistol included an extremely strong recoil spring and
often a strong hammer spring as well. This action—i.e., the spring exerting pressure in order to resist
the rearward motion of the slide immediately after firing—keeps the breech closed long enough for
the chamber pressures to drop to a safe level. Otherwise, the shooter could be in danger or the cartridge case rim could tear off, leaving the cartridge casing hopelessly jammed in the firing chamber.
The disadvantage of using such strong springs to close the breech is that loading and cocking the gun
before firing requires the shooter to work the slide. If the springs are too strong to operate the slide by
hand, then the gun is useless. In attempts to do away with this problem, the makers of 9mm pistols
sought ways to get rid of the pistol's locked breech.

Stallard's Maverick, however, was able to fire the 9mm round safely, due to an extremely heavy
slide—some 22 ounces on early examples. This weight, which is more than twice as much as that of
the slides used on many competing 9mm pistols, provided the slide with enough inertia to resist its
rearward motion after firing. Because of its low cost, the Maverick became moderately successful. Its
name was later changed to "Stallard" (followed by numerous others, including Iberia, Hi-Point,
Beemiller and MKS); and its grip was given a more rounded, ergonomic shape.

Currently, Hi-Point makes a full-sized 9mm pistol and two compact 9mms, one with a
lightweight alloy frame and the other with a polymer frame that's three ounces lighter. Full-sized .45
ACP and .40 S&W versions and a polymer-framed .380 ACP version complete Hi-Point's line.

Despite differences in size, caliber and magazine capacity, these guns all operate identically. When
handling any Hi-Point pistol, the first thing a shooter notices is its massive slide, which is the major
factor in controlling the pressures of the full-powered cartridges commonly used with this pistol. That,
in turn, allows a recoil spring that's weaker than normal. The slides on all Hi-Point pistols are difficult
to draw back when loading the first round and cocking the striker. The retraction serrations at the rear
of the slide are slick and shallow, making it difficult to grasp the slide firmly. Many other automatic
pistols with stiff slides have an exposed hammer that the shooter can cock, lessening the pressure on
the slide and making it easier to pull back. Hi-Point pistols instead employ a striker concealed within
the slide, thus offering little help. One simply must have enough hand strength to grasp the rear of the
slide and pull it firmly to the rear. These heavy slides, combined with the Hi-Point's light frame, make
these pistols top-heavy, amplifying their recoil as well.

Due to their low cost, Hi-Point pistols lack refinements, nor do they incorporate a hold-open device to lock back the slide after firing the last round. The undersized manual safety is located on the left side of the slide only. And, since the slide is connected to the frame by a retaining pin, before the parts can be separated for disassembly, this pin must be driven out of the frame with a punch. The magazine release on Hi-Point's compact models is located on the frame behind the trigger guard; on full-sized models, it's mounted on the bottom rear (heel) of the grip. The button-type magazine release found on the compact 9mm and .380 models is hard to reach; and when depressed, it doesn't

The Hi-Point Model C costs about 10 percent of what a Walther P5 Compact sells for, yet in some applications it can perform almost as well. Here it displayed impressive accuracy when matched with compatible ammunition. This five-shot offhand group fired from a distance of 25 feet measures only .9 inch across.

always drop the empty magazine entirely free of the grip.

On a more positive note, both Hi-Point 9mm pistols tested for this book, one alloy-framed, the other polymer-framed, proved completely reliable with a variety of ammunition. Their single-action trigger pulls are acceptable and smooth. The sights, set a little too low to minimize the chances of snagging, are easy to see. And the manual safety, though small, is accessible for right-handers.

The two compact 9mms tested shot surprisingly well, outperforming some far more expensive guns. The best five-shot offhand group fired from 25 feet went into a pattern only .9 inch across; and another five-shot offhand group fired from a distance of 50 feet spanned 1.6 inches. Although the guns functioned reliably with all ammunition tested, including hollowpoints, the factory recommends jacketed ammunition. The recoil experienced when using Cor-Bon P ammunition—widely regarded as one of the best stoppers in 9mm Parabellum caliber—was unpleasant and caused accuracy to suffer as well. Shooters are well advised to use only standard-pressure ammo when firing Hi-Point pistols.

HI-POINT MODEL C

Manufacturer	Years Produced	Caliber/Capacity	Dimensions
Beemiller, Inc., Mansfield, OH	1987–Present	9mm/8 rounds	Barrel Length: 3.5" O.A.Length: 6.8" Height: 4.9" Width: 1.3" Weight: 32 oz. (polymer frame) 35 oz. (alloy frame) Add 4 oz. for loaded weight

INTRATEC CAT-9

Although Intratec introduced this gun as recently as 1995, the original design dates back to the Israeli-made Sirkis pistol made between 1982 and 1986. While the Sirkis pistol was produced almost entirely from sheet-sheet stampings, the CAT-9 (short for "Category 9") has a polymer frame similar to those of the Glock and Smith & Wesson-made Sigma pistols (*see* separate listings). Like these pistols, the CAT-9's slide also rides on stainless-steel rails inserted into the frame.

Intratec's CAT-9 is a blowback-operated (unlocked breech) automatic pistol, similar to Hi-Point's Model C (*see* previous listing). Whereas the Model C's ability to handle the 9mm cartridge in a blowback mechanism is obvious, the function of the CAT-9 is something of a mystery. Disassembling a CAT-9 and weighing all its parts, the following results were observed:

The Intratec CAT-9 disassembles into the following components (top to bottom): barrel and breechblock group, recoil spring and guide rod, magazine, retainer pin and frame.

Barrel weight:
  3 oz.
Breechblock weight:
  3 oz. (stripped)
Slide weight:
  6.5 oz.
Frame weight:
  5 oz.
Magazine weight:
  5.5 oz. (unloaded)

Especially puzzling is how this lightweight pistol can sustain the high pressures of the 9mm pistol and still be comfortable to shoot. Its slide is not heavy, nor is the recoil spring stiff. In short, it seems to violate with impunity all the traditional rules of how to make a blowback 9mm pistol. And yet, it works quite well.

Interestingly, the slide on the CAT-9 pistol is made of stamped sheet steel. The firing pin, extractor and other operating parts are all placed in a machined breechblock, which is inserted into the slide as a separate piece. The slide and frame are held together by a large retaining pin, made accessible only with a specialized punch. It's removed simply by working it out of the frame with a nail. Once the slide has been removed from the frame, all that's needed to gain access to the working parts for cleaning and maintenance is to push the breechblock down and out of the slide.

Among the CAT-9's most appealing features is the utter simplicity of its operation. One merely

The Intratec CAT-9 is strictly a short-range pistol. This five-shot off-hand group fired from a distance of 15 feet measures 1.9 inches across. Beyond this distance, the gun's lack of sights and long trigger pull combine to make hits a matter of luck.

points the gun and pulls the trigger. Unlike the single-action Hi-Point, it comes with a trigger mechanism that is double action for every shot, making it as safe as a double-action revolver. The CAT-9 has no manual safety devices, further smoothing its contours. The magazine release, located on the upper portion of the left grip, is easy to depress with either hand. It's shielded, though, and consequently not likely to be released by accident.

Although it comes close to being the ideal pocket 9mm pistol, not all is perfect with the CAT-9. Its magazine has a large finger rest at the bottom, which, while helpful to large-handed shooters, adds almost half an inch to the pistol's height, making it a bit tall for most pockets. The original Sirkis design had a smaller magazine that held one less shot and contained no extended finger rest. And, because it lacks sights, the CAT-9 is capable of point firing only. Beyond 25 feet, the chance of hitting a target with this gun is mostly a matter of luck. On the other hand, shooting beyond 20 feet or so with accuracy is really not expected in most self-defence handguns. Within that distance—and perhaps a little beyond—the CAT-9 is more than adequate. Because it lacks a slide hold-open latch, the only way to know if the gun is empty is when it quits firing—and that could be a problem when it is called for in an emergency.

No doubt about it, Intratec's compact yet powerful CAT-9 pistol is eminently suitable for the compact, powerful 9mm cartridge. Moreover, it's half a pound or so lighter than the Kahr K9 and actually weighs less than Smith & Wesson's Model 940 Centennial revolver. The CAT-9's ease of handling and reasonable price are additional selling points.

For those who dislike the 9mm cartridge, Intratec offers the same basic design in .380, .40 S&W and .45 ACP calibers. The .380 version is exactly the same size as the CAT-9, while the .40 and .45-caliber versions are only slightly larger (3.25-inch barrels). They include locked breeches, a magazine with one less round, and slightly higher unloaded weights.

INTRATEC CAT-9

Manufacturer	Years Produced	Caliber/Capacity	Dimensions
Intratec Miami, FL	1995–Present	9mm/7 rounds	Barrel Length: 3.0" O.A.Length: 5.75" Height: 4.6" Width: 0.95" Weight: 18 oz. (unloaded); 22 oz. (loaded)

LLAMA MINIMAX

The Spanish-made Minimax has emerged as one of the best among the new breed of compact, full-caliber pistols. Its modest size makes it eminently suitable for concealed carry in a modern inside-the-waistband or shoulder holster. This latest in a long series of Llama pistols is based on the seemingly ageless Colt Model 1911 designed by John Browning nearly a century ago.

Llama Gabilondo has been making similar pistols since 1931, and the Minimax may well be the best yet. It includes all the latest features, including a skeletonized, rounded hammer, 3-dot sights (the front "dot" is actually a rectangle), soft neoprene grips, and an extended slide release. There's also an internal passive safety which locks the firing pin (unless the grip safety is activated), a squared trigger guard to facilitate two-handed shooting, and a choice of three popular calibers and two finishes, matte blue and satin chrome.

As a departure from the M1911, the Minimax's muzzle end of the barrel is slightly flared or belled, and the M1911-style muzzle bushing has been dropped. Instead, the front end of the Minimax's recoil spring fits into a removable, cylindrical steel plug that closes up the open space between the muzzle and recoil spring. Still another departure from M1911 practice is Gabilondo's use of an exposed extractor (as opposed to the M1911's internal extractor). This exposed, pivoting extractor is, for most shooters, an improvement because it is less prone to malfunction and breakage. One good feature the Minimax shares with the Model 1911/Government Model, however, is its magazine interchangeability. Because it is slightly longer, the M1911 magazine protrudes slightly at the bottom of the Minimax grip. Nevertheless, this magazine interchangeability remains a desirable feature.

According to *American Rifleman*, which reported the results of its tests on the Minimax in the June 1996 issue, the new pistol exhibited only mediocre accuracy, occasional unreliability, and a tendency to throw empty cartridge cases back into the shooter's face. The Minimax

Like all Llama-brand pistols, the Minimax, upon disassembly, looks much like the classic Colt Model 1911 Government Model.

This five-shot offhand group fired from 25 feet with a Minimax measures 1.1 inches across. Another five-shot offhand group fired from 50 feet spanned only 1.4 inches—that's accuracy.

pistol tested for this book, however, must have been better than the one *American Rifleman* used. Ours showed excellent accuracy for a defensive pistol and perfect reliability after only one jam in the first magazine. The test pistol did—but only rarely—display a tendency to eject spent cartridge casings toward the shooter's face, but in our testing this amounted to only once out of approximately 200 shots. In the past, Llama had earned a reputation for making its guns out of excessively soft steel, causing the guns to "shoot loose" after a few hundred rounds. But Gabilondo has advertised extensively its "upgraded new steel design" for the Minimax; and based on our test firing of nearly a thousand rounds, no discernible wear or loss of performance, in terms of reliability or accuracy, was noted.

However, the Minimax safety lever is not ambidextrous, as is Star's Firestar, but then the Minimax is much less expensive. A lightweight, alloy or polymer-framed version would be welcome at some point in the future, and thin wooden grips would provide better concealment than the thick neoprene types now offered on the Minimax. The added weight of the steel frame and the large, resilient rubber grips do, however, help make this a comfortable gun to shoot. In sum, the Minimax is a modern, well-appointed pistol, one that is capable of competing seriously in the U.S. market.

LLAMA MINIMAX

Manufacturer	Years Produced	Caliber/Capacity	Dimensions
Llama Gabilondo y Cia. Vitoria, Spain Imported by S.G.S. Wanamassa, NJ	1995–Present	9mm/8 rounds .40 S&W/7 rounds .45 ACP/6 rounds	Barrel Length: 3.7" O.A. Length: 7.3" Height: 5.1" Width: 1.4" Weight: 35 oz. (unloaded); 41 oz. (loaded)

PARA-ORDNANCE P12·45

The Para-Ordnance P12•45, which dates from 1990, is a high-capacity adaptation of the Colt Government Model design, though it most closely resembles the smaller Officer's ACP. The P12•45's original 11-round magazine, however, holds nearly twice as much ammunition as the Officer's ACP. The gun gets its name, incidentally, from the fact that it could be carry cocked and locked with an additional round in the chamber. (Now only 10 rounds are allowable for sporting purposes.)

The P12•45, like its larger cousin— the P14 (*see Complete Guide to Service Handguns*), uses a firing-pin lock, a grip safety, and a thumb safety that's pushed down to fire and up to safe. The ejection port is slightly relieved (beveled) to enhance reliability and to spare the shooter's brass for reloading purposes. The workmanship throughout is excellent. The pistol tested had a businesslike matte black finish that looked much like the parkerizing on a Colt M1991A1. Para-Ordnance also offers a pistol in stainless steel with a silvery finish. The sights are high-profile and use a 3-dot sighting system—much like the improved sights used on Colt Government Models, rather than the skimpy sights of old military M1911A1 models.

The features of the Para-Ordnance P12•45 are basically the same as the P14•45, except the P12•45 is slightly smaller. Its trigger pull is not as smooth as the P14•45's, but otherwise it's much the same, including the smoothly operating controls and excellent sights. Its

The magazine for the Para-Ordnance P12•45 (left) is similar in concept and execution to the Browning High Power magazine (right).

Even though at long ranges the Para-Ordance P12 tested had poor accuracy, at short ranges it is reasonably accurate. This five-shot offhand group fired from 25 feet measured 1.9 inches.

shorter grip, though, does present a problem. During tests with the P12, several jams occurred because it was difficult to keep a firm grasp on the pistol. Our best 25-foot, five-shot offhand group measured 1.9 inches, but at 50 feet the group enlarged to an unacceptabe 7.1 inches.

In general, the P14 with its larger grip seems preferable to the P12, but that opinion is wholly subjective. Anyone interested in Para-Ordnance pistols should try them all first before deciding which model provides the best fit.

PARA-ORDNANCE P12•45

Manufacturer	Years Produced	Caliber/Capacity	Dimensions
Para-Ordnance Mfg., Inc. Scarborough, Ontario, Canada	1990–Present	.45 ACP/10 rounds	Barrel Length: 3.5" O.A. Length: 7.2" Height: 5.1" Width: 1.3" Weight (unloaded): 24 oz. (alloy frame) 33 oz. (steel frame) (loaded) Add 11 ounces

SIG P225 AND P239

While SIG (of Neuhausen am Rhinefall, Switzerland) is not well-known as a manufacturer of compact pistols, the company does in fact make three excellent large-caliber pistols that are suitable for concealed carry: the 8-shot Model P225 (1978); the 10-shot Model P229 (introduced in 1991 as a 13-shot model— *see* following listing); and the 8-shot P239 (1995). A compact small-caliber model, the P230, is also available (*see* page 185).

The 9mm P225 (or P6, as it is known in European military and police circles) has become Europe's top police pistol (*see* photo above). It was made small to suit West German police requirements for a pistol that could be carried on a belt holster or for concealed carry by plainclothes officers.

Despite its excellent reputation overseas, the P225, however, never established itself solidly in the United States, for three reasons. First, other compact SIG models are available in high-capacity formats. The P225 has only an 8-round magazine, while the P228 and P229, both pistols of the same length, originally were produced with 12- and 13-round magazines (now limited to 10, except for

Although SIG's Model P225 has not sold well in the U.S., it is an excellent concealable compact, with outstanding reliability and accuracy, as this 25-foot offhand group demonstrates.

law-enforcement use). Second, the P225 failed to take hold in the U.S. because of its relatively high cost. Other 8-shot compact 9mm pistols from such competitors as Beretta and Smith & Wesson are readily obtainable at a considerably lower price. Finally, SIG's own introduction of a smaller, less expensive 8-shot pistol— the P239— rang the death knell for the P225 in terms of U.S. sales.

In addition to a better price, the newer P239 has other advantages of the P225. It is built mostly in the U.S.; that is, only the lockwork and other small internal parts are produced for SIG at the J.P. Sauer & Sohn plant in Germany. SIGARMS, the U.S. subsidiary in New Hampshire, locally manufactures the slide, then assembles the pistols using domestic and imported components; this allows SIGARMS to sell the P239 in the U.S. for considerably less than the P225. The P229 and P239 are both made from a slide milled from a single solid block of stainless steel. As such, they are considered more attractive and functional than the three-piece SIG slides produced in Germany, which consist of two pieces of heavy sheet steel welded together with a machined steel breechblock, then pinned in place. The P239, moreover, is noticeably lighter and slimmer than either the P225 or P229.

All SIG compact pistols have excellent accuracy because of their high-visibility sights and smooth, light trigger pull in either double- or single-action modes. As for reliability, both the P225 and P239 pistols, when used with clean, fresh factory ammunition made by a reputable manufacturer, proved flawless. When worn in a well-designed, inside-the-waistband or shoulder holster under a jacket or overcoat, the P225 and P239 are among the finest automatic pistols in terms of concealability, quality, accuracy and reliability.

SIG P225 AND P239

Manufacturer	Years Produced	Caliber/Capacity	Dimensions
J.P. Sauer & Sohn Eckenförde, Germany for SIG of Switzerland SIGARMS Exeter, NH	1978–Present (P225) 1995–Present (P239)	9mm/8 rounds .357 SIG/8 rounds* *(P239 only)	(P225/P239) Barrel Length: 3.9"; 3.6" O.A. Length: 7.1"; 6.7" Height: 5.15"; 5.2" Width: 1.33"; 1.25" Weight (unloaded): 29 oz.; 24 oz. (loaded) Add 4 oz.

SIG P229

The Model P229, which dates from 1993, is based on earlier SIG-Sauer P220-series designs, but it differs in one important aspect: it has a new slide assembly. Other P220-type pistols use a three-piece slide made of two stamped sheet metal components welded together, then mated to a forged, machined steel breechblock. The P229 instead uses a one-piece forged and machined slide made of stainless steel. This design change gives the P229 a heavier slide, which is needed to control the high pressures of the 9mm and .40 S&W cartridges. While the .40 S&W is the dominant caliber for this pistol, SIG also markets a proprietary cartridge—the .357 SIG—made by Hornady and Federal for the P229, and a 9mm version is slowly supplanting the P228.

The right-side view of the SIG P229 shows a clean profile devoid of protruding levers or controls (the magazine release button, if desired, can be switched to operate from the right side).

Like all the other SIG-Sauer pistols—including Models P220, P225, P228 and P230—the Model P229 combines the instant readiness to fire that marks a good double-action revolver with the kind of accuracy found in the best automatic pistols. It features a double-action trigger pull for the first shot that is fairly heavy but quite smooth, combined with crisp and certain single-action follow-up shots. SIG also offers a P229 with a trigger capable of double-action shooting only. This variant omits the decocking lever on the frame. Some police departments prefer guns with this so-called DAO trig-

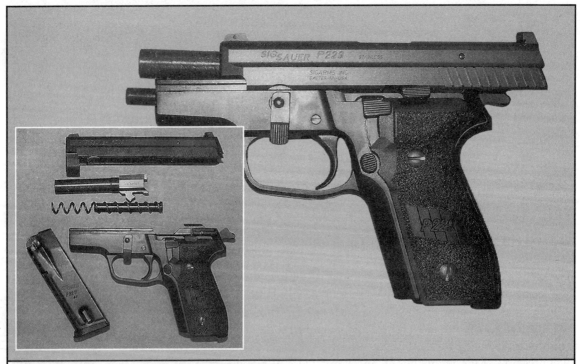

The SIG P229 can be easily disassembled for cleaning. After removing the magazine, the slide locks back into position, using the slide stop. The disassembly latch located above the trigger guard is rotated straight down, as shown. The slide stop is then depressed and the slide pushed forward off the frame. The SIG P229 disassembles into the following components (top to bottom): slide, barrel, recoil spring and guide rod, magazine and frame.

The SIG P229 is a formidable close-range handgun. This well-centered five-shot offhand group fired from a distance of 25 feet demonstrates performance close to that of the legendary .357 Magnum.

ger because they handle more like the revolvers many of these officers were trained originally to use.

All SIG pistols are made to extremely high standards of fit, finish and workmanship; indeed, the P229, with its one-piece slide, is arguably the most attractive pistol of the company's entire line; and with the sole exception of the ultra-expensive P210, it's unquestionably the sturdiest as well. Compared to older 9mm models, though, it has stiffer springs, which cause a heavier trigger pull and require more effort to work the slide. But that is a relatively minor drawback; in fact, the P229's only real impediment is its high price.

SIG P229

Manufacturer	Years Produced	Caliber/Capacity	Dimensions
J.P. Sauer & Sohn Eckenförde, Germany for SIG of Switzerland Imported by SIGARMS Exeter, NH	1991–Present	9mm, .357 SIG, .40 S&W/10 rounds 12 rounds (as designed, for law-enforcement only)	Barrel Length: 3.9" O.A. Length: 7.1" Height: 5.5" Width: 1.4" Weight: 30.5 oz. (unloaded) 39 oz. (loaded)

S&W MODEL 3900 SERIES

Over the past few years, Smith & Wesson has greatly expanded and improved its automatic pistol line. With the advent of the company's modernized "Third Generation" of automatic pistols in 1989 has come a renewed commitment to quality control and innovative thinking on the part of this long-established gunmaker.

Smith & Wesson's first 9mm handgun was the Model 39 (*see Complete Guide to Service Handguns*), which, upgraded, became the new Third Generation 3900 series. Four guns from this series have been tested for this book: the Model 3906, a full-sized duty gun; the Model 3913 LadySmith, a compact version; the Model 3914, featuring dual ambidextrous safety levers and blued finish; and the Model 3953, a double-action-only gun that combines the easy handling of a revolver with the slimness and rapid reloading features of an automatic pistol.

All four guns have a stainless (or blued) steel slide and lightweight aluminum-alloy frame with slim, one-piece checkered Delrin plastic grips. The breech-locking mechanism found in all 3900-series guns is a modified Browning system pioneered long ago by FN's classic High Power. All are equipped with a magazine safety and a firing-pin lock that can be deactivated only by pulling the trigger all the way to the rear. In addition, the Models 3906 and 3913 have manual safeties that move down to decock the hammer. Following are brief descriptions of each gun in S&W's 3900 Series:

Model 3906. This was conceived as a duty pistol for belt-holster wear by those who prefer the size and handling of the 15-shot Model 5900 series but with a slimmer grip. Nevertheless, this pistol offers such "big gun" features as optional adjustable sights, an ambidextrous safety, and a curbed backstrap as that found on Models 39, 439 and 639. The satin stainless Model 3906, along with its blued steel equivalent Model 3904, remained in production from 1989 until late 1991, when Smith & Wesson reduced its product line by some 70 models.

The 3906 is a comfortable gun to carry and shoot, its size making it somewhat easier to handle than the other, smaller

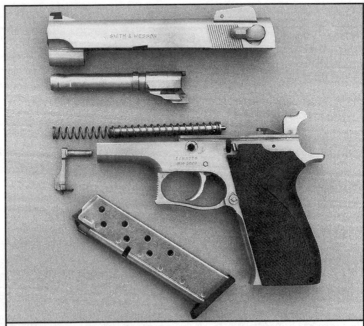

The Smith & Wesson Model 3906, shown here disassembled, uses a modified Browning short-recoil locking mechanism.

3900-Series guns. It has proved extremely reliable with all types of FMJ and hollowpoint ammunition, a typical five-shot offhand group running 3.0 inches at 25 feet and 3.7 inches at 50 feet.

S&W MODEL 3906

Manufacturer	Years Produced	Caliber/Capacity	Dimensions
Smith & Wesson Springfield, Ma	1989–1991	9mm Luger/8 rounds	Barrel Length: 4.0" O.A. Length: 7.5" Height: 5.5" Width: 1.25" Weight: 34 oz. (unloaded); 38 oz. (loaded)

Model 3913 LadySmith. This compact is probably the most attractive of all Smith & Wesson handguns. Its clean lines make it an excellent concealed-carry gun, leaving little to catch on a holster or clothing should a rapid draw be necessary. Introduced in 1990, this series includes, beside the LadySmith, S&W's J-frame and K-frame revolvers and the Model 3914LS (now out of production). All offer somewhat lighter trigger pulls, improved grip profiles for small hands, and other features designed to make the guns more comfortable for women to carry and shoot. Although the original Model 3913 featured an ambidextrous safety, the LadySmith version omits the right-side lever; it's also slimmer and sleeker in profile than the earlier version. Fortunately, the Model 3913 LadySmith uses the Novak Lo-Mount design, which is virtually snagproof. These sights are usually marked with the three-dot system (luminous tritium night sights are also available).

The Model 3913 LadySmith excels in accuracy and reliability with all 9mm bullet types tested. Our best five-shot offhand group measured 1.4 inches at 25 feet with Winchester 115-grain Silvertip hollowpoints. Because the pistol tested had a pronounced tendency to throw the double-action first shot well away from the others, these groups were actually a lot more impressive than those reported above. For example, one five-shot group fired at 25 feet using Winchester Silvertips put its four single-action shots into one ragged hole measuring

The sleek, clean lines of the Model 3913 LadySmith (top) are preferred by many to the standard Model 3914 (bottom). Note the non-ambidextrous safety lever on the LadySmith designed to slim down its slide. Each gun comes with one finger-rest and one flat-bottomed magazine as shown.

The Model 3913 series pistols feature a hammer dropping safety mechanism. With the safety lever up in its fire position (left), a red dot is exposed on the frame and the bobbed hammer is flush with the rear end of the slide. But when the safety lever is down in its safe position (right), the red dot is covered and the hammer protrudes slightly from the back of the slide.

With the M3913 LadySmith, this five-shot 25-foot offhand group measures 1.4 inches across. Three hits of the powerful Cor-Bon +P load went into a single hole .25 inch in diameter.

just .75 inch across, but the double-action first shot opened up the five-shot pattern to 2.1 inches. Similarly, at 50 feet, the best five-shot pattern was only 1.6 inches across when the double-action first shot was discounted. Given this pistol's mission as an emergency defensive piece, its first-shot accuracy is more than adequate for the ranges most likely to be used.

The blued Model 3914 is virtually identical to the Model 3913 LadySmith, except that its frame contours are slightly different in the area in front of the trigger guard. It also has an ambidextrous safety lever with arms on both sides of the slide. The Model 3914 we tested was equipped with a set of excellent Hogue rubber grips with curved backstrap, replacing the one-piece grip (with straight backstrap) supplied by Smith & Wesson on all its compact Model 3900s. The Hogue grips, which are easily installed, greatly improve this gun's handling. Slimmer than Astra's competing A-75, and only slightly larger than the single-action-only Star Firestar (*see* page 265), this fine Smith & Wesson LadySmith pistol is a top candidate for concealed carry.

MODEL 3913 LADYSMITH

Manufacturer	Years Produced	Caliber/Capacity	Dimensions
Smith & Wesson Springfield, MA	1990–Present	9mm Luger/8 rounds	Barrel Length: 3.5" O.A. Length: 6.9" Height: 5.0" Width: 1.25" Weight: 25 oz. (unloaded); 29 oz. (loaded)

Model 3953. This pistol in the 3900 series boasts a number of clever and innovative designs. Its contours resemble the original Model 3913 more closely than the LadySmith. It has the same concealability in a 9mm pistol for which the LadySmith is noted. Thanks to its concealed-hammer and double-action-only design (with no external safety levers), the Model 3953 is very sleek, with no sharp edges or corners to snag on a holster or clothing during a fast draw. Other so-called compact 9mm models offering similar features, such as Walther's P5 Compact and Beretta's Model 92 Type M, are appreciably larger, especially in width, than the Models 3913 and 3953. The only other 9mm pistols that are smaller have either reduced magazine

Because of its concealed-hammer and double-action-only design, the 9mm Model 3953 is very sleek, with no sharp edges or corners, which means good carry-ability.

capacities or poor "shootability" and handling qualities, such as the Detonics Pocket 9. Still others lack the double-action capability many people want in a small carry pistol, such as the Astra A-70 or Star Firestar.

The Model 3953, which evolved from the basic Model 3913, was made sleeker by having its trigger mechanism work only in double-action. This innovation simplifies handling by giving the shooter only one trigger pull to learn, and it also eliminates the manual safety lever, which has been replaced by a cylindrical plug flush with the slide. Gone also is the finger-rest extension of the Model 3913 magazine, having been replaced by a much thinner pad in one magazine and a flush-mounted bottom plate in the other (note that Smith & Wesson has the wisdom to sell each of its automatic pistols with two magazines). As shown in accompanying photos, the stainless steel Model 3953 (The Model 3954 is the blued version) is hardly bigger than a Walther PPK, but yet it holds two more rounds of a much more powerful cartridge.

In attaining its compactness, the Model 3953 remains a fine performer that compromises nothing. Its double-action-only trigger is easy to handle, like that of a revolver, with a smooth travel and reasonable pull. As for accuracy, the Model 3953 is truly sensational. In test-firing at 25 feet, one five-round string of Winchester USA 115-grain FMJ bullets went into a single ragged hole less than .75 inch across. At the same distance, two premier hollowpoint brands—Winchester's Silvertip and Federal's 9BP, both with 115-grain bullet weights—gave five-shot offhand groups of 1.3 and 1.4 inches, respectively. Even at 50 feet, a distance not really conducive to pinpoint accuracy, two 3.2-inch off-hand groups resulted, both using Winchester Silvertips (one with 115-grain bullet weight and another with 147-grain subsonic bullet weight). Despite its small size, the Model 3953 has a low level recoil, making it pleasant to shoot, even with hot Remington +P loads and 147-grain Winchester Silvertips. The grip is quite thin for ease of concealment, yet it feels quite good in the hand. Even with the shorter magazine in place, there's enough grip length for the average-sized hand to grasp. In test-firing a dozen rounds, using everything from military surplus to hot +P, reliability was flawless.

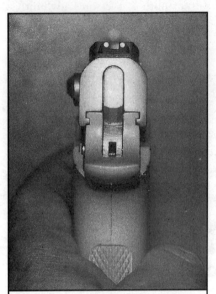

Model 3900 series pistols owe much of their accuracy to their acceptable trigger pulls (in both single and double action) and their fine sights. Shown here is the Model 3913LS with the Novak Lo-Mount rear sight. Note also the one-sided manual safety lever.

Apart from its good handling, comfortable concealed carry, accuracy and reliability, the Model 3953 has two short-comings. First, the gun is not quite small enough for convenient carry in an ankle holster or in a pocket. Smith & Wesson should reduce the height and length of its Model 3900-series pistols even more, perhaps by shrinking the magazine capacity a round or two if necessary. And second, the Model 3953's double-action-only mechanism can be reset only when the slide is moving back. This mechanism is the same type used by Glock with its "Safe Action" design. Should a round not fire when the trigger is pulled—which can happen even with top-quality, factory-loaded ammunition—the hammer "hides" in the slide recess and won't recock itself no matter how many times the trigger is pulled. Only after the slide has gone back about 1/8 inch will the trigger and hammer reset. Thus, when using a Model 3953 or a Glock, a person under attack who experiences a misfire has no other option than to pull the slide back to eject the failed cartridge, bring up a fresh cartridge from the magazine, and reset the mechanism—the same procedure one uses when a single-action automatic pistol misfires.

That leads to a teaching method used by the best schools of combat shooting, called the "tap-rack-bang" method: (1) tap the bottom of the magazine to make sure it's seated firmly, (2) draw back

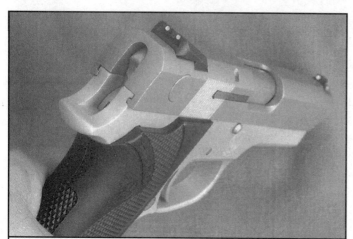

The hammer on this Model 3953 is smooth and cannot be cocked for single-action firing. Note the three-dot Novak sights and the absence of a manual safety lever.

the slide to eject the failed cartridge; (3) pull the trigger. The problem with using this method whenever a misfire occurs is that it goes against human instinct, which says that whenever something doesn't work, the action must be repeated to make sure it was done properly the first time. Because the "tap-rack-bang" method goes against this natural instinctive reaction, extensive training is required. This method also dictates that the shooter have both hands on the gun, which is not always possible in a close-quarters struggle.

Because Glock's safe action mechanism is reset only when the slide moves to the rear—whether by the recoil of a fired cartridge or by manual recycling—the U.S. Army refused to consider that company's pistol because it couldn't create multiple strikes on a misfired cartridge without using a second hand to clear the malfunction. For that reason, many people do not use Glock or Smith & Wesson double-action-only pistols as defensive sidearms, despite their highly rated designs. They prefer a gun with a trigger mechanism that allows a second strike on a misfired cartridge. Most double-action automatic pistols—including Smith & Wesson's conventional double-action/single-action pistols, such as the Models 3913 and 3914—do offer this capability. With these so-called "traditional double-action" pistols (i.e., those that convert to single action after the initial shot), when a shooter brings up his support hand to execute the tap-rack-bang drill in the event of a misfire, he simply pulls the trigger a second time.

But shooters who use a double-action-only gun like the Model 3953 or the Glock should stay away from low-budget ammunition and hand loads. In fact, when choosing ammunition for any gun that could save your life, it's good advice to use only top-quality ammunition from reputable sources. Then inspect every single round you load into your handgun with great care. Don't assume that the ammunition is good, for even a reputable company can make a mistake.

The original Model 39 was an excellent gun in its time, and its descendants in the Model 3900 series are still excellent. Which one you choose depends on finish, trigger function and perhaps aesthetics. Indeed, these compact Smith & Wesson pistols are reliable and well-tested, the end result of more than 40 years of conscientious development and widespread use.

SMITH AND WESSON 3953/3954

Manufacturer	Years Produced	Caliber/Capacity	Dimensions
Smith & Wesson Springfield, MA	1991–1995	9mm/ 8 rounds	Barrel Length: 3.5" O.A. Length: 7.0" Height: 5.0" Width: ??? Weight: 25 oz. (unloaded); 29 oz. (loaded)

SMITH & WESSON MODEL 4013

Many of the .40 S&W-caliber pistols—including Ruger's P91, Glock's 22 and Smith & Wesson's own Model 4006—are full-sized duty sidearms. The Model 4013, however, is a noticeably smaller gun, giving it a major caliber punch in a compact 9mm-sized pistol. One of the earliest guns introduced in .40 S&W caliber, the Model 4013 remains one of the best. Although not quite as easy to control in recoil as a 9mm model, it's a reasonably good shooter.

The popular .40 S&W-caliber Model 4013 compact offers one of the best power-to-size ratios available. Like Smith & Wesson's other compact automatics, it comes with both a low-profile magazine and a slightly taller magazine with a finger-rest extension (for shooters with large hands).

The Model 4013 is slightly larger than the Model 3900-series Smith & Wesson 9mm pistols, but small enough for effective concealment in a holster or even a large overcoat pocket. This model has a smaller frame, however, and a correspondingly reduced grip size when compared with small .45 ACP-caliber handguns, such as Star's PD and the Officer's Model made by Colt. S&W's 4013 has a great deal of potential, though, and will doubtless appeal to many shooters who remain skeptical of the 9mm cartridge, yet are unable or unwilling to carry a really big handgun.

The Model 4013 is quite accurate. Using Federal Hi-Power 180-grain JHP in an off-hand group at 25 feet, five shots went into a group measuring 1.7 inches across. Another five-shot offhand group fired at 25 feet, using Winchester Super-X 180 gr JHP, went into 1.8 inches. At 50 feet, the best five-shot off-hand group, using the same ammunition, measured 3.7 inches across.

The Model 4013 has all the features of S&W's popular pistol line and is therefore much more conventional in operation and less likely to be controversial than, say, a Glock Model 23. The S&W gun makes the compromises necessary to create a powerful handgun in a truly compact package, more so than just about any gun now in production.

SMITH & WESSON MODEL 4013

Manufacturer	Years Produced	Caliber/Capacity	Dimensions
Smith & Wesson Springfield, MA	1991–Present	.40 S&W/8 rounds	Barrel Length: 3.5" O.A. Length: 7.1" Height: 5.2" Width: 1.25" Weight: 26.5 oz. (unloaded); 32.5 oz. (loaded)

SMITH & WESSON MODEL 6906

When it was introduced in 1989 as an updated version of the highly respected Models 469 (blued finish) and 669 (stainless finish), the 9mm Model 6906 represented a much-improved and updated version of Smith & Wesson's basic automatic pistol design that began with the classic Model 39 (*see Complete Guide to Service Handguns*). As such, this double-action pistol boasts an impressive pedigree. Granted, its 10-shot magazine makes the short grip rather chunky, but overall the pistol is still only slightly larger than a snubnosed revolver. In short, the Model 6906 has what it takes to serve as a rugged and capable defensive pistol.

The 6906 has a stainless steel slide and a matching silver-anodized aluminum-alloy frame, while its counterpart, the Model 6904, has a blued steel slide and black-anodized aluminum-alloy frame (*see* photo above). A third version of this pistol—the Model 6946—is a stainless slide/alloy-frame pistol with a double-action-only trigger mechanism similar in operation to the Model 3953 (*see* page 255).

The Model 6906/6904 features all of Smith & Wesson's "Third Generation" improvements, including a much-improved trigger pull, a more ergonomic grip design, and improved sights. Early versions of the Model 6906 featured a hooked, recurved trigger guard; but by 1992, S&W switched to a more sensible rounded style. One controversial feature of this series is the ongoing use of a prominent finger rest on the magazine bottom, making the gun undeniably easier to hold and fire. On the other hand, it also compromises concealment and creates an exposed, angular surface that could cause a snag on the draw.

The sights on the Model 6906 are the efficient Novak Lo-Mounts, which provide an excellent sight picture and practically eliminate the chances of catching on a holster or clothing (a luminous-sight version is available for improved sight acquisition in low-light conditions). And, like most Third Generation pistols, the Model 6906 is, with its two-sided safety lever, set up for ambidextrous operation. Other safety features include a firing-pin lock and magazine safety.

The Model 6946, another 9mm compact in the 6900 series, is a stainless slide/alloy-frame pistol with a double-action-only trigger mechanism similar in operation to the Model 3953.

Smith & Wesson's Model 6906, shown here with stainless steel slide and matching silver-anodized alloy frame, ranks among the best high-capacity compact 9mm pistols. It produced this 1.5-inch five-shot off-hand group from 25 feet.

The Model 6906 tested for this book handled well and was reasonably accurate. Our best five-shot offhand group fired from a distance of 25 feet measured 1.5 inches, with the four single-action shots that followed registering a much tighter .75 inch. A 50-foot group subsequently measured 3.4 inches. Both groups used Winchester Silvertips in the 115-grain bullet weight. No jams or other malfunctions resulted in the course of testing with a variety of ammunition types.

About the only negative feature found on this model, aside from its alloy frame, is the prominent finger extension on the magazine bottom. As discussed earlier, all sharply angled or protruding surfaces should be eliminated on concealed-carry pistols. Smith & Wesson should also be advised to install easily-removable stocks on their pistols, as most manufacturers now do.

Whether concealed deep inside pockets or against the skin, these defensive pistols require frequent cleaning. Unfortunately, though, the one-piece plastic grip on the Model 6906 can be removed only by driving out a pin at the heel of the grip— not the sort of thing one would choose to do on a regular basis.

Overall, though, the Model 6906 is well worth considering for those who desire a medium-sized, high-capacity 9mm pistol. Even with its most expensive options added, this highly capable pistol still costs less than a SIG P228.

SMITH & WESSON MODEL 6906

Manufacturer	Years Produced	Caliber/Capacity	Dimensions
Smith & Wesson Springfield, MA	1989–Present	9mm/10 rounds	Barrel Length: 3.5" O.A. Length: 7.0" Height: 5.5" Width: 1.3" Weight: 26 oz. (unloaded); 31.5 oz. (loaded)

S&W SIGMA COMPACT (SW9C)

When Smith & Wesson introduced its first Sigma pistol in 1994, the gun made an immediate and powerful impression within the world of handguns. By the following spring, Smith & Wesson announced the addition of a compact and .380-caliber Sigma variations, all featuring the same polymer frames, locking mechanisms and disassembly procedures inspired by the Glock pistol line.

The Sigma departs considerably from the Glock, however, in terms of its trigger design and ergonomics. The Sigma's trigger (double action for every shot) is smoother than the Glock's; and, unlike Glock's "Safe Action" mechanism, the Sigma trigger can be pulled more than once should the first strike fail to fire a chambered cartridge. The Sigma's grip angle (18 degrees) is less acute than the Glock's (22 degrees); indeed, the Sigma grip is considered more comfortable by most shooters who've tested it. The smooth contours also make it an easy-carry handgun.

Considered a striking innovation in design for Smith & Wesson, the Sigma SW9C has enjoyed commercial success during its early years. Note, however, that its 9mm and .40-caliber versions are limited to 10-round magazines only for civilian use as mandated by the Crime Bill of 1994.

SMITH AND WESSON COMPACT (SW9C)

Manufacturer	Years Produced	Caliber/Capacity	Dimensions
Smith & Wesson Springfield, MA	1995–Present	9mm/10 rounds 14 rounds (law-enforcement only)	Barrel Length: 4" O.A. Length: 6.9" Height: 5.5" Width: 1.2" Weight: 24.5 oz. (unloaded); 29.5 oz. (loaded)

SPRINGFIELD 1911A1 COMPACT

Introduced in 1989, the 1911A1 Compact was a good seller for Springfield Armory until the company went out of business in 1992. The following year, after Springfield, Inc., took over part of Springfield Armory's assets and product line, this model continued to do well.

Intermediate in size between the Colt Commander and the Officer's Model, the construction of the Model 1911A1 Compact is all steel, giving it heft with excellent stability and balance. The workmanship is outstanding, with standard blued finish plus optional dual-tone and all-stainless versions available at additional cost. The checkered wooden stocks fit the frame perfectly and offer a good gripping surface. The hammer is rounded in the same style begun in 1950 with Colt's Commander. The mainspring housing was straight on early Compacts, but has since reverted to the arched M1911A1 style, which many shooters prefer because it seems to point better.

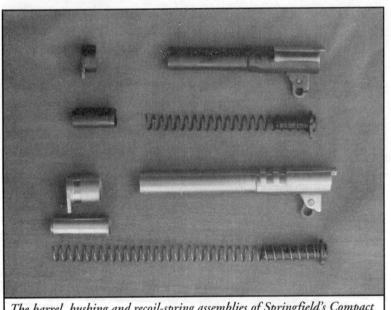

The barrel, bushing and recoil-spring assemblies of Springfield's Compact pistol (top) are similar in function, albeit smaller, than those of Colt's Government Model (bottom).

The 1911A1 Compact's box magazine is easily loaded to its advertised capacity of seven rounds. The sights are quite good, although the rear sight is not quite wide enough for rapid sighting in an emergency situation. The pistol's safety mechanisms, similar to those of a pre-Series '80 Colt pistol, do not include an automatic internal firing-pin block. It does have, however, every other Colt-style safety, including an inertial firing pin, a half-cock notch on the hammer, a frame-mounted manual safety lever ("up" for safe, "down" to fire), and a grip safety.

The 1911A1 Compact produced by Springfield Armory, Inc., is an excellent shooter. Despite its small size, the gun fits very well in the hand, is comfortable to hold and easy to conceal. The rear grip tang is generously sized to prevent hammer bites; that plus its substantial mass and rounded hammer make this a comfortable gun to shoot with surprisingly light felt recoil. In test-firing this fine pistol,

SPRINGFIELD

The Springfield Compact (right) is not much longer or taller than the .380-caliber Walther PPK shown at left. The Springfield model is appreciably wider and heavier, though, making it possible to accommodate the more powerful .45 ACP round.

our best five-shot offhand group measured only 1.3 inches at 25 feet, using Remington's +P 185-grain jacketed hollowpoints, and 2.8 inches at 50 feet, firing Federal's white label "American Eagle" 230-grain FMJ ammunition. Indeed, the test pistol's reliability was flawless with all brands fired in it, including Federal's Hydra-Shok 230-grain hollowpoints and Winchester's "USA" 230-grain FMJs.

The Springfield 1911A1 Compact is a superb shooter, as evidenced by this five-shot 50-foot offhand group, which measured only 2.6 inches. From 25 feet, the same pistol fired a pattern of merely 1.3 inches across.

SPRINGFIELD 1911A1 COMPACT

Manufacturer	Years Produced	Caliber/Capacity	Dimensions
Springfield, Inc. (formerly Springfield Armory, Inc.) Geneseo, IL	1989–Present	.45 ACP/7 rounds	Barrel Length: 4.0" O.A. Length: 7.75" Height: 5.1" Width: 1.3" Weight: 32 oz. (unloaded); 39 oz. (loaded)

STAR MODEL BM/BKM

Star's Model BKM made its first appearance in the early 1970s. At first, it was available only in a lightweight version with an aluminum-alloy frame. A heavier all-steel version—the Model BM—was added several years later (*see* photo below). A .45-caliber version, called the Model PD, was introduced in 1975 (*see* page 272). But by 1991, Star had ceased production of the BK/BKM in order to concentrate on its new Firestar pistol.

The BKM series is smaller but otherwise nearly identical to the famous Model B (*see Complete Guide to Service Handguns*). The Star pistols were based closely on Colt's M1911A1 but without a grip safety. They came usually in a blued finish, but late in the production run a chrome finish, called Starvel, was made available. Checkered wooden grips were standard, but Pachmayr made a set of wraparound rubber grips for this pistol series that are still found, particularly on the light, hard-recoiling Models BKM and PD.

Like Colt's M1911A1 and Government models, the manual safety lever on the BK/BKM models goes up to its safe setting and down to its fire setting. In fact, all handling drills on these small Star pistols are about the same as the larger Colts. Think of a Star BKM or BM as a smaller Government Model without a grip safety and you'll have a pretty good idea of what this pistol is all about.

Although the BKM and BM could use slightly larger sights, their accuracy is nevertheless acceptable. And while the alloy-framed BKM may be more than half a pound lighter than the all-steel BM, making it easier to carry, its recoil is considerably more than the BM, which, consequently, is easier to shoot. But neither gun is compact enough for pocket or ankle holster carry. Both guns are now discontinued, of course, but they still appear occasionally as used guns. They lack the ambidextrous features of Star's Firestar, but the BKM and BM remain excellent choices for those who like the way the Government Model operates but seek a smaller, handier gun.

STAR MODEL BM/BKM

Manufacturer	Years Produced	Caliber/Capacity	Dimensions
Star Bonifacio Echeverria Eibar, Spain	1970s–1992	9mm/8 rounds	Barrel Length: 4.0" O.A. Length: 7.0" Height: 5.2" Width: 1.1" Weight (unloaded): 35 oz.(BM);26 oz.(BKM) (loaded): add approx. 4 oz.

STAR FIRESTAR (M43, M40, M45)

Firestar M43. In 1990, Star introduced its much-advertised seven-shot 9mm Firestar. Mechanically, the Firestar is a Star Model 31 (CZ 75) breech-locking type scaled down to the smallest size possible. Its slide sits inside of, rather than atop, the frame. To make the Firestar even more compact, Star elected to use a single-action-only mechanism. Like other Star pistols, it comes in either a matte blued finish or Star's own Starvel hard-chrome finish.

The Firestar's controls, which are well thought out, go a long way toward alleviating any objections a shooter might have toward the cocked-and-locked method of carrying a single-action pistol. The ambidextrous manual safety levers are slightly oversized and quite positive in operation, wiping down easily to the fire position. Putting them back up into their safe position is, however, considerably more difficult, mostly because the grip interferes with the shooter's thumb as it tries to push the safety levers from below (a little work with a sharp razor or a hobbyist's X-Acto knife on the rubber grips can quickly eliminate this problem). In any event, it makes more sense to own a gun that goes off safe more easily than it goes on safe. After all, taking off the safety must at times be done in a hurry, as under the stress of mortal combat. By contrast, pushing the safety on is generally done under less stressful conditions.

Like the CZ 75 and Star's own Model 31, the magazine release on the Firestar does not drop the magazine completely clear of the gun. It also has a magazine safety, which prevents the gun from firing with the magazine removed. Still another safety feature on the Firestar is a firing-pin lock of modern design.

As for accuracy, the Firestar is surprisingly good, particularly for its small size. In addition, the gun's excellent sights at least partially compensate for a mediocre trigger. Our best five-shot offhand efforts measured 1.7 inches at 25 feet using Norinco 124-grain FMJs, and 4.4 inches at 50 feet with Federal 9BP 115-grain jacketed hollowpoints (JHP). Like other Star pistols, the Firestar's reliability is flawless, and it does not seem to be at all choosy about

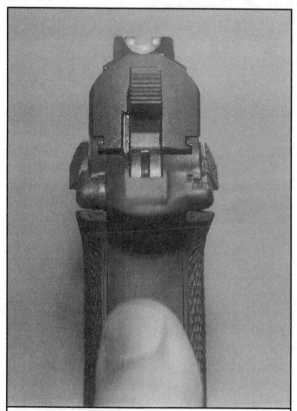

The rubber grips used on the Firestar improve rapid fire control and shooting comfort. The raised upper rear surfaces, however, make it difficult to push the ambidextrous manual safety levers back up to their safe setting.

Despite its small size, Star's Firestar M43 pistol handles well and shoots like a full-sized service pistol. This five-shot offhand group fired from 25 feet measures 1.7 inches.

what types of ammunition are used.

In our opinion, a lightweight version of the Firestar with an aluminum-alloy frame—or better still, a frame made out of equally light, but much stronger titanium—would make this pistol more easily carried in a pocket or in an ankle holster. At just over two pounds fully loaded, the Firestar is too heavy for these carry modes. Star (and its importer, Interarms) should also supply its pistols with at least two magazines, rather than the single magazine now standard. A chief advantage of an automatic pistol over a revolver is, after all, the pistol's more rapid reloading. This advantage is lost when there's only a single magazine. In addition, the magazine spring is under tremendous pressure in a loaded magazine. Having replacement magazines would eliminate these problems.

For those who insist on the smallest possible 9mm automatic pistol (discounting the five-shot 9mm revolvers now available) the Firestar ranks among the best choices for a defensive pistol. Although heavier than other comparably sized firearms, that extra weight contributes to the Firestar's pleasant handling characteristics. As an eminently concealable and reliable small automatic pistol for wear in a shoulder holster or an inside-the-waistband holster, the Firestar makes an excellent choice.

STAR FIRESTAR M43

Manufacturer	Years Produced	Caliber/Capacity	Dimensions
Star Bonifacio Echeverria Eibar, Spain Imported by Interarms Alexandria, VA	1990–Present	9mm/7 rounds	Barrel Length: 3.4" O.A. Length: 6.5" Height: 4.7" Width: 1.25" Weight: 30 oz. (unloaded); 33 oz. (loaded)

Star Firestar M40. In 1991, Star added a .40 S&W version of the M43 to its Firestar lineup; in 1992 a slightly larger .45 ACP Firestar made its appearance (*see* following listing). The Firestar has since become a tremendous success for Star and its U.S. importer, Interarms (Alexandria, VA). So good has the Firestar been that it has nearly supplanted Star's excellent BM and PD pistol series.

The 9mm and .40-caliber Firestars are identical in size and appearance, the only major difference is their magazine capacities (the .40-caliber M40 magazine holds only six rounds). Like the M43, the M40 uses the reversed slide-to-frame relationship made popular by the Czech CZ 75, in which the slide sits inside the frame rather than atop it.

To keep dimensions to an absolute minimum, Star decided to make the Firestar in a single-action version only. It has succeeded admirably in making the 9mm and .40-caliber versions of its Firestar compact, their length and height measuring no more than those of the .380-caliber Walther PP. The Firestar is wider, though, and its unloaded weight tops 30 ounces, making it almost half a pound heavier than Walther's classic concealment pistol. Nevertheless, the .40-caliber Firestar M40 remains a top choice for a defensive pistol. It boasts an excellent safety system, combining a passive firing-pin block with ambidextrous safety levers that push down easily to the fire position. There's also a magazine disconnect that prevents firing when the magazine has been removed from the grip. The safety levers are, unfortunately, much harder to move up to the safe setting, but cutting away a small portion of the rubber stocks can easily correct this deficiency.

The Firestar, disassembled, is an extraordinarily well-conceived package. The slight swelling at the barrel enables it to return to battery (forward firing position) after each shot without a separate barrel bushing.

Considering its small size, the Firestar M40 shoots surprisingly well. The sights are good (although the rear sight notch is a bit too narrow) and the trigger pull, albeit heavier and grittier than it needs to be, releases with an acceptable amount of effort. Thanks to the gun's substantial weight and somewhat top-and muzzle-heavy balance, recoil is acceptable, making possible rapid-fire, close-in shooting. In testing, the Firestar demonstrated that double taps fired at 15 feet could be placed as close as one inch apart. Increasing the distance to the target to 25 feet, our two smallest five-shot offhand

The Firestar M40, like other single-action pistols, offers easy transitions from one shot to the next, making double taps easy. This two-shot, rapid-fire burst measures just one inch apart, fired from a distance of 15 feet (left photo). Most double-action automatic pistols would give a wider double tap. At 25 feet, the same pistol produced this 2.4-inch five-shot offhand group (right photo).

groups measured 2.4 inches across, using Federal 180-grain JHPs and similar Winchester jacketed hollowpoints.

In an era of double-action high-capacity automatic pistols, the M40 Firestar, with its single-action design and six-shot capacity, may seem a bit anachronistic. However, it's easily concealed and easy to fire rapidly and accurately. The .40 S&W round is, moreover, far more powerful than the .38 Special and offers less recoil and muzzle flash than a .357 Magnum. These characteristics make the .40-caliber Firestar an especially good candidate as a defensive handgun, especially for shooters who are used to a revolver.

STAR FIRESTAR M40

Manufacturer	Years Produced	Caliber/Capacity	Dimensions
Star Bonifacio Echeverria Eibar, Spain Imported by Interarms Alexandria, VA	1991–Present	.40 S&W/6 rounds	Barrel Length: 3.4" O.A. Length: 6.5" Height: 4.7" Width: 1.25" Weight: 30 oz.(unloaded) 34.5 oz. (loaded)

The magazine release on the Firestar M45 ejects the magazine only a fraction of an inch, as shown. Note that the manual safety lever is on its safe setting even with the hammer uncocked.

Star Firestar M45. The Firestar M45 pistol introduced by Star in 1992 represents a growing trend toward truly compact .45-caliber handguns made to compete on even terms with compact pistols in 9mm and other calibers. Naturally, a compact .45-caliber pistol has strong appeal for shooters who prefer it over a 9mm, .40 S&W and other smaller calibers.

Even though the M45—in reality an ex-model PD—had to be strengthened to handle the .45 ACP cartridge, the gun is still remarkably compact, though noticeably thicker and heavier (by about five ounces) than its 9mm and .40 S&W counterparts. Even so, the M45 Firestar is not much longer or higher than a .380-caliber Walther PPK and is, overall, a remarkable example of design engineering and gunmaking.

Like the Model PD it replaces, the M45 Firestar is a six-shot, single-action design; i.e., the hammer must be fully cocked to the rear before the trigger can release it to fire the gun. A seven-shot extension magazine, available as an option, may well be a better choice for large-handed shooters despite a slight compromise in concealability resulting from the bigger magazine. The M45 Firestar features a Browning short-recoil locking system with lugs on the top of the barrel that lock into grooves machined into the top underside of the slide. Instead of a link (or lug) under the barrel to unlock it from the slide during recoil, an enclosed cam serves the same purpose. To stabilize the muzzle at the end of each recoil stroke, the M45 Firestar employs a barrel that is slightly bell-shaped at the muzzle, much like the Colt Officer's ACP (*see* page 213). The Firestar improves on the Colt design, though, by eliminating the latter's separate muzzle bushing. In the same manner pioneered in the SIG P210 (and later copied in the CZ 75 and Star's own Models 28, 30 and 31), the slide on the Firestar travels inside the frame, rather than on top, thereby providing a longer bearing surface and offering better support. The result is superior accuracy and improved longevity. To eliminate glare, lines have been machined into the upper surface of the slide.

The Firestar's safety features are plentiful, including a firing-pin safety and an ambidextrous manual safety lever that locks the hammer. A half-cock notch on the hammer adds another safety element should the thumb slip in the process of cocking the hammer. Finally, a magazine disconnect safety keeps the gun from firing whenever the magazine has been removed from the pistol.

Like many modern automatic pistols, the M45 Firestar provides ease of operation. For example, aggressive checkering on the grip allows the shooter to get a firmer hold on the pistol. The rear of the grip also has a slight curve, or palm swell, so that this rather thick pistol fits the hand well. The grip tang is longer than usual to prevent the shooter's hand from being pinched between tang and hammer upon recoil ("hammer bite" is an extremely painful experience we can all live without!). The oversized safety lever, magazine release and slide stop all allow for easy operation and go a long way towards eliminating shooters' objections concerning single-action pistols.

The M45 Firestar is available in either a blued or Starvel chrome finish. Checkered rubber grips are standard. The slide flats and the upper portion of the frame are highly polished, while the lower frame and the top of the slide come in a nonreflective matte finish.

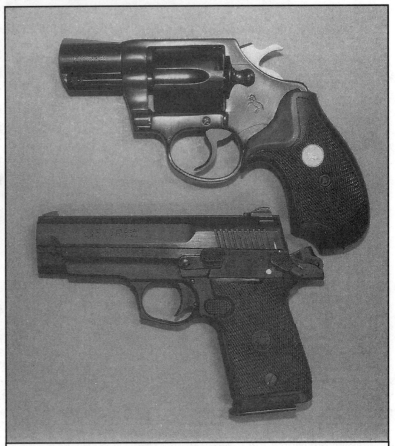

The Firestar M45 (bottom) poses a challenge to such small concealment revolvers as Colt's famous Detective Special (top). Those who prefer automatic pistols for concealment purposes will find one of the Firestars in 9mm, .40 S&W or .45 ACP much to their liking.

On the negative side, the magazine on Star's .45 pistol is tough to load, especially the last two rounds. The magazine lips are sharp, requiring careful attention to what one is doing. After a loaded magazine has been put into the pistol, the slide is drawn all the way back, with the safety down in the fire position, and then released so it can be shoved forward by the recoil spring. With the hammer now cocked and the safety off, the gun can be fired immediately. To delay firing, simply push the thumb safety up into the safe position; the pistol can then be carried cocked and locked until firing resumes.

Not surprisingly, few other shortcomings were discovered in testing the M45 Firestar. For one, the safety lever does not move easily to the on-safe position (although it's easily taken off the safe setting prior to firing). Also, its release button functions sloppily; and because of the magazine disconnect safety, the magazine is prevented from dropping more than a fraction of an inch, which can complicate reloading. Finally, only a single magazine comes with the gun, reducing its overall efficiency. It also restricts one to the ammunition available in the pistol itself—a potentially dangerous situation in the event one lacks the time or opportunity to reload loose rounds.

The M45 Firestar is an acceptably accurate pistol. Although several millimeters of creep occur before the trigger releases the sear to fire the pistol, it trips crisply at about eight pounds of pressure. Many shooters prefer a trigger about half that weight, but the Firestar's heavy trigger can certainly be mastered. Moreover, its weight—only 3 to 4 ounces less than most M1911-type pistols—and its wide grip (made of recoil-resistant rubber) help reduce recoil despite the powerful .45 cartridge. In test-firing the M45, a five-round 25-foot offhand group measured 1.8 inches, using Winchester's American Eagle 230-grain FMJ round. The same ammunition also produced at 50 feet a group measuring 3.7 inches. Several different brands of ammunition were used during the tests with absolutely no trouble experienced with fully-jacketed rounds or hollowpoints. Nor did any "breaking-in" jams occur, as is common initially among even the most reliable and well-conceived pistol designs.

Those who choose the M45 Firestar will own a fine compact .45-caliber pistol suitable for both standard issue and concealment. In any event, when acquiring this very capable pistol, be sure to add an extra magazine to supplement the one supplied by Star.

STAR FIRESTAR M45

Manufacturer	Years Produced	Caliber/Capacity	Dimensions
Star Bonifacio Echeverria Eibar, Spain Imported by Interarms Alexandria, VA	1992–Present	.45 ACP/6 rounds	Barrel Length: 3.6" O.A. Length: 6.9" Height: 4.9" Width: 1.3" Weight: 35 oz. (unloaded); 41 oz. (loaded)

STAR FIRESTAR PLUS

This version of the Firestar pistol, which was introduced by Interarms in 1995, features a high-capacity magazine and ambidextrous safety levers. To hold down the weight, an alloy frame has replaced the Firestar's steel frame. It is an interesting concept, but tests with an early specimen (using one 13-round magazine) were not impressive. Although the earlier Firestars proved quite accurate in testing, the Firestar Plus did not. Its trigger also seemed rougher than the original Firestar. In any event, the Firestar Plus faces an  uncertain future. What's more, with the 10-round magazine limit imposed by the Crime Bill of 1994, this Star pistol loses three rounds of magazine capacity to the standard mode. A more productive concept for Star, it seems, would be to apply the lightweight alloy frame technology created for the Firestar Plus to the regular Firestar series—particularly the 9mm M43—as an "airweight" option. That would make the standard Firestar, which is heavy for its compact dimensions, light enough to become a practical pocket or ankle-holster pistol.

Although the earlier Firestars proved quite accurate in testing, offhand groups with the newer Firestar Plus were not impressive.

STAR FIRESTAR PLUS

Manufacturer	Years Produced	Caliber/Capacity	Dimensions
Star Bonifacio Echeverria Eibar, Spain Imported by Interarms Alexandria, VA	1995–Present	9mm/10 rounds	Barrel Length: 3.4" O.A. Length: 6.5" Height: 4.9" Width: 1.30" Weight: 30 oz. (unloaded); 35 oz. (loaded)

STAR PD

Star's Model PD, which unfortunately is now out of production, was at one time arguably the finest compact .45-ACP pistol on the market. An excellent, innovative gun, it became something of a cult classic. Although the PD itself was made only in .45 ACP, Star also built the similar Models BK and BKM in 9mm Parabellum caliber (*see* page 264).

Like the M1911, which it closely resembles, the Star PD is a single-action automatic pistol. To hold down its weight, the PD has an alloy frame, giving the gun a stiff recoil but also making it eminently concealable. Unfortunately, the workmanship is spotty, varying from only fair to extremely good, depending on Star's quality-control program at whatever time a particular pistol had been manufactured.

Most PDs sport a blued finish, but late in Star's production run the "Starvel" chrome finish came

The Star PD compact (bottom), although out of production now, still presents a competitive challenge to Springfield's M1911A1 Compact (top). Note the Starvel finish on this late Model PD, which lacks the grip safety found on M1911 variants.

into use. Checkered walnut grips are standard on the PD, though Pachmayr once made an excellent set of recoil-absorbing wraparound rubber grips. These are occasionally found on PDs and a variety of other handguns.

The PD's breech-locking mechanism is slightly modified from the Browning short-recoil system used in the Colt M1911/Government Model. The PD's modified barrel has only a single locking lug atop the barrel, but function is unimpaired. The thumb safety operates the same as Colt's; a magazine safety has been added, however, and the Colt's grip safety omitted. Oddly, the PD includes an adjustable rear sight, probably to gain points with the BATF and thus allow its importation. The sights on all but the lat-

In a test-firing, Star's PD pistol produced this five-shot 50-foot offhand group measuring slightly less than 5.0 inches. Note the Pachmayr grips added to help tame the recoil.

est models are slightly undersized, but accuracy remains acceptable.

Despite the heavy recoil, the PD shoots well. Trigger pull, while not sensational, is light (7–8 pounds) and smooth even with the magazine safety. Our best five-shot 25-foot offhand effort from 25 feet put five Federal American Eagle brand 230-grain FMJ bullets into 1.4 inches, while from 50 feet out the group measured 4.9 inches, using Remington's +P 185-grain JHPs.

Unfortunately, Star discontinued production of the Model PD in 1991, concentrating instead on its Firestar production, discussed earlier. While this decision made sense within the company, many shooters lamented the loss of this fine pistol.

STAR PD

Manufacturer	Years Produced	Caliber/Capacity	Dimensions
Star Bonifacio Echeverria Eibar, Spain	1975–1991	.45 ACP/6 rounds	Barrel Length: 4.0" O.A. Length: 7.5" Height: 5.0" Width: 1.3" Weight: 25 oz. (unloaded); 31 oz.(loaded)

STAR ULTRASTAR

The Ultrastar was formally introduced by Star in 1995, although prototypes had appeared earlier in European gun exhibitions. In its attempt to combine the compact but relatively powerful 9mm round with a platform that can be readily concealed, the Ultrastar ranks high among the more innovative 9mm designs now in production. Its appeal to "special" agents, undercover police officers and legally armed civilians is tremendous. Star has indeed succeeded in creating a gun capable of fulfilling most of these missions.

The secret of the Ultrastar's success is its polymer frame, which allows the strength and durability of a steel frame but with much less weight. In addition, the Ultrastar uses several traditional concepts found in previous Star handguns. These include a forged steel slide that sits inside the frame (inspired by the CZ 75); an ambidextrous manual safety; and a smooth double-action trigger. The Ultrastar offers in addition its own manual safety with a third (decocker) setting that lowers the cocked hammer mechanically to its rest position. The pistol also comes with two magazines, unlike former Star models, which traditionally were supplied with only one.

Tests conducted on the Ultrastar proved its accuracy and reliability with a wide variety of 9mm commercial brands. Although it's not the smallest 9mm service pistol available, the Ultrastar is among the smallest to offer such amenities as ambidextrous controls, substantial sights and a hold-open latch on the slide. It is without a doubt the equal of the Astra Model A-75 or the S&W Model 3900 series.

STAR ULTRA STAR

Manufacturer	Years Produced	Caliber/Capacity	Dimensions
Star Bonifacio Echeverria Eibar, Spain Imported by Interarms Alexandria, VA	1995–Present	9mm/9 rounds	Barrel Length: 3.6" O.A. Length: 7.0" Height: 5.0" Width: 1.25" Weight: 26 oz. (unloaded); 31 oz. (loaded)

WALTHER P5C COMPACT

In 1988, having heard enough complaints about the
size of its P5 (*see Complete Guide to Service Handguns*),
Walther introduced a slightly smaller version, called the P5
Compact, or P5C. The P5C differed from the P5 with its
rounded bobbed hammer, straighter rear gripstrap, and lack of a
heel-mounted magazine release. Mechanically, though, the two pistols are identical in function and operation.

Aside from a slight reduction in length and weight, the P5C differs from the
P5 chiefly in the location of its magazine release. The P5's is in the lower rear portion of the frame, while the P5C uses a conventional magazine release button
mounted at the rear of the trigger guard. The location of the magazine release on the
P5 is more popular with Europeans, generally speaking, while most American shooters prefer the
magazine release setup on the P5C.

An attractive gun with excellent workmanship and clean, simple lines, the P5C features a combi-

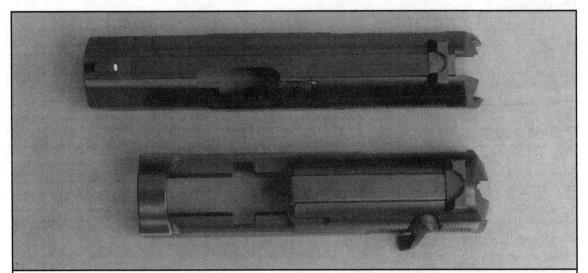

The enclosed slide with small ejection port on the Model P5C (top) differs greatly from the slide of the "classic" Walther P.38 (bottom). Note also that the P5C's front sight is mounted directly on the slide.

nation matte and high-polish blued finish on the steel slide, with its aluminum-alloy frame anodized
black. Grips are either checkered wood or checkered black plastic. Like the P5, the P5C has a sensible
trigger guard large enough to accommodate a gloved hand. And although it is nicely rounded at the
front, the trigger guard used on the compact version has horizontal grooves for shooters who use the
finger-forward hold.

The P5C is an excellent shooter, one that is highly accurate and reliable with a wide selection of
different ammunition brands. Its trigger pull is typical of a Walther handgun; i.e., heavy on the first

The Walther P5C (bottom) is highly competitive with other compact 9mm pistols, such as the Smith & Wesson Model 3953 (top) but its price is more than twice that of its closest competitors.

shot when fired double action with the hammer down, and with single-action follow-up shots coming smooth and easy. For that reason, the first shots in many of the groups test-fired for this book went wide, while the next four shots made a tight pattern. Our three best five-shot 25-foot offhand groups measured 1.4, 1.5 and 1.6 inches, respectively, using (in order) Remington 115-grain +P JHP, Winchester "USA" white label 115-grain FMJ rounds, and Federal 9BP. The best target shot at 50 feet, using Winchester USA 115-grain FMJ, placed all five rounds in a sensational 1.6-inch group.

Because of Walther's continued use of the underbarrel locking block, which the P5C inherited from the P.38, it remains a thick, chunky handgun. Indeed, the wide slide on this gun makes the P5C as tough to conceal as a good-sized revolver. In fairness, though, the gun is compact in its other dimensions—and no wider than other P.38-type "compacts," such as Beretta's Model 92FC or the PT-92C made by Taurus. Unlike those pistols, the P5C has a dauntingly high price, though it has attracted considerable military interest in Europe and Asia, causing its price to drop. If you can afford one, the P5C is an excellent gun. If you can't afford one, try a Taurus PT-908 or a Smith & Wesson Model 3913/3914 for similar features at a considerably lower price.

Despite its heavy double-action trigger, the Walther P5 Compact is capable of extraordinary accuracy. This five-shot offhand group fired from 25 feet measures a mere 1.6 inches.

Manufacturer	Years Produced	Caliber/Capacity	Dimensions
Carl Walther Waffenfabrik Ulm, Donau, Germany	1988–Present	9mm/8 rounds	Barrel Length: 3.1" O.A. Length: 6.6" Height: 5.1" Width: 1.45" Weight: 27.5 oz. (unloaded) 31.5 oz. (loaded)

WALTHER P88 COMPACT

Walther's original P88 pistol was created to compete in the U.S. military XM9 pistol trials of 1984. The gun was a radical departure from traditional Walther designs in that it used the short-recoil system and tilting barrel design of John Browning's; it was also the company's first pistol to use a double-column, high-capacity magazine. Built with exacting care, the P88 was also superbly accurate, despite its heavy double-action trigger pull.

Walther introduced the P88 Compact in 1990 in Germany, but not until 1992 did Interarms import a limited quantity into the U.S. In addition to being slightly smaller than the full-sized P88 (*see Complete Guide to Service Handguns* for a full discussion), the P88 Compact does not have an operating lever, but instead uses a ambidextrous, hammer-dropping safety lever mounted on the slide, similar in function to that of Walther's older Model PP.

Like the regular P88, the P88 Compact is incredibly accurate, but has enjoyed little sales success, forcing Walther to consider halting production altogether in favor of its new Glock-influenced Model P99. Its design seems well-conceived, though, making it somewhat better shaped to the hand than its full-sized counterpart.

WALTHER P88 COMPACT

Manufacturer	Years Produced	Caliber/Capacity	Dimensions
Carl Walther Waffenfabrik Ulm, Donau, Germany	1990–Present	9mm/10 rounds	Barrel Length: 3.9" O.A. Length: 7.5" Height: 4.9" Width: 1.4" Weight: 28 oz. (unloaded); 36 oz. (loaded)

HANDGUN SAFETY

Every time you pick up a gun, you're risking your life and that of anyone who falls within range. Remember, some handgun bullets can travel a mile or more. It stands to reason that we all need to take reasonable precautions to avoid accidents. One of these precautions is avoidance. "An ounce of prevention is worth a pound of cure" may be old advice, but it's still valid. By avoiding situations that foster illegal use of handguns, you'll have gone a long way toward achieving gun safety. Take precautions that include handling guns yourself in a safe and sane manner, and seeing to it that members of your family do likewise.

JEFF COOPER'S FOUR RULES FOR SAFE GUN HANDLING

Jeff Cooper, whose teachings and writings on handgunning have contributed more to the development of combat pistolcraft than any other expert in the field, has developed four easy-to-learn safety rules. If faithfully followed, they can make accidental shootings virtually impossible. Cooper's rules are:

1. **Always assume that all guns are loaded**, and that there's no such thing as an unloaded gun. Observing this simple rule can provide the proper sense of awe and respect for the potential dangers that gun ownership engenders. Always remember that any type of gun—no matter how small, old or worthless it may be—can cause death and tragedy.

2. **Never point a gun at anyone or anything you don't intend to shoot.** Remember, not only is every gun presumed to be loaded, it's always pointing somewhere. Unless you've determined that your life depends on shooting your handgun, keep the muzzle pointed away from all innocent persons and valuable property.

3. **Keep your finger off the trigger until you're ready to shoot.** The fact is, your trigger finger is most comfortable when it's resting on the trigger. Guns are designed that way. To avoid a needless tragedy, teach yourself never to put your finger on the trigger until the moment you're ready to fire a shot. Until then, your finger must stay off the trigger, usually alongside the frame next to the trigger, or resting with its tip on the leading edge of the trigger guard. In fact, the trigger guard is a safety device designed to prevent foreign objects from catching against the trigger and causing the gun to fire. Following this one rule alone can greatly reduce the number of accidental shootings.

4. **Before you shoot, identify your target.** Once a bullet begins its deadly flight, you cannot recall it. No amount of hand-wringing can restore a lost life. Make certain you know who or what lies in the path of a bullet before you fire your gun.

Some corollaries to these four basic rules are also worth mentioning:

Become Thoroughly Familiar with Your Firearm. Know how it works and what it can—and cannot—do. Know all the features it possesses, then practice firing it under safe conditions. When target shooting, check the backstop before firing. Is it adequate to stop the kind of bullets you're using? In general, it's better to shoot in an approved shooting range rather than out in the woods, because you'll have the added protection of established safety regulations and procedures, plus an approved backstop. Practice different "styles" of shooting in addition to target shooting.

Keep Your Gun Clean. Keep your handgun scrupulously clean, and make sure the barrel is clear of obstructions before you begin shooting. Always make sure the gun is completely unloaded before cleaning it. Removing the magazine of an automatic pistol, remember, does not fully clear the weapon. There could still be a round left in the firing chamber. To be sure, always remove the magazine fully from the pistol, then draw back the slide to its fullest extent. This will eject any round that's left in the chamber.

Use Safety Features to the Fullest. If there's a decocking lever or hammer-dropping safety, for example, use it—not the trigger—to lower the hammer onto a loaded firing chamber. And when using the decocking control, remember Cooper's rule about pointing the muzzle in a safe direction. With a round in the firing chamber, do not carry an automatic pistol on the half-cock hammer setting. Even with revolvers that are mechanically safe, with a loaded cylinder and the hammer down (uncocked) over a loaded round, never cock a loaded revolver for a single-action shot unless you're absolutely certain you will fire. With the hammer of a revolver cocked, there's no way to unload the gun safely.

And don't assume that all firearms of similar make or type have the same safety features. For instance, many owners of Smith & Wesson's Safety Hammerless or Model 40/42 "Centennial" revolvers elect to have a grip safety pinned or deactivated. The point is, don't assume your gun has all the designed safety features fully operational.

Wear Safety Glasses and Hearing Protection When Shooting. Guns have been known to blow up and eject metal parts at high speeds back into the shooter's face, so the glasses must be sturdy and impact-resistant. Ear plugs or earmuff-type hearing protectors are fine for the ears; and using both at the same time is better still.

Use the Proper Ammunition. Some guns will operate effectively with different cartridges, but it's always a good idea to use the type of ammunition marked on the gun. Inspect carefully each round of ammunition as it's placed in the gun. Cartridges that are dented, scratched or otherwise deformed should not be fired.

Buying Previously Owned Firearms. When buying a gun secondhand, insist that all papers that initially came with the gun be given to you as a condition of sale. Having all the original paperwork (and packaging, if possible) increases the value of the gun and helps ensure your safety—provided you stop long enough to read the owner's manual! If the seller of a secondhand gun does not have an owner's manual, then contact the manufacturer. Most reputable gun companies will send you an owner's manual free of charge. It's also a good idea to read up on handguns in general before buying one. Look through some of the trade magazines and gun annuals to find out what the experts recommend.

Be Cautious About Gunsmithing. In general, it's unwise to have a gun worked on unless something is obviously wrong with it, or you've handled and fired it enough to know exactly what's needed. Most guns work reasonably well as they come from the factory, and the "break-in" period is probably as useful for shooters to accustom themselves to the gun as it is for the gun to "wear in" properly. A great deal of money can be spent on custom work in some cases, far more than the gun itself costs. Frequently extensive gunsmithing can invalidate a factory warranty on a new gun. Aside from changing a grip or a stock for a more comfortable fit, and perhaps replacing the sights or marking the front sight with bright paint, not much more is needed.

On the other hand, some people want "action jobs" to smooth the trigger pull or "carry bevel" work to break sharp corners or edges. These improvements are fine, within reason, but they can also cost serious money. Whatever custom work you decide to have done, make sure your gunsmith is capable of doing quality work. Just because he's an expert on M1911-type pistols doesn't make him one with a Browning High Power.

How to Learn More About Safe Gun Handling. To learn more about safe handling of a gun, contact a local gun store, many of which conduct classes on their premises or know about someone in the area who provides qualified instruction. The NRA encourages safe gun handling and can provide the names of certified instructors in your area also.

CARRYING A HANDGUN

The decision to carry a handgun should not be made lightly. Owning a firearm itself carries with it great responsibilities, but the decision to actually carry one is even more extreme. Most people should be encouraged to carry a non-lethal weapon instead, such as gas or an expandable baton, reserving the right to carry a handgun for emergency use only. Law-abiding citizens who have demonstrated mature and responsible behavior should not be denied the right to carry a weapon when doing so might save a life.

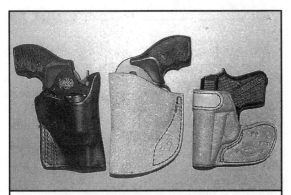

Although pocket carry sounds convenient and easy, it is generally best to carry a small pocket-sized gun in a holster specifically made for the purpose. Shown here are (left to right) a Smith & Wesson Model 37 in a Kramer holster; a Smith & Wesson Model 38 in a Thad Rybka holster; and an Intratec Protec in a Mitchell Leatherworks Pocket Pal.

CARRYING A HANDGUN WITHOUT A HOLSTER
Without a holster, the most obvious way to carry a handgun is in a briefcase, backpack or some kind of luggage that is easy to pick up and move around. A disadvantage of this method is that a briefcase—and the gun that's inside—can be stolen or tampered with. The gun may also be too hard to grab in an emergency. The same applies to keeping a handgun in the glove compartment of an automobile. The point is, a handgun is useless unless it's available when you need it.

Carrying a handgun in a pocket sounds logical enough, and in some instances it may work reasonably well. Make sure the pocket is large enough, though, and that it's strong enough to hold a gun for several hours or more. Even a tiny .25-caliber automatic pistol weighs a lot more than a wallet or a set of keys. Moreover, a handgun, because of its weight, has an annoying habit of settling into a pocket upside down or in some other awkward position that makes it difficult to reach in a hurry. The popular Mini-Revolver (made by North American Arms) is suitable for unholstered pocket carry because it weighs only six ounces fully loaded and is just four inches long. At the same time, accuracy and handling qualities of such a gun are limited. Unfortunately, such handguns—the kind that are the best suited for pocket carry—are also the most vulnerable. Another weakness is that any protrusions—an exposed hammer or a manual safety lever—can catch in the inner lining of a pocket at a time when one most desperately needs to draw the gun. Pockets also have a nasty habit of collecting dirt and lint, which can work their way into a gun and gum up its mechanism.

Probably the best way to carry a handgun of decent size and power without a holster is inside a waistband. The gun can go anywhere around your waist, although most people find it easiest to conceal the weapon behind the hipbone on the strong side (i.e., the dominant gun hand side). Holsterless carry offers a wide range of creative possibilities, but most lack real security. A gun not carried in a holster tends to move around, making it difficult to withdraw the weapon in a hurry when needed. For these and many more reasons, various types of handgun holsters have been developed over the centuries.

HOLSTER CARRIES
The secure carry of a handgun becomes much easier with a holster than without one. A gun

owner, however, must match a holster carefully to one's missions, needs, and the handgun itself. Unfortunately, too many handgunners skimp on their holsters when, in fact, they should select the very best for their particular needs. In general, the more effectively a holster conceals a gun, the longer it takes to draw the weapon. Another consideration involves comfort, for often a person must carry a handgun/holster combination close to the body for long hours at a time.

The following safety admonitions concerning holsters should be observed.

1. Be realistic about how much time you need to draw your gun from its holster. Too many handgunners have false notions about how quick they are on the draw.

2. Don't rush when you reholster your gun. Be sure your index finger is off the trigger while returning a handgun to its holster. Help guide the gun into the holster by placing the index finger alongside the slide of an automatic pistol or the cylinder of a revolver (hopefully one equipped with a rounded trigger guard rather than one of the modern recurved types). Too many people shoot themselves while reholstering their handguns.

3. Always choose a holster design that covers the trigger area and trigger guard. The last

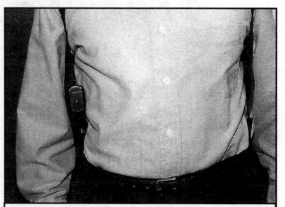

The shoulder holster allow shooters to carry full-sized handguns such as this Browning High Power. Note that a jacket or other outer garment would be needed to conceal the holster.

thing anyone needs is for a gun to go off because something outside the holster catches against the trigger and fires the gun.

Several different types of holsters are available to accommodate various needs:

Wrist Carry. Wrist holsters are popular, requiring a very small gun (.25 caliber or less) and a long-sleeved shirt or coat with wide cuffs. Wrist carry probably works better for women wearing wide, puffy sleeves. However, this type of carry limits women to a relatively weak gun/holster combination. The problem with small handguns is that they do not offer an optimum level of protection. No handgun is an ultimate weapon, but the more powerful it is, the more effective it's likely to be. With that in mind, gun owners should carry the most powerful handgun they can handle and conceal with safety.

Ankle Carry. Ankle holsters are surprisingly popular and quite versatile, so long as the owner is careful not to select a gun that's too large. Some can conceal a gun as large as a Smith & Wesson 3900-series automatic pistol, or even a 15-shot 9mm Glock 19, but for most a Walther PPK automatic pistol or a Smith & Wesson J-frame revolver is probably a more realistic choice. Weight and the size of one's calf muscle

The ankle holster is a popular (but controversial) method for carrying a small handgun. Shown here is a Walther PPK in a Ken Null ankle holster.

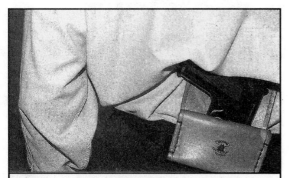

This versatile concealment holster worn in the small of the back is made by Law Concealment Systems; it holds a Browning High Power.

Waist Carry. One of the best ways to carry a large, powerful handgun is at the waist, and a variety of holsters have been created for just that purpose. Most standard military holsters consist of a holster attached to a belt that buckles around the waist (some use cross-chest carries). The more concealable holsters of this type usually attach to the waistband by a clip, or they attach to a belt. The so-called "belly-band" holster is an elastic strap fastened under the shirt, usually around the waist, and attached with Velcro, which makes the holster adjustable. It can then be worn as high or as low as necessary for maximum comfort and concealment. The belly band is surprisingly concealable—even guns the size of an S&W Model 65, Glock Model 19 or Browning High Power disappear under a shirt.

When carrying a handgun at the waist position, the gun should be kept behind the hip or in front of it (some even prefer wearing the holster at the small of the back). While highly concealable, this position risks serious injury should the shooter fall. A gun carried in this manner is also likely to "print" against the shooter's upper-body garment when he or she bends forward.

are important considerations as well. A Star Firestar in 9mm or .40 S&W caliber is small enough to conceal effectively in an ankle holster, but its weight (almost two pounds unloaded) can cause most people to walk in such a way that it attracts unwanted attention. The main disadvantage, however, aside from limiting the size of the gun, is that it can be more difficult to withdraw a gun from an ankle holster than from other types. As for the best gun to carry in an ankle holster, an S&W Model 37 Airweight Chiefs Special or Model 38 Bodyguard is tough to beat. These five-shot revolvers pack a real punch with .38 Special hollowpoints, yet they are extremely light and comfortable to carry at the ankle. They're unlikely to malfunction even under hot and dusty conditions.

Shoulder Carry. Shoulder holsters have become popular in spy thrillers and can actually be quite concealable. Given proper attention to detail and quality, even a large handgun can be hidden in a shoulder holster. Moreover, this type of carry also allows easy accessibility for the shooter but not for an assailant. On the negative side, shoulder holsters lack comfort and require wearing an outer garment, which in warm climates are sure clues that you're carrying a gun. Depending on one's physique, shoulder carry can be extremely good or, conversely, utterly unsuitable. For those with large chests or short arms (or both), shoulder carry is not advisable.

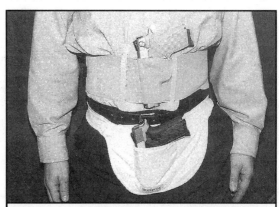

Two relatively new methods of concealing a handgun under clothing are (top) the belly-band holster and the Thunderwear holster. Both guns shown are Smith & Wesson 3900-series pistols (the holsters are worn outside the clothing for illustrative purposes only).

DISASSEMBLING COLT MODEL 1903-TYPE PISTOLS

The Browning-designed Colt Model 1903 pistol and its many clones require periodic disassembly, just as other handguns do. In general, all pistols should be disassembled and cleaned as soon as possible after firing, or about once a month in storage, on a daily basis if the gun is being carried in a holster or immediately after it has been dropped into water, mud or sand. Since the Colt-type pistol has been widely copied throughout the world, the example used here is a Spanish "Venus" model made by Tomas de Urizar around 1922. Basic field-stripping is quick, convenient and easy, without the need for any tools (unless the grips are removed with a screwdriver).

1. Make certain the gun is completely unloaded by removing all ammunition from the magazine and firing chamber. Remove the magazine by pressing the magazine release, then drawing the magazine completely out of the frame.

2. Draw back the slide as far as it will go, ejecting any round that remains in the firing chamber. Using the manual safety, draw back the slide, until it is again locked in the fully open position.

3. Grasp the barrel by its front end and rotate it about 1/4 turn clockwise until the locking ribs are free of the locking recesses in the frame.

4. Draw the barrel out of the front end of the slide. The barrel can now be cleaned.

5. If further disassembly is needed, hold the slide firmly against the forward pressure exerted by the recoil spring, then release the manual safety and ease the slide forward off the frame.

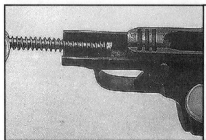

6. Finally, draw the recoil spring assembly out of the frame.

7. There are only five major parts to this gun: slide, barrel, recoil spring assembly, magazine and frame.

Accu-Tek, 103
  AT-380 Pistol, 103,106,138
Action Arms, 221, 223
Alkartasuna, 89
  Ruby Pistol, 90
American Arms Pistols
  CX 22, 105
  Model 40, 105
  Model 79K, 105
  P-98, 105
  PK 22, 105, 108
  PX 22, 105, 107
  PX 25, 107
American Derringer, 183
AMT Pistols
  .45-caliber Backup, 204
  .380 Backup, 193
  Single-action Backup, 204
Astra Pistols
  A-70, 205, 208, 209,255
  A-75, 255, 274
  A-75 Featherweight, 209
  A-75 Firefox, 208
  A-80, 205, 208
  A-100, 235
  Constable, 205
  Model 200 Firecat, 64, 65
  Model 300 Series, 77, 205
  Model 400 Series, 77, 205
  Model 600 Series, 77, 205
  Model 900, 205
  Model 2000 Cub, 64
  Model 5000 Constable, 65
  Ruby, 205
  Victoria, 205

Baikal Pistols
  IJ-70, 80, 111
  IJ-70-01, 111
Bauer Baby Pistol, 169
Beemiller, Inc., 153, 241
Beretta, Pietro, S.p.A., 116, 119, 120, 212
Beretta, 67, 113, 114, 116, 120, 210
  Pistols
  Centurion, 210
  Model 20, 113, 120
  Model 21, 113, 120, 194, 196
  Model 34, 226
  Model 70, 114, 139, 140
  Model 70S, 115
  Model 71, 115
  Model 72, 115
  Model 73, 115
  Model 74, 115
  Model 75, 115
  Model 76, 115, 116
  Model 84, 197
  Model 84/85, 113, 116-118, 120, 124
  Model 84F/85F, 116
  Model 86, 114, 120
  Model 92, 114,117,197, 210, 237
  Model 92 Type M, 210, 255

Beretta Pistols (cont.)
  Model 92F, 79, 113, 116, 117, 120
  Model 92FC, 210, 276
  Model 92FM, 211, 212
  Model 92FS, 210, 211
  Model 92S, 210
  Model 92SB, 210, 211
  Model 92SBC, 210
  Model 92SBCM, 211, 212
  Model 950, 113, 114, 120
  Model 950BS, 114
  Model 951, 115
  Model 1934, 21, 67, 74, 80, 114, 115, 138, 139, 140
  Model 1935, 67, 68
Bersa Pistols
  Model 23, 121
  Model 83, 121
  Model 85, 121
  Model 86, 121
  Model 644, 69
  Model 844, 69
Browning, John M., 71, 75, 76, 78, 87, 114, 125, 129, 130, 132, 168, 169, 188,238, 244, 278
Browning Pistols
  Baby, *see* FN Browning
  BDA, 124, 197
  BDA-380, 124
  Buck Mark, 125, 163, 164
  High Power, *see* FN Browning
  Micro Buck Mark, 126
  Model 1900, *see* FN Browning
  Model 1906, *see* FN Browning

Calibers, Pistols listed by
5.4x18mm
  Russian PSM, 179
9mm
  Astra A-70, 205
  Astra A-75 Firefox, 208
  Beretta Model 92FC, 210
  Beretta Model 92 Type M, 210
  CZ-75 Compact, 221
  Detonics Pocket 9, 226
  EAA FAB-92 Compact, 229
  EAA Witness Subcompact, 228
  FEG GKK-92C/P9RK, 230
  Glock Model 19 Compact, 232
  Glock Model 26, 237
  Hi-Point Model C, 240
  Intratec Cat-9, 242
  Llama Minimax, 244
  Semmerling LM-4, 183
  SIG P225, 248
  SIG P229, 249
  SIG P239, 248
  S&W Model 469, 92
  S&W Model 3953, 255
  S&W Model 3954, 256
  S&W Model 6906, 259
  S&W Compact (SW9C), 261

9mm (cont.)
  Star BM/BKM, 264
  Star Firestar M43, 265
  Star Firestar Plus, 271
  Star Ultrastar, 274
  Walther P5C Compact, 275
  Walther P88 Compact, 278
9mm Luger
  S&W Model 3906, 252
  S&W Model 3913 LadySmith, 253
9x18mm Makarov
  Baikal IJ-70, 111
  FEG PA-63, 142
  FEG SMC-918, 145
  Makarov Model PM, 79
.22 Long Rifle
  American Arms PK 22, 105
  American Arms PX 22, 107
  Astra Model 5000 Constable, 65
  Beretta Model 21, 113
  Browning Buck Mark, 125
  Colt Woodsman, 132
  Jennings J-22, 158
  Mitchell Arms Trophy II, 161
  Navy Arms TT-Olympia, 165
  Ruger Mark II Government Target Model, 175
  S&W Model 41, 187
  S&W Model 2213, 188
  S&W Model 2214, 188
  Taurus Model PT-22, 194
  Walther PPK, 97
  Walther Model TPH, 200
.22 Short
  Astra Model 2000 Cub, 64
.25 ACP
  Astra Model 2000 Cub, 64
  Beretta Model 21, 113
  Intratec Protec 25, 154
  PSP-25, 168
  Raven, 172
  Taurus Model PT-25, 194
  Walther Model 8, 94
  Walther Model 9, 96
  Walther PPK, 97
  Walther Model TPH, 200
.32 ACP
  Astra Model 5000 Constable, 65
  Beretta Model 1935, 67
  Bersa Model 844, 69
  Colt 1903 Pocket Model M, 71
  CZ Model 27, 73
  FN Browning Model 1900, 75
  FN Browning Model 1910/1922, 76
  Mauser Model HSc, 82
  Ortgies Pistol, 85
  Remington Model 51, 174
  Ruby Pistols, 89
  Seecamp LWS-32, 181
  Walther Model 4, 93
  Walther PPK, 97

Calibers, Pistols listed by (cont.)
.357 SIG
  AMT Backup, 204
  SIG P229, 249
  SIG P239, 248
.38 Special
  Davis D38 Derringer, 136
.38 Super
  AMT Backup, 204
.380 ACP
  Accu-Tek AT-380. 103
  AMT Backup, 204
  Astra Model 5000 Constable, 65
  Beretta Model 70, 114
  Beretta Model 84F, 116
  Beretta Model 85F, 116
  Beretta Model 86, 120
  Beretta Model 1934, 67
  Bersa Model 83, 121
  Bersa Model 85, 121
  Bersa Model 86, 121
  Browning BDA-380, 124
  Colt .380 Government Model, 128
  Colt 1903 Pocket Model M, 71
  Colt Mustang, 128
  Colt Mustang Plus II, 128
  Colt Mustang Pocketlite, 128
  CZ Model 83, 134
  Davis P-380, 137
  EAA .380 European, 139
  FEG AP9, 142
  FEG Model B9R, 141
  FEG PMK-380, 142
  FEG SMC-380, 145
  FN Browning Model 1910/1922, 76
  Grendel P-12, 148
  Heckler & Koch P7K3, 150
  Hi-Point Model CF, 152
  Jennings/Bryco Model 38, 157
  Iver Johnson (AMAC) Pony, 160
  Mauser Model HSc, 82
  Ortgies Pistol, 85
  Remington Model 51, 174
  SIG-Sauer P230, 185
  Smith & Wesson Sigma, 192
  Taurus Model PT-58, 197
  Walther PPK, 97

.40 S&W
  AMT Backup, 204
  Astra A-70, 205
  Astra A-75 Firefox, 208
  EAA FAB-92 Compact, 229
  EAA Witness Subcompact, 228
  Glock Model 23, 235
  Glock Model 27, 237
  Llama Minimax, 244
  SIG P229, 249
  S&W Model 4013, 258
  Star Firestar M40, 267
.45 ACP
  AMT Backup, 204

.45 ACP (cont.)
  Astra A-75 Firefox, 208
  Colt Double Eagle Officer's ACP, 215
  Colt Double Eagle Lightweight Officer's
    Model, 217
  Colt "Enhanced" Officer's ACP, 213
  Colt M1991A1 Commander, 218
  Colt M1991A1 Compact, 220
  Detonics CombatMaster/MC-1, 224
  EAA Witness Subcompact, 228
  Llama Minimax, 244
  Para-Ordnance P12 45, 246
  Semmerling LM-4, 183
  Springfield 1911A1 Compact, 262
  Star Firestar M45, 269
  Star PD, 272
Calibers, Revolvers listed by
9mm
  Ruger SP101, 40
  S&W Model 940, 47
.22 Long Rifle
  NAA Mini-Revolver, 30
  Rossi Model 518, 35
  Ruger SP101, 40
  S&W Model 34, 42
  Taurus Model 94, 57
.22 Magnum
  S&W Model 651, 52
  Taurus Model 941, 60
.32 H&R
  Ruger SP101, 40
.32 S&W
  S&W Safety Hammerless, 20
.357 Magnum
  Rossi Model 971 Comp, 38
  Ruger SP101, 40
  S&W Model 640, 47
  Taurus Model 65, 53
  Taurus Model 605, 59
.38 S&W
  S&W Safety Hammerless, 20
.38 Special
  Charter Arms Off Duty, 28
  Colt Detective Special, 14
  Rossi Model 68, 33
  Rossi Model 88, 34
  Ruger SP101, 40
  S&W Chiefs Special Model 36, 16
  S&W Model 37, 44
  S&W Model 38, 46
  S&W Model 60, 18
  S&W Model 442, 47
  Taurus Model 85, 54
  Taurus Models 85CH & 85CHS, 55
  Taurus Model 605, 59
.44 Special
  Charter Arms Bulldog, 12
  Rossi 720 Covert Special, 37
Century Arms, 111
Century Int'l. Arms, 141, 143, 230
Ceska Zbrojovka, 134
Charco, 12, 28

Charter Arms, 12, 28, 105
  Revolvers
  Bulldog, 12, 22, 29, 37
  Off Duty, 12, 28, 81
  Pit Bull, 26
  Undercover, 12, 28
Colt, 14, 71, 128, 132, 213, 215, 217,
  218, 220
  Pistols
  Automatic Colt Pistol, 71
  "Camper," 65
  Challenger, 132, 133
  Commander 213, 217, 262
  Double Eagle, 180, 215, 216, 217
  Double Eagle Lightweight Officer's Model,
    217
  Double Eagle Officer's Model ACP, 215,
    217
  "Enhanced" Officer's ACP, 213
  Government Model, 213, 214, 215, 217,
    218, 246, 262, 264
  Huntsman, 132, 133
  Junior, 64, 65
  M15 General Officer's Handgun, 213
  M1911, 129, 213, 214, 216, 218, 239,
    244, 272, 273
  M1911 Government Series, 224
  M1911 Series, 21, 226
  M1911A1, 71, 79, 129, 206, 213, 218,
    246, 264
  M1991A1, 129, 213, 214, 215, 217, 218,
    220, 246
  M1991A1 Combat Commander, 218
  M1991A1 Commander, 218, 220
  M1991A1 Compact, 214, 218, 219, 220
  Match Target, 132
  Model 1911, 244, 246
  Mustang, 90, 128, 160
  Mustang Plus II, 128
  Mustang Pocketlite, 128, 182, 193
  1903 Pocket Model, 76
  1903 Pocket Model M, 71
  Officer's ACP, 213, 215, 216, 217, 220,
    224, 246, 262, 269
  Officer's LW, 213
  Pocket Model 24, 76, 78
  Sport, 132
  Target, 132
  .380 Government Model, 128, 160
  .380 Government Pocketlite, 129
  Woodsman, 125, 127, 132, 166
  Revolvers
  Detective Special, 14, 81, 99, 270
  Navy Model 1889, 23
  Pocket Model Automatic, 24
  Police Positive Special, 14
  Single Action Army, 20
CZ Pistols
  vz 22/24 Series, 73
  vz 27, 73
  vz 45, 154
  vz 52, 134

CZ Pistols (cont.)
  vz 75, 21, 134, 135, 221, 222, 228, 265, 267, 269, 274
  vz 75 Compact, 221, 228, 229
  vz 82, 134
  vz 83, 119, 134, 186, 197
  vz 85, 134, 135, 221, 222

Davis Pistols
  D38 Derringer, 136
  P-32, 136, 137
  P-380, 136, 137, 172
Detonics Pistols
  CombatMaster/MC-1, 224, 226
  Pocket 9, 226, 255
  Pocket 9 LS, 226

EAA (European American Armory), 139, 209, 228, 229
  Pistols
  .380 European, 139
  FAB-92 Compact, 228, 229
  Witness, 229
  Witness Compact, 223, 229
  Witness Subcompact, 228
Eagle Imports, 123
Eibar-type Pistol, 89
Erma E.P. 25 Pistol, 86
Erma-Werke, 105, 107
Excam TA-90 Pistol, 228

Fabbrica d'Armi Fratelli, 229
Fabrica de Armas, 70
FEG Pistols
  AP9, 142
  B9R, 141, 197
  GKK-92C/P9RK, 230
  Model 48 (Attila), 142
  P9R, 230
  P9RK, 141
  PA-63, 142, 145
  PJK-9HP, 231
  PMK-380, 142, 145
  RK-59, 145
  SMC-380, 145
  SMC-918, 145
FIE Pistols
  Titan II, 139
  TZ-75, 228
FN (Fabrique Nationale) Browning, 76, 124
  Baby, 32, 157, 168, 169, 170, 171, 193
  High Power, 21, 79, 80, 124, 206, 226, 246, 252
  Model 140 DA, 124
  Model 1900, 75, 77, 188, 189
  Model 1903, 71, 77, 89, 205
  Model 1906, 154, 168, 170, 171
  Model 1910, 75, 76, 124, 205
  Model 1922, 76
  Type 64, 75
Forgett, Val, 166
Frankonia Jagd, 180
French Model 1935T, 206

Gabilondo y Cia, Llama, 89, 244
Gabilondos y Urresti, 89
  Ruby Pistol, 70, 89, 94
Gamba, Renato, SpA, 83
Garcia Model D Pistol, 160
Glock Pistols
  Model 17, 232, 233, 238
  Model 19 (Compact), 135, 232, 235, 238
  Model 21, 235
  Model 22, 235, 258
  Model 23, 235, 238
  Model 26, 237
  Model 27, 237
  P-80, 232
Grendel Pistols
  P-10, 148
  P-12, 148

Hämmerli AG Pistols
  Model 200, 165
  Model 201, 165
  Model 202, 165
  Model 203, 165
  Model 204, 165
  Model 205, 165
  Model 206, 165
  Model 212, 165
  Model 230 Series, 165
Heckler & Koch Pistols
  HK 4, 83, 150
  P7, 88
  P7K3, 150
  P7M8, 150, 151
  P7M10, 150
  P7M13, 150
  PSP, 150
Hi-Point Pistols
  Maverick, 152
  Model C, 152, 240, 242
  Model CF, 152
  Stallard, 152

Interarms, 33, 36, 37, 39, 83, 98, 99, 100, 132, 200, 266, 267, 271, 274, 278
Intratec Pistols
  Cat-9, 204, 242
  Protec 25, 154, 181
Izhevsk Ordnance Factory, 180

Jennings Pistols
  /Bryco 38, 138, 157, 159
  J-22, 158
  J-25, 158
Johnson, Iver, (AMAC) Pistols
  Pony, 160
  TP-22, 107
  TP-25, 107
  X-300 Pony, 160

Kahr K9, 237, 243
K.B.I., 111, 143, 144, 145, 146, 169, 230
Kel Tec P-11, 237

Llama Minimax Pistol, 244
Luger P08 Pistol, 80, 93

Magnum Research, 134, 221
Makarov Pistols
  Pistole M (East German), 80
  PM, 79, 111, 112, 143, 147, 179, 180, 184, 186
  Type 59 (Chinese) Pistol, 80
Manurhin, 100
Mauser Pistols
  C.96 "Broomhandle," 148, 205
  HSa, 82
  HSc, 82
  Model 1914, 82
  Model 1934, 82
Mauser-Werke, 84
Mitchell Arms Pistols
  Citation, 161
  High Standard, 125, 127, 176, 177
  Olympic I.S.U., 161
  Sharpshooter, 161
  Sport King, 161
  Trophy, 161
  Trophy II, 161, 188
  Victor, 161

Navy Arms TT-Olympia Pistol, 165, 177
New Detonics Corp., 225
Norinco, 11, 132, 166
North American Arms Revolvers
  Black Widow, 31
  Mini-Revolver, 30, 182

Ortgies Pistol, 85

Para-Ordnance Pistols
  P12•45, 246
  P14•45, 246
Pedersen, John, 174
Poland vz.63 Pistol, 145
PSP-25 Pistol, 168

Ranger Manufacturing, 99, 200
Raven Pistol, 97, 137, 159, 172
Remington Arms Model 51 Pistol, 174
Rossi Revolvers
  Model 68, 33, 34
  Model 88, 33, 34
  Model 88 "Lady Rossi," 35
  Model 518, 35
  Model 720, 37
  Model 720 Covert Special, 37
  Model 971 Comp, 38
Ruby Pistols, 89
Ruger, 40, 175
  Pistols
  Mark II, 127, 162, 163, 164, 188
  Mark II Government Target Model, 175
  Mark II Target Model, 175
  P91, 258
  Standard, 175

Ruger (cont.)
 Revolvers
  GP100, 40
  SP101, 40, 49, 59
  Speed-Six, 40
Russian PSM Pistol, 179

Saive, Dieudonne Joseph, 168, 169
Sauer Model 38H Pistol, 185
Sauer, J.P., & Sohn, 249, 251
Seecamp LWS-32 Pistol, 181, 193, 204
Semmerling LM-4 Pistol, 183
S.G.S., 245
SIG-Sauer Pistols
 P6, 248
 P210, 269
 P220, 206, 208, 249
 P225, 208, 248, 249
 P228, 248, 249, 260
 P229, 248, 249
 P230, 80, 185, 249
 P230SL, 186
 P239, 248
SIGARMS, 249, 251
Sirkis Pistol, 242
Smith, Horace, 20
Smith & Wesson, 16, 18, 20, 42, 44, 46,
 47, 52, 92 187, 188, 192, 252, 258,
 259, 261
 Pistols
  Model 39, 92, 252, 257, 259
  Model 39 Series, 92
  Model 41, 164, 176, 177, 187, 188
  Model 41-1, 187
  Model 46, 187
  Model 59 Series, 92
  Model 422, 188, 189
  Model 422/622 Series, 188
  Model 439, 252
  Model 469, 92, 259
  Model 639, 252
  Model 669, 259
  Model 2204, 188
  Model 2206, 188
  Model 2213, 188
  Model 2214 "Sportsman," 127, 188
  Model 3900 Series, 209, 212, 233, 252,
   274
  Model 3904, 252
  Model 3906, 252
  Model 3913, 253, 255, 257, 276
  Model 3913 LadySmith, 208, 252, 253,
   255, 256
  Model 3914, 252, 253, 255, 257, 276
  Model 3914LS, 253
  Model 3953, 234, 252, 255, 259, 276
  Model 3954, 256
  Model 4006, 258
  Model 4013, 258
  Model 5900 Series, 252
  Model 6904, 92, 259
  Model 6906, 259

Smith & Wesson Pistols (cont.)
  Model 6946, 259
  Sigma, 192, 242, 261
  Sigma .380 (SW380), 182, 192
  Sigma Compact (SW9C), 192, 261
 Revolvers
  Centennial Series, 46, 55, 57
  Chiefs Special, 16, 24, 28, 44, 46, 99
  Chiefs Special Airweight, 16, 44
  J-frame, 13, 15, 16, 17, 28, 42, 43, 54,
   55, 81, 99, 253
  K-frame, 253
  "Lemon Squeezer," *see* Safety Hammerless
  Military & Police, 24, 53
  Model 10, 21, 79
  Model 13/65 Series, 53
  Model 19 Combat Magnum, 53
  Model 32 (Terrier), 24
  Model 34, 36, 42
  Model 36 Chiefs Special, 16, 18, 33, 54,
   79, 155
  Model 37 Chiefs Special Airweight, 16,
   44, 46, 47, 48, 49, 54
  Model 38 Bodyguard, 17, 28, 30, 44, 46,
   48, 49, 55, 57, 82, 148
  Model 40 Centennial, 47
  Model 42 Centennial, 16, 17, 25
  Model 49, 46, 57
  Model 60, 17, 18
  Model 60 LadySmith, 19
  Model 442, 47
  Model 640, 25, 47, 59
  Model 642 Centennial Airweight, 16, 48
  Model 649, 46, 57
  Model 651, 52, 61, 62
  Model 940, 47, 243
  Model 1880 (.38 DA), 20
  "New Departure," *see* Safety Hammerless
  Safety Hammerless, 12, 17, 20-26,47
Springfield Armory Pistols
  Model 1911A1 Compact, 262, 273
  P9, 228
Stallard Maverick, 240
Star, 89, 160, 264, 265, 271, 272, 274
 Pistols
  B, 264
  BK, 272
  BKM, 264, 272
  BM, 264, 267
  DK (Starfire), 160
  Firestar, 223, 245, 255, 264
  Firestar M40, 267
  Firestar M43, 206, 207, 265, 267, 271
  Firestar M45, 238, 267, 269
  Firestar Plus, 271
  Model 28. 269
  Model 30, 269
  Model 31, 265, 269
  PD, 264, 267, 269, 272
  Ultrastar, 274
Stoeger, A.F., 97
Stoeger 1932 Pistol, 165

Tanfoglio, Fratelli, 139
Tanfoglio SpA, 229
Taurus, 53, 54, 55, 57, 59, 60, 194, 197
 Pistols
  PT-22, 113, 194
  PT-25, 113, 194
  PT-57, 197
  PT-58, 142, 197
  PT-92, 197
  PT-92C, 276
  PT-908, 276
 Revolvers
  Model 65, 53
  Model 85, 33, 54, 55, 56, 57, 59
  Model 85CH, 55
  Model 85CHS, 55
  Model 94, 43, 57, 60, 61, 62
  Model 605, 49, 59
  Model 605 Custom, 59
  Model 941, 60
Thompson, Leroy, 145
Tokarev Pistol, 79

Waffenfabrik Walther, 93, 95, 96, 100
Walther, Fritz, 165
Walther Pistols
  Model 1, 96
  Model 3, 93
  Model 4, 93
  Model 8, 94, 97, 137
  Model 9, 96, 99, 157, 159, 172, 200
  Funfkampfmodell, 165
  Jagermodell, 166
  KPK, 98
  Olympia-Pistole, 165, 166, 188
  P5, 275
  P5 Compact (P5C), 241, 255, 275
  P.38, 79, 80, 96, 99, 105, 275, 276
  P88, 278
  P88 Compact, 278
  PP, 79, 82, 86, 93, 97, 117, 123, 142,
   143, 144, 145, 165, 185, 200, 201, 234,
   267, 278
  PP Super, 80, 185, 186
  PP/PPK Series, 95, 96, 105, 107, 112,
   121, 143, 185, 188
  PPK, 24, 65, 66, 79, 82, 97, 103, 104,
   105, 107, 123, 141, 142, 145, 146,
   147, 157, 179, 185, 186, 200, 201, 206,
   208, 224, 227, 256, 263, 269
  PPK/S, 98, 99, 100, 200
  Sport-Pistole, 165
  Sportmodell, 165
  TP, 97, 200, 201
  TPH, 30, 97, 99, 193, 200
Webley No. 2 Revolver, 12
Wesson, Daniel B., 20